WHAT HAPPENED TO SIN?

*Dedicated to all the married People of God
who have suffered down the ages
from the flawed teaching of Augustine
which usurped the teaching of Christ.*

Seán Fagan SM

What happened to sin?

the columba press

First published in 2008 by
the columba press
55A Spruce Avenue, Stillorgan Industrial Park,
Blackrock, Co Dublin

Cover by Bill Bolger
Origination by The Columba Press
Printed in Ireland by ColourBooks Ltd, Dublin

ISBN 978-1-85607-633-3

Table of Contents

Introduction

In 1977 I wrote a book called *Has Sin Changed?* It was written in two months and was published by Michael Glazier, Wilmington, Gill & MacMillan, Dublin, Doubleday, New York, and was the Thomas More Book Club selection, USA in 1978. It sold 65,000 copies worldwide and is a Talking Book for the Blind in the United States. I still receive requests for it and queries about it, so I thought it worthwhile to re-write it totally in the light of developments during the thirty years since it first appeared. There have been very considerable developments in the church and world in that time. Although many of the giants in theology have gone to their heavenly reward and now enjoy the fullness of life for which they were created, their research, lectures, writing and wisdom live on for the enrichment of contemporary Catholics. Thousands of lay men and women have discovered the joys of theological study and are excited about the experience. But they are saddened that their talents are so often ignored by the clerical church. While the church in the Third World is full of enthusiasm and growing in numbers, its place in developed countries continues to shrink, with massive reductions in Mass attendance, and an ever-growing drop in vocations to priesthood and religious life. It is so easy to blame outside forces like relativism, materialism, individualism and the general sinfulness of the secular world for our current misfortune, but the first Christian converts who moved out of Palestine and into Europe had to cope with the sophisticated paganism of Greece and Rome, and later the savage barbarism of the scattered tribes looking for fresh conquests. The problems of today's church are not all caused by outside influences.

There is no simple answer to the problem of renewal. More than just organisational management of personnel, we need a renewal of spirituality and vision, a new effort to take seriously the insights of the Second Vatican Council in our understanding and living of the meaning of church and mission. A helpful step in this direction is to recognise and discard so much useless and at times dangerous baggage from the past, so that our gospel message can shine out clearly in its own light. A wider interest in, and knowledge of, theology can be of help and we should make more room for those laity who have begun to discover the riches of their faith and how it helps them to make godly sense of the complicated world we live in. So many committed lay Catholics find it difficult to live in our clerical church, and women are still waiting to have more than lip-service paid to the equality of the sexes.

But the major stimulus to my re-writing this book has been my experience of hearing confessions in many countries and listening to so much heart-break in marriage counselling since 1968. Like me, many clergy will have encountered the intense pain suffered by hundreds of thousands of married women around the world, while others alas seem to have ignored that intense pain when those women came to the confessional asking to be absolved from a 'sin' which, with sincere and well-formed responsible conscience, they knew could not be proved sinful. This situation becomes critical when the woman's health precludes a further pregnancy. The most poignant example of this was just one of many, that of a woman who had two children followed by eleven miscarriages (with the agonising worry about the mysterious Limbo). As a good Catholic, she and her husband conscientiously tried so-called natural family planning with no success, except that the strain of abstinence and repeated unwanted death-threatening pregnancies almost destroyed their marriage. Her doctor told her that she could easily become pregnant, which she did, but because of her medical condition she could never bear a live child, and her abnormal blood-clotting problem meant that each pregnancy could easily cause death. Her problem was solved by tubal ligation. Only God knows the number of those refused absolution by priests who felt they were just doing their job. An extreme example was an English woman who never missed Sunday Mass for almost thirty years but felt she could not receive communion because two priests had refused her absolution. She was overjoyed just recently to be able to have communion again. Clerics who have the privilege of daily celebration of the Eucharist have no idea of the intense suffering of devout Catholic couples who love the Mass but have been told for years that they cannot accept the invitation of Jesus when he offers his body and blood with the words 'Take and eat, take and drink.' Most of them are convinced that this cannot be God's will, but they are saddened to know that the church can do nothing to help them. Those in second unions have the same suffering.

This tragic experience sharpened my interest in their problem. The first step in my research was the discovery of the masterly study of Professor John T. Noonan Jr, of Notre Dame Law School: *Contraception, How the Catholic Church has viewed birth control, from the earliest times to the present day*.[1] He was special consultant to the papal commission in Rome set up to study the question of birth control. His book is a magnificent presentation and discussion of statements of popes, theologians and canonists from the Roman Empire to the present day. It is doubtful that Pope Paul VI ever read this extraordinary book, written in English, and it has been said that many bishops dismissed it as not being 'reliable', without ever looking at it. An equally enlightening book was Robert McClory's: *Turning Point, the inside story of the Papal Birth Control Commission*.[2] The book is called after the extraordinary moment when none of the Commission could point out why contraception was contrary to Natural Law. Much has been written about contraception and church teaching during the past forty years, but not a single convincing argument has emerged to prove that artificial contraception is 'intrinsically evil'. Cardinal Heenan, who was a member of the Second Vatican Council and also a member of the papal commission, told Dr John Marshall, a fellow member, during the long wait for the encyclical: 'It does not matter now what the Pope says. It is too late. The people have made up their minds.' Dr Marshall voted with the majority of the commission that contraception was not intrinsically evil, while Cardinal Heenan was one of three abstaining bishops.

Cardinal Wojtyla was a member of the Commission but

1. *Contraception*, Harvard University Press, Cambridge, Mass, 1965.
2. *Turning Point*, Crossroad, New York, 1995.

never attended a single session, possibly because of the high view of papal infallibility he expressed in his book *The Theology of the Body* (p 389) where he says that 'Even if the moral law formulated in *Humanae vitae* is not found in Sacred Scripture, nonetheless, from the fact that it is contained in Tradition, and as Paul VI writes, has been "very often expounded by the Magisterium" (*HV* 12) to the faithful, it follows that this norm is in accordance with the sum total of revealed doctrine contained in biblical sources.' This unfounded view is far from the First Vatican Council's understanding of 'infallibility' and 'revealed doctrine.'

Humanae vitae teaches that 'every act of marriage must, in itself, stay destined towards the chance of human procreation.' (n 11). Apart from cases of low sperm count, this happens only in male intercourse, because God has created female human nature differently. A woman is fertile for only 48 to 72 hours each month from puberty to menopause, so most of her acts of intercourse throughout life are not open to procreation. The obvious conclusion is that God has attached procreation to the marital relationship itself, the two-in-one-flesh which is the essence of marriage, and not to all acts of intercourse.

Although women are still excluded from Holy Orders, since late in the last century many of them have been able to study theology and have excelled in it. What I found most enlightening and heart-warming since 1968 has been to listen to the voices and experience of some of these women. who are far more qualified in this area than most celibate clerics. Their contributions to my thinking and understanding are beyond number, but I mention just three to record my admiration, appreciation and deep gratitude. Their help will be apparent in chapter 5. The first is Kim Power, an acknowledged world expert on Augustine, his culture and his writings, author of *Veiled Desire, Augustine on Women*.[3] She points out the irony in the fact that it was Augustine, the man who argued so powerfully, and eventually persuasively, that sexuality belonged in Eden, who also made the desire to be loved by the beloved so suspect and so shameful, rendering it so tainted and dangerous that the erotic could

---

3. *Veiled Desire, Augustine on Women*, Continuum, New York, 1996.

never be permitted to symbolise divine love. So much for the Song of Songs in the Bible. She brilliantly shows how Augustine legitimised the split between love and sex so that sexual intercourse is depersonalised, and it wasn't until Paul VI that papal teaching accepted that intercourse had a unitive meaning. I was also encouraged and enriched by correspondence and conversations with Angela Hanley, an Irish married woman well qualified in theology, a coordinator with the Priory Institute Distance Education Programme in Theology, Tallaght, Dublin, author of *Justified by Faith*,[4] and co-editor of *Quench not the Spirit*.[5]

A special source of inspiration and understanding was Elizabeth Price of the UK, also an avid student of Noonan's *Contraception*. She noted that Paul VI said of the Pontifical Commission that 'The conclusions to which they came the Pope cannot accept; for they are not conclusive in themselves, and some of their proposals went much too far away from what the Teaching Church has always said.' (*HV* 6) Having read Noonan, she saw that this was indeed true of contraception, but that the wider understanding of the physiological and psychological aspects of marital sexuality had changed beyond all recognition since the middle of the twentieth century. Up until the sixteenth century this misunderstanding had led to many acts of intercourse in marriage being seen as mortal or venial sin, then after argument between rigorist and pastoral theologians were seen as innocent. Feeling that this should be true of contraception, she wrote an article prior to the Synod on the Family in 1980, and published it in the May edition of the *Clergy Review* that year. It was expressively called *Sexual Misunderstanding – The true reason for the Magisterial Ban on Contraception*. The points it raised are still being ignored. They will be discussed in chapter 5 of this book.

In 2000 Elizabeth wrote a pamphlet called *Seeing Sin Where None Is*,[6] which was published by Catholics for a Changing Church, a group which had come into being in 1968 to protest at what they saw as the moral injustice of *Humanae vitae*. Frank

---

4. *Justified by Faith*, St Patrick's Missionary Society, Kiltegan, 2002.
5. *Quench not the Spirit*, eds Angela Hanley & David Smith, Columba Press, Dublin, 2005.
6. *Catholics for a Changing Church*, 14, West Halkin Street, London SW1 8JS.

Pycroft, co-founder and current chairman of CCC, has recently described it as one of the group's most important publications. As one of the group's vice-chairmen, Elizabeth was given the task of writing letters to the Catholic Press on marriage matters. Her main point in these letters is to say that given the need for 'responsible parenthood', this can be achieved in two ways: either by altering the act of intercourse by removing its potential fertility with the use of contraception, or altering the very relationship of marriage itself by removing an act intrinsic to it – sexual intercourse. She argues that no moral authority has the right to do this, because Christ's teaching in Mt 19:4-6, which has been used by the church throughout history in an almost fundamentalist way to ban divorce, is also in fact Jesus himself revealing that the initial and continuous purpose of intercourse is to bring about a change between the couple, and to sustain them as no longer two but one. This special relationship forms the background security both for the couple and for any children born to them. Chapter 5 will hopefully show not only why this beautiful teaching of Christ has been ignored until the present day, but also how this text ought to be used to change our whole understanding of human sexuality and of how our Catholic Church could better engage in preparation for, and ministry to marriage.

It is a well-known fact that 80% of Catholics disregard the ban on contraception. It will be clear from our discussion of the subject that this is not the result of lust, selfishness, materialism or secularism among the laity, but rather that the fault arose from the ignorance of the close advisors of Paul VI who disregarded the informed advice and lived experience of the married People of God on the Pontifical Commission. The advice of these married people was rejected simply because it did not accord with a flawed and untried theory passed down from one generation of celibate clerics to the next, which had never been put to the test in their own lives.

The contraception debate gets only brief treatment in chapter 5, but fuller information is available in my earlier book *Does Morality Change?*[7] – chapters 5-9: Does Nature Change? Conscience Today, Moral Discernment, Responsible Parenthood, and Church Teaching.

7. Seán Fagan SM, *Does Morality Change?* Columba Press, Dublin, 2003.

CHAPTER ONE

What Happened to Sin?

I am now 81 years old and since 1953 I have heard confessions in 12 different countries and five languages. I also have my own experience of personal sinfulness. This does not make me an expert on sin, but for the past 53 years I have lectured on moral theology to adults, so I have given serious thought to the subject. It is neither a fashionable word nor a popular subject in today's world. For non-religious people it is simply irrelevant, a carry-over from a bygone age. Even in religious circles it has not the common currency it once had. Among Christians its meaning has become confused to such an extent that preachers tend to soft-pedal it. The loss of the sense of sin may well be a reaction against overemphasis on sin in the past, both in its hell-fire punishment aspect and in the detailed labelling that attached a degree of sinfulness to even the simplest of human activities. Until a short time ago a single act of sexual self-gratification was considered a mortal sin meriting eternal punishment. It was common church teaching that to miss one Sunday Mass deliberately without sufficient reason meant hell for all eternity, and for centuries it was a mortal sin for married couples to have intercourse during menstruation or pregnancy, although for hundreds of years the church only recognised murder, adultery and apostasy as mortal sins. Today's common sense rejects this kind of thinking, but the rejection is often accompanied by impatience with any talk of sin, so the real meaning of sin is weakened or lost.

The worldwide decline in respect for authority is another factor. Sin has traditionally been preached as disobedience to God's law expressed in the Bible, church teaching and the commands of lawful authorities. But people are nowadays more alert to the abuses and exaggerations of authority, and find it difficult to see any convincing link between obedience to rules and fidelity to God. This too can be a healthy reaction, rejecting the notion of

13

God as primarily legislator and taskmaster, but it can blunt our sensitivity to God's invitation and call, and blind us to the possibility of sinful refusals.

A new, but not always correct, understanding of conscience may also lessen the sense of sin. Reacting against the blind obedience often preached in the past, many people now confuse personal conscience with simply doing as they please, without any reference to guidance from authority. 'What is right' very easily becomes 'what I like or want', and since there is no strong urge in human nature to do what one dislikes, the lines between right and wrong become blurred, moral conflict disappears, and with it the whole notion of sin.

A more general reason for the weakening of the notion of sin is the lessening of the sense of God in today's world. Western society is becoming more and more secularised, with little direct reference to God, so that human wrongdoing is seldom understood as a religious reality, as sin. Affluence is a factor here, insofar as riches often bring a spirit of independence and self-sufficiency, with little room for God. Jesus himself warned us about this: 'How hard it will be for rich people to enter the kingdom of heaven' (Mt 10:23).

Freedom and responsibility
In the area of freedom and responsibility, the discoveries of psychology about subconscious motivation and the influence of heredity and environment tend to lessen people's sense of guilt and consequently their admission of sin. It is frequently believed that because a motive for an action can be identified that the action was not fully free, and so the evils in the world can be attributed to outside forces and circumstances beyond our control. It is too easily forgotten that no human action can be without a motive, that our motives are freely chosen, notwithstanding outside influences, and they are often sinfully selfish, without regard for our true good or for the needs of others.

Paradoxically, a somewhat similar form of escapism may be our greater sensitivity nowadays to collective responsibility for sinful situations and structures, for social evils like discrimination, racism, and economic exploitation on national and international levels. We can become so righteously indignant about these social injustices not of our making that we forget the personal sins in our own lives. The enormity of some of these unjust structures and our helplessness in the face of them make our personal misdeeds seem trivial by comparison.

Psychologists have discovered a great deal in recent decades about neurotic guilt and the influence of what Freud called the 'super ego'. The general acceptance of these findings by the public at large has tended to weaken the sense of sin, since sin is usually associated with guilt. But writers of popular psychology often fail to distinguish between the irrational guilt feelings produced by infantile conscience and the real guilt acknowledged by morally mature people who have acted against their conscience. Psychiatrists and counsellors sometimes undermine our morale and sense of personhood by telling us that we were not responsible for our actions, instead of helping us to accept our responsibility and real moral guilt. There is a sure-fire remedy for the pain of real guilt, namely acknowledgement, repentance, atonement. To treat it as neurotic, in those cases in which it is clearly not such, is to ask for trouble. A rehabilitation of the word 'sin' and a greater understanding of how to cope with it through repentance and forgiveness would be more helpful to many people than the guesswork and groping of some psychiatrists.

An over-optimistic view of evolution and human progress can also blunt the concept of sin. It is possible to contrast today's moral sensitivity to human rights with the barbarism and cruelty of former times, but it would be a mistake to conclude that human beings are therefore less sinful. Our greater awareness of certain moral values and our deeper insight into our human dignity do not mean that we are morally better than our grandparents. The developments of technology that have made life more comfortable and offer us possibilities for a new humanism, have also opened new roads to unprecedented forms of inhumanity. The old are often lonelier today than in most times in the past, people are less capable of coping with the problem of death in today's society, and the living conditions in modern cities have not produced greater friendliness or neighbourliness. We can feel self-righteous in condemning apartheid abroad, but what happens to our convictions when we are in a

15

position to do something about racial discrimination in our own neighbourhood or in our business? The torture and oppression practised by so many governments throughout the world should be a warning against a too easy optimism. Sin is still a reality in our world, and the world might be a healthier place if it were more sincerely and realistically admitted.

Large numbers of Catholics lived happy and holy lives with an over-simple understanding of sin and morality, and there may be some for whom that is still meaningful, or at least not too harmful. But growing numbers are dissatisfied with such an over-simplified picture. It does not speak to their condition, and it raises too many questions for which they have not been given convincing answers. There is a reaction against a legalistic, formalistic, juridic notion of sin as a thing, the breaking of an external law, a disruption of order and stability. We now have a greater awareness of our personal responsibility, a realisation that the established order itself, whether in church or state, may be an obstacle to full human development, and so not in accordance with God's will. The dissatisfaction with the older presentation is not always clearly defined or understood, but there is real need for a new understanding of sin. Such a new understanding has indeed developed over the past few years. There is no question of a 'new theology' to do away with sin or encourage the so-called 'permissiveness' of modern society. There is continuity between the old and the new, though a considerable shift of emphasis has taken place, and in many ways the whole question is seen in a new light. Sin is as much a reality as ever, and is taken quite seriously by the new theology. In a sense, the new understanding makes far more demands than the old.

It could be objected that what is needed for the renewal of the church is a positive theology of love rather than a negative theology of sin. This is certainly true, but there is room for a book which will meet people where they are, which will take what understanding they already have, and help them to see where it needs to be corrected and developed. A book on sin need not be a negative treatment. The good news of the gospel is that God loves us with an infinite and everlasting love, and that this love became incarnate in Jesus through whom we have the forgiveness of sins. We cannot repent and be converted unless we take sin seriously. But a defective notion of sin can produce distorted ideas of God, the church, conscience, law, sacraments (particularly penance), and Christian morality itself. It may be helpful, therefore, to take a critical look at those aspects of the common understanding of sin which need correcting and development. To identify and admit the negative influence of our past can in itself be a liberating experience.

Problems from the past

The old 'sin-grid' focused attention on measurement, both of the matter of the sin and of the degree of responsibility and guilt. This needs re-examination today. Are the old categories sufficient? They emphasised law, which was always clearly defined, and therefore easily measured. But with the multiplication of church laws, people felt that where there was no clear-cut law, there was no moral obligation. Besides, many came to believe that things were wrong because they were forbidden instead of seeing that they were forbidden because they were wrong. This is hardly moral maturity. Among the commandments, the two relating to sex were singled out for such disproportionately special treatment that many people today automatically think of sex when the word 'sin' is mentioned. If sin was feared, it was often because of the punishment attached to it, but the over-simplified traditional notions of purgatory and hell are unconvincing to modern Catholics, so their sense of sin is affected. Not only can parents no longer instil the fear of God into their children by invoking the threat of hell-fire, but they are at a loss when it comes to explaining and handing on the moral principles they themselves were brought up on. They feel particularly helpless in trying to form the consciences of their children, because they themselves were seldom encouraged to explore the full meaning of conscience or to use it in a really personal way. The teaching church, as a loving mother concerned for the safety of her children, at times developed an over-protective attitude amounting to a nervous distrust of the presence of the Holy Spirit in the faithful. A narrow view of the 'teaching church' restricted it to church leaders, and it was forgotten that the whole church is both a teaching church and a learning church. Before there is any reference to how the church is organised or ruled, the Second

Vatican Council defines it as the People of God, all God's holy people, equal in our baptism. Because of an individualistic notion of sin, the sacrament of penance became, for many people, a private guilt-shedding process with little reference to the church itself as a community of reconciliation. Preoccupation with law and measurement, coupled with this individualistic notion of sin, left Catholics less conscious of collective responsibility and the general sinfulness of the community itself. Likewise, individual sinful actions were often assessed in isolation from the overall pattern of one's life. Bits of behaviour were often given moral labels merely in terms of their physical component, without reference to the full human meaning of the action.

Change in the church
While these various factors have left many Catholics with an inadequate or even distorted notion of sin, it is also true that the confusion they experience is part of the general upheaval in the church since the Second Vatican Council. Changes were not limited to dogmatic theology, liturgy or ecclesiastical organisation, but affected some of the basic principles of Christian morality. The interpretation of the Bible, the nature and extent of the church's teaching authority, and modern insights about human nature, all gave rise to new questions in the area of morality. The old black and white answers were no longer convincing, the lines became blurred, and soon people were confused as to what could be labelled sin, or indeed what sin really meant.

Traditional theology taught that sin was an offence against God. This was a dangerous half-truth because it left people with an ungodly understanding of God. He was feared as the all-seeing eye examining our behaviour to pounce on every last ounce of guilt, with special focus on sexuality. This left us not only with an unhealthy understanding of God's beautiful gift of sexuality and relationship, but with a totally false notion of God, who is essentially infinite love, compassion and forgiveness, not a task-master spying on the intimate lives of his holy people created in his own image and likeness.

Sin is a religious concept
Sin is the word used to describe moral evil when seen in the con-

18

text of religion, as distinct from ethics or civil or criminal law. The Christian ideal is to do everything as done to the Lord, so shortcomings are considered as against a divinely given law, as grieving the Holy Spirit. It is a symbol which expresses our alienation from God. As a symbol it was subject to historical and cultural development, from biblical times to the present day. The cultural conditioning of past centuries was so strong that it almost trivialised the meaning of sin in today's world. The popular press uses the word in reference to sexual misconduct, but seldom applies it to economic oppression or the abuse of power. The catechism definition was clear and workable within the framework of stable, classical culture. But today's Christians are more questioning and critical, less passively accepting of rules and regulations binding 'under pain of sin', especially mortal sin with its implication of eternal punishment. They would like it to make sense in the light of modern experience and without the legalism inherited from the past.

The healthy fear of sin as displeasing to God could often degenerate into a crippling and scrupulous fear of self and a doubting of one's own self-worth. Preoccupation with law and measurement and a kind of lust for certainty left people illequipped to live creatively with tension or to keep a balanced Christian attitude in ambiguous situations. The scandal of 'good-living' Christians supporting an unjust social system, even economic exploitation and cruel repression, raises questions about the primacy of obedience. Since Vatican II the emphasis has changed in our thinking about sin. The starting point is no longer the sinfulness of the creature needing pardon, but the incredible love of God our Creator, Mother and Father, who treasures each of us infinitely, and sees in each one of us the image of Jesus his Son.

The central insight here is that we are most like God in our freedom, that we are created to be free, to grow and develop into the fullness of the maturity of Christ. We do this by saying Yes to the world, to life, to our neighbour, and in and through all of this to God. To say No is to sin, to alienate ourselves from the world, from life, from our true selves, from our brothers and sisters in the human family, and ultimately from God who created us for life, for friendship and love. If the glory of God is the human person fully alive, sin can be seen as anything that violates our human dignity, anything that restricts or blocks our freedom, in ourselves or others.

The negative forces and actions that offend human dignity and lessen human freedom are seen as bad, as evil, as realities to be avoided, to be fought against, but they are not *moral* evils until associated with deliberate human action, the outcome of free human choice. Since sin is moral evil, all that is said of moral evil applies to sin, but is understood in a wider context. It is seen in the context of Christian faith in a God who is love, a God who is not indifferent to how we live our lives and treat our brothers and sisters, how we care for the universe God created as our home. King David's sins of adultery and murder were certainly against a fellow human being and the order of society, but in the moment of conversion he acknowledged them as sins against God, in the words of the psalm: 'Against you, you only, have I sinned and done what is evil' (Ps 51:4).

The Old Testament describes sin as iniquity, guilt, rebellion, disorder, abomination, a lie and folly, but it is always clear that it was essentially a break in the love-relationship with God, a failure to live up to the dignity and destiny intended for us by God. Sin has meaning only in the context of faith. The Jewish people, our ancestors in the faith, continually experienced the presence of God in their history, and in that sense knew God as a wife knows her husband and is known by him. But their response was often one of infidelity, provoking God to complain with all the heartbreak of a deserted husband or wife: 'My people, why do you turn away from me without ever turning back? Not one of you has been sorry for his wickedness ...' (Jer 8:5-7). This is the essence of sin, each one going their own way, seeking their own private ends regardless of others, forgetting that we are members of one family, parts of a greater whole.

Sin and God's forgiveness

The history of Israel's infidelities is a history of sin, but it is equally the story of God's continual never-ending forgiveness and love. No matter how often or how far God's children go whoring after false gods, God is always there gently drawing them back to forgive and heal them. The New Testament does

not enter into details about sin, but presents Jesus as the incarnation of God's love capable of overcoming sin and death. His
healing miracles are signs of his mission. He drew sinners into
fellowship with himself, restored their dignity, and assured
them of full status in his Father's house. St Paul's letters have the
most developed treatment of sin, with the word occurring sixty
times. They stress the results of sin: a hardening of the heart, a
dulling of the moral sense, and a kind of death, because sin is the
denial of life, and sinners die to their own better, potential selves
each time they sin. But Paul equally affirms our freedom in the
face of sin, repeatedly assuring us that we can resist and overcome it by Christ dwelling in our hearts, by his spirit taking possession of our lives.

We cannot be fully Christian unless we feel a real need for
Christ, and it is our sinfulness that brings this home to us. The
English mystic Julian of Norwich was not ashamed to write: 'We
need to fall, and we need to realise this. If we never fell, we
should never know how weak and wretched we are in ourselves, nor should we ever appreciate the astonishing love of our
Maker ... We sin grievously, yet despite all this it makes no difference at all to his love, and we are no less precious in his sight.
By the simple fact that we fall, we shall gain a deep knowledge
of what God's love means ... It is a good thing to know this.'
Indeed, it is a very good thing. It makes all the difference between knowing *about* God and actually knowing God. St Paul
assures us that 'All things work towards good for those who
love God.' Commenting on this, St Augustine added: 'Yes, even
sin', and he knew what he was talking about.

CHAPTER TWO

What does the Bible say?

However weak the sense of sin may be in the world or whatever the distorted notions of it to be found among Christians, one thing is clear. Evil or wrongdoing is described as sin only when it is understood as directed against God. This is a notion that comes from the Bible, where it is a basic concept in both Old and New Testaments. Before considering the areas of inadequacy or confusion in the modern understanding of sin, therefore, it will be necessary to see what the Bible has to say about it. But we must be careful how we interpret the Bible. It is a misleading oversimplification to think of the Bible as God's revelation dictated to the sacred writers. It is more correctly understood as the written account of the religious experience of the Jewish people in the Old Testament and of the Christian communities in the New Testament. These writings are culturally conditioned and must not be interpreted in a fundamentalist way. They were divinely inspired in the sense that not only the experience, but the understanding and recording of it were under the influence of the Holy Spirit. That experience was primarily of the special relationship of intimacy to which they believed God had called and introduced them.

God's love

It involved a worldview that saw the whole of creation, their political history and their personal lives as a working out of that relationship. For them, God was the infinitely-loving, ever-faithful Father who never went back on his word, who allowed them to renew the covenant he had made with them over and over again, in spite of their repeated infidelities. Down through the centuries they had gone 'whoring after false gods'. The Old Testament is the record of their sins, their missing the mark, their continual failure to live up to what God wanted them to be.

22

But it is also the story of God's love, of his initiative in choosing them, and of his loving-kindness in continually caring for them, in spite of their failures. Sin is the foil which manifests God's incredible goodness, his never-ending forgiveness.

Their experience of God reached its peak in their encounter with his incarnate son Jesus, and it is significant that his very name, as explained by Matthew, refers to the forgiveness of sins: 'You shall call his name Jesus, because he will save his people from their sins' (1:21). He began his mission by a call to repentance: 'Be converted from your sins.' He spent much of his time with sinners and outcasts, and just before his death he summed up his mission in the sublime words: 'This is my blood which seals God's covenant, my blood poured out for many for the forgiveness of sins' (Mt 26:28). The good news preached by the early church was not simply that Jesus had risen from the dead, but that in his death and resurrection he had overcome sin, that in him we have the forgiveness of our sins. We ask now: what does the Bible tell us about the nature of sin that it is such a fundamental concept?

God and sin

There is no special word in Hebrew for the theological notion of sin, but the Old Testament uses different words to describe what the Jewish people understood by sin. The most common is the verb meaning to 'miss the mark', not simply a mistake in judgement, but a failure to reach a goal, and this could also be a non-action, an omission. Other words used were iniquity, guilt, rebellion, disorder, abomination, lie, folly. From the contexts in which these words occur it is clear that sin was not simply the transgression of a law, but caused a break in the relationship between God and his people. Israel understood this relationship as a covenant, alliance or pact of love, initiated by God himself. Because of this special choice of God, they were his people and were expected to act as the people of God. The laws they devised for their conduct and for the ordering of their society, whether discovered through their own experience or borrowed from the surrounding peoples, were understood as the law of God, coming from God himself. Failure to observe them meant to miss the mark of God's love. It meant to bring about iniquity, a deviation

23

from how things ought to be, and this meant guilt, the distortion produced by sin. Guilt was thought of as a burden too heavy to bear, a rust that eats into a person's soul and remains engraved on the sinner's heart. The description of sin as rebellion is not to be understood in terms of today's political relationships. In the ancient world the relationship between sovereign and servant was one of beneficence, so rebellion was ingratitude and personal insult, much like the rebellion of a child against the goodness of its parents. When sin is described as folly, this is not meant to excuse the sinner with a 'fool's pardon'. The word foolishness is used not to imply diminished responsibility, but to indicate that the sinner becomes foolish by his sin.

But the basic notion of sin throughout the Old Testament is that of a break in the relationship between God and his people. The relationship in question is not primarily between creator and creature, but that between the divine and human partners in a personal union, a mutual relationship of belonging. Israel actually experienced the ever-present love of God through the long years of its history, and in that sense knew God, as a wife knows her husband and is known by him. In the regular ceremonies for the renewal of the covenant, the people were sprinkled with the blood of the animal offered to God, to signify a kind of blood-relationship between God and his people, to emphasise that they were his family. But sin separates them from him. The prophet thundered: 'It is your sins that separate you from God when you try to worship him. You are guilty of lying, violence, and murder' (Isaiah 59:2-3). Hosea, Jeremiah and Ezekiel describe the people's sins as marital infidelity, disobedience, and pride. Though no action of the creature can really hurt the creator, Jeremiah speaks in God's name with all the sorrow and heartbreak of a deserted husband:

My people, why do you turn away from me without ever turning back? You cling to your idols and refuse to return to me. I listened carefully, but you did not speak the truth. Not one of you has been sorry for his wickedness; not one of you has asked: 'What have I done wrong?' Everyone keeps on going his own way, like a horse rushing into battle. Even storks know when it is time to return; doves, swallows, and

24

thrushes know when it is time to migrate. But, my people, you do not know the laws by which I rule you. How can you say that you are wise, and that you know my laws? Look, the laws have been changed by dishonest scribes. Your wise men are put to shame; they are confused and trapped. They have rejected my words; what wisdom have they got now? (Jer 8:5-9).

The New Testament
This is the background which the New Testament writers took for granted. They used the classical Greek noun *hamartia* and the verb *hamartanein* for sin, but turned them into theological terms by giving them a meaning not found in profane sources. To the Old Testament understanding they added new elements: that sin is not only an individual act, but also a state or condition, that it is a power at work in the world, but it is finally overcome by Jesus. Matthew, Mark and Luke have little to say abut sin, but it is significant that what they do have is usually in reference to forgiveness. They present Jesus as the friend of sinners, embodying by his patience, delicacy and tact, the mercy of God. In these gospels, it is made clear that ritual impurity is not a sin, that sins come from the heart and they alone defile a person (Mt 15:18-19). Sin is compared to the wandering of a son from his father's house (Lk 15:18), but he need only ask for forgiveness and he is immediately received back.

In the writings of John, sin is described as lawlessness, unrighteousness. He who sins is from the devil and is the slave of sin. Sin is the lust of the flesh, the lust of the eyes, and the pride of life. The sinner loves darkness rather than the light. More often than not, John uses the word sin to describe a state rather than a single act.

The Greek word for sin occurs sixty times in the letters of Paul, and it is he who has the fullest theology of sin in the New Testament. For him, sin is universal, something in which every human being is involved. It is first and foremost a state or condition of human nature from which sinful acts come. It is a power which has us in its grip. We are 'under sin' in the same way that a child is said to be under its parents, or an army under its commander. Sin 'lords it over us' like a despot. Sin 'takes us captive' as prisoners are taken in war. It is not merely an external power, but gets right inside us, into our every fibre, so that we become the 'slaves of sin'. But Paul also affirms our freedom in the face of sin. We can resist and overcome sin by Christ dwelling in our hearts, by his spirit taking possession of us (Rom 8:1-17). The New Testament speaks of the consequences of sin. Sin results in a hardening of the heart, a dulling of the moral sense, so that there is less and less reluctance to sin, and thus sin begets sin. It also results in 'death'. According to Paul it was sin that brought death, both physical and spiritual, into the world. Finally, it brings eternal damnation. In Christ's picture of the last judgement, the wicked are sent out of God's sight: 'Depart from me, you condemned.' Jesus himself speaks of the 'unquenchable fire' of Gehenna (Mk 9:43), of the 'eternal punishment' in store for sinners (Mt 25:46), and Paul warns of 'the punishment of eternal destruction, separated from the presence of the Lord and from his glorious might' (2 Thess 1:9). Of course these expressions, even from the lips of Jesus, are not to be taken literally in a fundamentalist sense, as we shall see in chapter 8.

Sins and sinfulness
Throughout the Bible, therefore, sin is taken seriously in all its aspects. It is not the mere transgression of a law, but a mysterious reality at work in the world, a dark power that can be overcome only by God himself, an evil that is finally conquered by the death of Christ. But this mysterious force is also described in terms of its concrete manifestations, in the sinful actions and omissions of individual people and of groups of people.

Though sin was always understood by the biblical writers as 'against the Lord', it was not restricted to religious failures in the narrow sense. It extended to all forms of selfishness, deceit, and exploitation. In the eighth century BC the prophet Amos was quite specific when, in the Lord's name, he castigated Israel for their sins:

Listen to this, you that trample on the needy and try to destroy the poor of the country. You say to yourselves: 'We can hardly wait for the holy days to be over so that we can sell our corn. When will the Sabbath end, so that we can start sell-ing again? Then we can overcharge, use false measures, and tamper with the scales to cheat our customers. We can sell worthless wheat at a high price. We'll find a poor man who can't pay his debts, not even the price of a pair of sandals, and we'll buy him as a slave' (Amos 8:4-6).

Likewise, though the Bible speaks of individual sinful actions, it lays more stress on the sinful attitudes behind them. Paul told the Colossians: 'You must put to death the earthly desires at work in you such as sexual immorality, indecency, lust, evil passions and greed (for greed is a form of idolatry)' (Col 3:5).

Jesus made it quite clear that sin comes from the heart, that it is not a mere surface action: 'The things that come out of the mouth come from the heart, and these are the things that make a person unclean. For from the heart come the evil ideas which lead people to kill, commit adultery, and do other immoral things: to rob, lie and slander others' (Mt 15:18-19). Indeed, the greatest sin is the uncircumcised or stony heart, the hard, obdurate neck that makes people unteachable, impervious to God's call, insensitive to a neighbour's need.

Psychology of sin
The Bible is also quite perceptive on the basic psychology of sin. The third chapter of Genesis, interpreted by Paul and succeeding generations of Christians as a description of the first, or original, sin, is really the story of every sin. The early chapters of Genesis tell us nothing historically about the first humans or what happened at the beginning of time, but they give us the religious meaning of what is happening all the time, not just to the first humans but to all human beings throughout history. We know nothing of the historical condition of the first humans on earth (who appeared over 40,000 years ago), but the paradise story describes God's plan for all people of all times. He created us 'in his own image and likeness'. Our human nature is basically good. Male and female he created us and he sees that we are basically good, that until we mess things up we have no reason to hide or be ashamed. He shares with us his 'dominion over all the creatures of the earth'. He invites us to intimacy with him,

wishes to treat us as friends who 'walk with him in the garden'. But sadly we are not satisfied simply to accept his goodness; we want to be like him in deciding for ourselves what is good or evil. The one thing we cannot have, to be gods, is the one thing we envy and want. This is the essence of all sin, to put self before God, to want something which is not ours, to want it so much that we ignore the consequences to ourselves or others. This, of course, is deception. We are blinded by our selfishness, and it is only afterwards that our eyes are opened, we discover that we are naked and have to hide, from God and from each other. Not only have we turned from God, but we are no longer at peace within ourselves, we are at odds with our neighbour and even the material world itself seems to turn sour on us.

The Vatican Council's key document, on the *Church in the Modern World*, refers to this and relates it to all people:

> People abused their freedom at the very beginning of history. They lifted themselves up against God and sought to attain their goal apart from him ... What revelation makes known to us is confirmed by our own experience. For when we look into our own heart we find that we are drawn towards what is wrong and sunk in many evils which cannot come from our good creator. Often refusing to acknowledge God as our source, we have also upset the relationship which should link us to our final destiny; and at the same time we have broken the right order that should reign within ourselves as well as between ourselves and other people and indeed all creatures. We are therefore divided within ourselves. As a result, our whole life, both individual and social, shows itself to be a struggle, and a dramatic one, between good and evil, between light and darkness (*GS* 13).

Historical development

This is the concept of sin we get from the Bible: our refusal to live according to God's plan, to behave as his children. Because of the special covenant of love which God had established with his chosen people, every deliberate failure to be fully human, to be hospitable, social and just was seen not simply as a misdemeanor, but as sin, as an offence against God himself. Of course, it would be an over-simplification to imagine that a theologically-

"man fully alive"

28

refined notion of sin was present from the beginning of human history, that the concept had no historical development. In fact, all religion is historically and culturally conditioned. God's word in the Bible comes to us in human words, and every word from the moment when humans first learned to speak is culturally conditioned, reflecting the experience and culture of the speakers.

There is no word of God in pure unadulterated form, a-temporal and a-cultural. The biblical descriptions of the creation of the world and the beginnings of the human race are not historical facts, literally true, but stories that teach profound religious truths dressed in the simple thought-patterns of primitive people.

The Israelite understanding of sin developed in keeping with their notion of God. The Jewish people had a special experience of God as a personal being who consecrated them as his chosen ones:

> I am almighty God, obey me and always do what is right and I will make my covenant with you ... I will keep my promise to you and to your descendants in future generations as an everlasting covenant. I will be your God (Gen 17).

This is clear from the earliest of the sacred writings. But, just as every adult still carries within him the infant and adolescent he once was, the Israelites down through the centuries continued to be influenced by more primitive notions of an autocratic, enforcing God, a rewarding and punishing God, a God more interested in his own laws and decrees than in people. Keeping the law brought the material rewards of long life and wealth, while failure brought God's punishment in the form of poverty, misfortune, sickness and death. The modern version of this attitude is the Christian who avoids sin primarily because of the fear of hell, or who does good 'to get to heaven'. Besides, a shift of emphasis often took place. Since all laws (even of hygiene, social order and liturgical services) were interpreted as God's laws, the Jewish religion was in constant danger of being reduced to legalistic formalism: law for its own sake, the letter of the law even at the expense of its spirit.

In this context, sin became an offence against the law rather than a break in one's personal relationship with God. Though originally seen as God's will, God's word, mediating his love, the law at times became almost a barrier hiding the real God from his people. Since one was perfect by the observance of the law, especially as interpreted by the Pharisees, all who did not follow Pharisaic observances were deemed sinners, and in the time of Christ the great majority of simple country people who could not understand or even remember those observances were considered beyond redemption. This attitude trivialises the whole notion of sin, divorces it from responsible morality. Jesus reacted strongly against this legalistic approach and condemned the Pharisees for straining at gnats and swallowing camels whole. Speaking of the Sabbath observance, he reminded them that the law was made for people, not *vice versa*. Over-emphasis on law can stunt moral growth. There are still people today who see morality in terms of what is allowed or forbidden, who seldom ask why, who never wonder whether the laws in question are really God's law in the particular circumstances.

Moral codes in the Bible?
This last point raises another important question with regard to what the Bible has to say about sin. When there is question of 'God's law', we look to the Bible as the revelation of God's will, expecting to find a code of revealed morality, God's own list of what is right and wrong. This over-simplified approach has led to no small confusion in contemporary discussion of moral issues. Biblical quotations are used as arguments against, for example, masturbation, homosexuality and contraception, although it is quite clear that the biblical writers had no conception of these problems as understood today. This 'fundamentalist' approach to scripture is not limited to ordinary Catholics, but is to be found even in official documents of the church.

The clearest and simplest example is in *Casti Connubii*, Pope Pius XI's encyclical on marriage, referring to Genesis 38. The text says:

> Those who, in performing the conjugal act, deliberately deprive it of its natural power and efficacy, act against nature and do something which is shameful and intrinsically immoral. We cannot wonder, then, if we find evidence in the

Sacred Scriptures that the Divine Majesty detests this unspeakable crime with the deepest hatred and has sometimes punished it with death, as St Augustine observes: 'Sexual intercourse even with a lawful wife is unlawful and shameful if the conception of offspring is prevented. This is what Onan, the son of Juda, did, and on that account God put him to death' (nn 54-55).

The text referred to here describes how Onan, in fulfilment of the levirate law, should have raised up children for his dead brother by sleeping with his sister-in-law, but instead spilled his semen on the ground every time he had intercourse with her. Scripture scholars have long since shown that this text says nothing whatever about sexual morality as such; it condemns Onan for his failure to carry out his duty to his dead brother. None of the more recent Vatican documents quote this text when discussing contraception, but neither have they ever explained that Pius XI was simply wrong. This kind of 'reform by amnesia' does real harm to the credibility of 'church teaching'.

The mere fact that a particular practice is related in the Bible as 'God's law' does not mean that it is still binding on today's Christians. In fact, those who quote scriptural texts as the primary basis to approve or condemn various kinds of human behaviour today must read the Bible very selectively. In the Genesis story, Onan is condemned by God for not doing what would be regarded today as totally immoral, namely having an adulterous relationship with his sister-in-law, Tamar. Furthermore, God's design in the story is realised by Tamar tempting her father-in-law into having intercourse with her by pretending to be a prostitute. This is only one of the many cases in the Bible where incest, fornication, polygamy, deceit, etc are presented as part of the divine plan. The same chapter of Deuteronomy which formulates the levirate law obliging a man to sleep with the wife of his dead brother and produce children for him, also has Moses, in God's name, commanding: 'If two men are having a fight and the wife of one tries to help her husband by grabbing hold of the other man's genitals, show her no mercy; cut off her hand' (Deut 25:11).

Even in the matter of obedience there is a Bible text which is revolting to a modern Christian conscience. As lawgiver speaking in God's name, Moses commands:

> Suppose a man has a son who is stubborn and rebellious, a son who will not obey his parents, even though they punish him. His parents are to take him before the leaders of the town where he lives and make him stand trial. They are to say to them: 'Our son is stubborn and rebellious and refuses to obey us; he wastes money and is a drunkard.' Then the men of the city are to stone him to death, and so you will get rid of this evil. Everyone in Israel will hear what has happened and be afraid (Deut 21:18-21).

Old Testament law strictly forbade sexual intercourse during the seven days of the menstrual period, and anyone in violation was to be 'extirpated', executed by stoning, burning, strangling or flogging. The punishment for adultery was death by stoning for both the man and the woman (Deut 22:22) and a woman found not to be a virgin on her marriage night was to be stoned to death by the men of her town (Deut 22:21).

The Ten Commandments

Of course, common sense will immediately see that these barbaric precepts can in no way be accepted as 'God's law'. But the traditionally-minded will go on to explain that we must distinguish between man-made laws which reflect the mentality of a particular age and culture (like those just quoted) and the revealed law of God as expressed in the Ten Commandments. Certainly, there are distinctions to be made between the meaning and importance of different biblical texts, but it does not follow that we can find in the Bible a literal code of 'revealed morality' handed down by God himself, a list of moral laws directly revealed. Most people are aware that the story of Moses being given the stone tablets containing the Decalogue on Mount Sinai is not to be taken literally, but how many realise that, in terms of material content, most of the Ten Commandments were widely known centuries earlier by non-Israelite peoples, and were the common law of Mesopotamia? In formulating the Decalogue, the Israelites drew on the accumulated wisdom of the surrounding peoples as well as on their own experience. Their laws reflect popular morality of the time, and derive from a variety of circumstances and backgrounds. Scripture scholars tell us that in the early history of Israel, the common law concerning the institution of marriage was not very different from what it was in the neighbouring civilisations. Polygamy, legalised concubinage, divorce prevailed there as elsewhere. There was no sociological break with the rest of the ancient Near East. The only real distinction was the specifically religious one, namely the basic values of the society and its understanding of God.

This applies also to the New Testament. Jesus left no detailed code of morality, so Paul and the early Christian communities simply fell back on the moral codes current at the time, which happened to come from the Stoic philosophers. The lists of virtues and vices in Paul's letters are largely the household rules common in his day (Col 3:18-4:1; Ephes 5:22-6:9; 1 Cor 6:9-10). What is special to Paul and the other New Testament writers is the new context in which they presented these lists. The vices and virtues then current in the Greek world were used to describe what is opposed to 'life in the Spirit' and what are the fruits of the Spirit for one who is 'in Christ' (Gal 5:1, 2, 6, 16-25). The New Testament, therefore, cannot give us a direct and simple answer to modern problems like the oil crisis, inflation and poverty, racial conflict, ecology, social justice, birth control, homosexuality, stem-cell research.

Insights from Scripture
The question then arises: if it is a mistake to go to the Bible for 'new bits of morality', specific moral laws directly revealed by God, how are we to use sacred scripture in our understanding of morality, or why bother with the Bible at all? There are many things we find in scripture to inspire and enlighten us in deciding moral issues: God's parenthood and the consequent fact that we are all brothers and sisters in God's holy family, infinitely and equally precious in his sight; the goodness of creation; the world entrusted to our stewardship and responsibility; God's care for all, especially the weak; the dignity of each human person, created in the image and likeness of God; God's patience and never-ending forgiveness; the example of Jesus in his relation to his Father and in his total availability to all people without

distinction; his attitude to evil and his acceptance of the cross; the sermon on the mount; the beatitudes; God's will for the salvation of all people. Any number of insights or themes can be gleaned from the Bible to influence us in our approach to moral problems, to sensitise us to certain values, to colour our outlook and attitude to daily life. We can also be enlightened and helped by studying how the people of God in times past dealt with particular problems, in both Old and New Testaments. But their solutions cannot be the last word for us. In the Bible we can find some concern about fundamental human values, the same values to which we ourselves subscribe. But something else altogether is the Bible's description of historically dated attempts to enshrine these values in laws for human behaviour.

The values are still meaningful and binding, but some of the laws embodying them have little meaning in today's world. Even the values themselves have undergone a change in many cases. For example, we still think that hospitality is a high moral value, but we shrink from the way Lot sacrificed his daughters for the sake of it. When the men of Sodom wanted to have their way with his two visitors, Lot entreated them:

> Friends, don't do such a wicked thing. Look, I have two daughters who are still virgins. Let me bring them out to you, and you can do whatever you want with them. But don't do anything to these men; they are guests in my house, and I must protect them (Gen 19:7-8).

These changes of attitude and understanding are not arbitrary, but are part of the normal process of human growth. From the time of Abraham or Jesus to our own day, there has been considerable development in the conscience of people, without extra bits of directly revealed moral knowledge. The prophets could summon the people of God to a holy war to exterminate enemies, including women and children, and Paul would be surprised at our modern abhorrence of slavery. For centuries popes, bishops and monasteries kept slaves without the slightest scruple. But today's Christians cannot afford to feel too superior, since we still have a long way to go in acknowledging in practice the full human rights of women, homosexuals, etc.

Why quote Paul to the effect that homosexuals are excluded

from the kingdom of heaven (e.g. 1 Cor 6:9), and forget that the Bible also says that 'women are not to wear men's clothing, and men are not to wear women's clothing; the Lord your God hates people who do such things' (Deut 21:5)? This is not meant as petty criticism of the biblical writers, but simply to make the point that the word of the Bible alone cannot give us God's revealed solution to a moral problem. People were confused when preachers labelled things as sins on the basis of a few words from scripture, and until recently they felt disloyal and guilty when tempted to criticise the preacher or the church. We are simply asking the wrong question when we ask: what does God say? and then search the scriptures for the appropriate quotation.

In fact, Jesus himself rejected the formal authority of the scriptures as absolutely binding. Interpreting scripture for his hearers, he did not treat it like other rabbis, drawing out its every implication, but instead opposed one passage with another to show what God's will meant in the present. The people of God in the Old Testament were not handed a code of morality from heaven, but had to discover and formulate it in the course of their experience, according to the varying circumstances of their lives. They refined and perfected it through the centuries. At times it lagged behind that of their pagan neighbours in some respects, while in others it reflected a more refined moral sense. The essential difference between their code and that of their neighbours was not that one was revealed and the other not. In terms of material content, they were practically the same. The distinguishing feature of the Jewish Decalogue was its religious meaning and context. For the Israelites, the Ten Commandments were not simply the rules for peaceful living in community, but the consequence of their being specially chosen by God, their response to his loving initiative in making them his chosen people. The commandments were the concrete expression of the way of life implied in the covenant situation of the whole people of Israel. In this context, the people came to see them, not as discovered by human wisdom through the ages, but as God's gift to them, and in that sense 'revealed'.

Bible not the last word

The ommandments themselves are quite general and flexible. They were sufficient for the needs of a simple nomadic people. But with the growing complexities of agricultural and town life, they needed to be further spelled out. Hence the proliferation of Old Testament laws. But these laws all reflected the circumstances and understanding of their times. Thus, for example, some of the laws governing sexuality are more concerned with justice, with the rights of husband and father, than with sexual life as such, and they consider the woman more a possession of man than a person in her own right. The same is true of the New Testament. Many of its moral precepts are coloured by the culture of the period. Our task is to disentangle the basic Christian attitudes and principles from the particular form in which they are embodied and presented. Jesus did not leave a detailed code of morality, and the New Testament writers did not adhere rigidly to the letter of what he said. Rather, they interpreted, adapted and applied his sayings to new situations. The early Christian communities had to formulate their own specific moral rules in the light of the new life in Christ which they believed they were called to live. The life and words of Jesus would always be a special challenge and example, but faith in him could never dispense his followers from the continuing search for God's will in the concrete. The same is true today. A Bible quotation can never solve a moral problem or end a discussion. The Christian community of today may get special help from the words of scripture, both Old and New Testaments. It will be enlightened, encouraged and strengthened by the presence of the Risen Christ and his Spirit in its midst. But it still has to discover the appropriate rules to meet new situations and needs, to discern God's will in the present.

Sin outside the church

The question: what does the Bible say about sin? could give the impression that sin is a reality only for believers. This is not the case. Sin is a reality for all people, just as redemption and grace are for all. The word sin is not used apart from a religious context, so unbelievers do not normally describe evil-doing as sin. Without belief in a personal God, they cannot see that their misdeeds are a break in the relationship with him. But it does not follow that the reality covered by the word 'sin' has no place in their lives. They are all part of God's plan of salvation. The Bible tells us of God's infinite love for all people. To make explicit his plan for humanity, he chose a special people to be the vehicle of his revelation and self-gift. In the Old Testament he chose a handful of nomads and fashioned them into a people, a close-knit community whom he set apart and consecrated for himself. They in turn consecrated themselves to him by accepting to be his people as he was their God. In founding his church, Christ renewed the covenant God had made with his people. In fact he made a new covenant, so that the church is the new people of God. The Christian community is a people consecrated by God in baptism, specially marked and set aside for a purpose in the world – to be his witnesses, a sacrament or sign of his presence among human beings, not just a sign pointing elsewhere, but an efficacious sign making his presence a here-and-now reality for those who believe. Christians respond to this call by consecrating themselves to him, accepting the challenge to be his witnesses, to try to reproduce in the world something of the life of Christ himself, individually and in community.

But the difference between them and the rest of humanity is not that God is present to them and not to the others, that they have grace and salvation denied to outsiders. The difference, rather, is between explicit and implicit. God is doing explicitly in the church what he is doing implicitly in the world at large. There is no world of 'mere nature', cut off from the supernatural world of God. God and his love and salvation are involved in the whole human world. In the depths of their conscience, all people are called to be good, to be fully human, to grow into the fullness of the maturity of Christ. Christians know this explicitly. Others hear it implicitly in the moral demands of their conscience, and they have the freedom to accept or reject it. To the extent that they respond to this call in fidelity to their conscience, that they go beyond their own selfishness and reach out to others in genuine concern, they are implicitly responding to God and thus growing in the Christ-life, even though the circumstances of their lives may cut them off from any explicit knowledge of God or Christ. Their moral consciousness can develop to a point at which it passes implicitly into religious consciousness, even without their being aware of it. Thus, there can be an implicit awareness of the divine reality even in some persons who profess themselves atheists. Such people are often called 'anonymous Christians'. Their morally good behaviour, therefore, is a growth in Christ and grace, and their evil deeds are sins, though of course they themselves would not describe them as such. There are many people who know little of Christianity but live God-filled lives that are the equal of our canonised saints.

In our discussion of the various factors affecting people's notion of sin in the following chapters, we confine ourselves to those who have a religious context to give meaning to the term. But this should not allow us to forget that non-believers can sin and are caught up in the mystery of sin in the world. On the other hand, we need to be reminded that if we speak of 'anonymous Christians' in the world outside the church, there are also a number of 'anonymous pagans' in the midst of our Christian communities. If 'belief' is to be measured by real commitment to Christ and his gospel rather than by pious practices and mere surface attachment to a church, the line between belief and unbelief may pass through each one of us rather than between classes of people. For that matter, the line between saint and sinner is not simply a division between two groups, but passes through each individual heart, since each one of us is a bit of both. This should cause no surprise, since every Christian is a sinner who is called to be a saint.

CHAPTER THREE

Is it allowed?

For centuries the catechism definition of sin was: any thought, word or deed contrary to the law of God. One of the most widely used summaries of moral theology introduced the chapter on sin with the statement: 'Sin is the free transgression of a divine law. Every law is, in a sense, a derivation from the divine law; therefore, the transgression of any law is sinful.' It is no wonder that for many people morality is often restricted to legality, and that right and wrong are understood in terms of what is allowed and what is forbidden. This infantile attitude was, if not created, at least encouraged, by much of the church's moralistic preaching. Textbooks of moral theology used precisely the kind of language that emphasised law as the primary criterion of morality, the measure of right and wrong. The following quotations are just a few examples: 'The direct taking of one's own life is a mortal sin if done on one's own authority. It is also forbidden to do something from which death will accidentally follow, if one has suicidal intentions in doing it, e.g. to smoke or drink immoderately in order to shorten one's life. Indirect suicide is in itself forbidden, but may be permitted for a proportionately grave reason.' 'Self-mutilation is allowed only to save one's life.' 'Dangerous tight-rope walking, etc. merely for motives of gain or vanity is forbidden, though if practice or skill make the danger remote there would be no mortal sin in such action.' With regard to the obligation of Sunday rest, the same text lists the forbidden servile works, and then goes on to say that 'custom justifies shaving, haircutting, knitting, etc, and it is also permitted to go walking, riding, driving, rowing, journeying, even though these be very fatiguing.' Another textbook uses the same language when speaking of the sixth commandment: 'It is permitted to take baths, to wash oneself, to mount a horse, etc, even if one foresees a possible pollution. In the same manner it is permitted to scratch an irritation of the genital region provided that the itching does not proceed from an excess of semen or the heat of passion. When the cause of the irritation is in doubt, scratching is permitted. If the irritation is slight, it is permitted to scratch even when the scratching may provoke slight sexual stirrings.'

Danger of law

With such an emphasis not only on law as such, but on the multiplicity of laws attempting to cover every conceivable situation, it is no wonder that so many Catholics were confused about the notion of sin. There have been so many changes in the church in recent years that people are no longer sure what is allowed and what is forbidden. Concerned parents complain that their children are no longer taught what is sinful and what is not, and that the commandments are seldom mentioned in religion classes. Some preachers are at a loss to explain the church's laws in today's world, and may even long for the black-and-white precision of the older approach. But this attitude to law is no longer sufficient for an understanding of morality and sin.

Certainly, law is an essential element in Christian morality, and sin is a breaking of God's law. 'Keep the law, and the law will keep you' has a certain attractiveness, and generations of good people have led holy lives with this simple attitude. It makes life easy and straightforward. You know where you stand. All-important decisions are made for you in advance; there is no doubt, indecision or agony of conscience. It also makes for uniformity; everybody is bound by the same law, with no messy exceptions. The good Catholic is easily recognised as the one who keeps the laws of the church. The church itself is clearly marked off from other Christian groups by its distinctive rules and regulations. A good system of laws can make for order, stability and efficiency in society, and the morally good person is normally a law-abiding citizen.

Sin and law

But an exaggerated emphasis on law gave rise to serious inadequacies in people's understanding of morality and Christian living. When sin is primarily seen as the transgression of a law, it is easy to feel that where there is no clear-cut law there can be no question of sin, indeed no moral obligation at all. For example, people often confessed to having missed Sunday Mass, even though they were sick and unable to attend. Although their illness excused them, they still felt obligation and a certain amount of guilt because of the specific law. On the other hand, their marriage could be falling apart because of some personality disorder recognised as the cause of their trouble, but they would not see any sin in their failing to get professional help, because there is no law to the effect that they should see a marriage counsellor on the first Monday after discovering their problem. Again, people might confess to using contraceptives, but fail to realise that sin, and indeed serious sin, may be involved in their savage driving habits, dangerous parking on a corner, their flirting with people at work, their lack of sensitivity towards their marriage partner, their failure to give time to their children, their obsession with their job or hobby. A priest might accuse himself of not praying his breviary, but see no sin in his authoritarian attitude to parishioners, his frequent failure to respect their intelligence or experience as he talks down to them from the pulpit, never listens to them, and generally behaves as though he owned the parish. All sin is idolatry, setting oneself up as the centre of one's world, suiting self without regard for God, for neighbours, for consequences. But in practice most sin consists in simply not bothering about patience, kindness, humility, temperance, and discretion. There is no precise law about these things, so people are inclined to regard them as optional extras reserved for those striving for perfection.

Over-emphasis on law also tended to reduce morality to mere obedience, so that little room was left for conscience and personal responsibility. All one needed was to discover the appropriate law for each situation and assess how far it was binding in the circumstances. Since this was the only exercise of conscience that many people were familiar with, it is hardly surprising that they were confused, and felt let down when confessors told them that they must 'follow their conscience' on a question where the law is a matter of controversy, as in the birth control issue.

When law becomes paramount in morality, the church as a

whole suffers. The church is a very large institution, and like every institution it cannot survive without law. But when law takes pride of place, the church tends to be identified with the institution, and people lose sight of the fact that the church is also a fraternity of brothers and sisters in the Lord, a sacrament of Christ, a herald of the kingdom of God, and a servant of the world that Jesus came to save. These are more than just titles. They are the reality of the church, and the church needs to be experienced in these ways by its members. But pre-occupation with law can block that experience. Over-concern with law is most damaging to pastors and bishops, who can become simply administrators hiding behind the law whenever a difficulty arises and refusing to dialogue with a brother or sister in distress.

Appreciation of law

Law can become impersonal, and its observance mechanical and empty. But its inadequacies and dangers should not lead us to a total rejection of it. For true religion and service to God, we need a real appreciation of it, combined with a critical awareness of its limitations and pitfalls. To savour it in its proper religious context, one should read psalm 119, the longest psalm in the Bible. Almost every one of its hundred and seventy-six verses is in praise of God's law, of its goodness and power, and of the protection it affords:

> Happy are those who live according to the law of the Lord ... I will obey your laws ... I take pleasure in your laws; your commands I will not forget ... Open my eyes that I may see the wonderful truths in your law ... Explain your law to me and I will obey it; I will keep it with all my heart ... Your word, O Lord, will last forever; it is eternal in heaven ... The rules that you have given are completely fair and right ... I will always praise you, because you teach me your law ...

This was the attitude of the early Israelites to law. It was not seen as a burden or an arbitrary imposition by a remote and angry God, but as a privilege and a gift revealed by the God who loved them. To obey it was to be faithful to the covenant, to prosper and be happy, to share in God's wisdom. In the law, God was offering himself, and therefore offering wisdom and life.

The law was wisdom, the knowledge of how true life was to be lived. The response was not so much to learn the law in all its details, as to accept God, to love and serve him with one's whole heart and mind in the concrete circumstances of daily life. As these circumstances varied through the centuries, the law changed and developed. It became a living tradition guiding and directing the people's response to God. The details were gleaned from experience and many of the formulations were copied from the surrounding peoples, but these were always incorporated into a context that lifted them onto a new level, the religious level of the people of God.

Legalism

With such high regard for the law, however, it was not easy to avoid the temptation to legalism and formalism. The law which was meant to be a free response to God, a share in his wisdom, often became an end in itself. It was looked on as God's word, revealing God's mind. But in the attitude of some, it actually became God's mind itself, then took on an objective life of its own within God's mind, and finally outside and even above God's mind. A Jewish rabbinical tradition at the time of Jesus maintained that the law was so sacred that even God himself studied it for a certain length of time each day. When the law became fixed in a canonical legal text, the temptation to absolutise and make it an end in itself became all the greater. The law was so sacred that no prophet, no new Moses could change or replace it. In practice, the law was God, more immediate and more concrete than the real God. The Lawgiver became bound, circumscribed by his own law. All of God was expressed in the law; he became reduced to the law. For the Jewish people, this was the letter at the expense of the spirit. The law had been given to make them free, with the freedom of the children of God. But they used it to avoid the complexity of life and the pain of decision. They abdicated their power to make personal moral decisions. The law decided all questions in advance; they had only to obey. The law was no longer valued because of its relation to God and the covenant, but because the people could rely on it, measure it, obey it and be in the clear before God. This was boasting and complacency. This was the attitude for which Jesus castigated the Pharisees. Likewise, when Paul inveighed against the law, it was not so much against the specific details of its content as against the place accorded it by the Jews, as though the law itself could justify them.

This was a constant danger throughout the whole of the Old Testament. The prophets continually warned against it, and in the liturgical ceremonies for the renewal of the covenant the people were reminded of the kind of God who had chosen them, and the kind of service he required. They were told that true religion was a matter of the heart, and that the Lord wanted worshippers in spirit and in truth. But the very multiplicity of laws tended to exaggerate their importance. It is easy to criticise the scribes and Pharisees for their six hundred and thirteen precepts, and forget that the Christian Church has continued the tradition, and in some ways outstripped the Pharisees, both in the multiplication of its laws and in the intricacies of its casuistry. No society can survive without some organisation, and the larger the society the more complex its body of law. The simple structures that kept the first Christian communities together would not suffice for today's Catholics, who number over a billion in our international church. But somewhere along the line a serious shift of emphasis took place as law developed. Laws which were formulated to guide people in their response to God often reached a stage where they defeated their purpose and became an obstacle.

Defeating its purpose
There are hundreds of examples, but a few will suffice. There is a Christian obligation to pray, and over the centuries the church developed the Divine Office in Latin, originally for choral recitation in the monasteries, but eventually imposed on all in sacred orders. The seriousness of the obligation was such that it was considered a mortal sin, punishable by an eternity in hell, to omit even three short psalms from it. Until the 1960s one could not fulfil the obligation by praying the office in English; it had to be in Latin to avoid mortal sin. This applied even to nuns who did not understand a word they were saying. One wonders how many of these good sisters and priests ever suspected that Jesus was trying to tell us something when he commanded: 'When

you pray, do not use a lot of meaningless words, as the pagans do, who think that God will hear them because their prayers are long' (Mt 6:7). Since the obligation was to 'say' the office, it could not be fulfilled unless the vocal chords actually vibrated, even though no sound was heard. It was further explained that internal attention was not necessary for the essence of the prayer, and that the obligation could be fulfilled even though the prayer was said with freely willed distractions. What a far cry from the teaching of Jesus (Mt 6:5-13).

Similarly, to promote reverence for the blessed Eucharist and dispose people to receive it with due reverence, the church imposed the law of total fast from midnight before holy communion, again under pain of mortal sin. As social conditions changed, people found this more and more difficult, until a stage was reached where the vast majority of Mass-going Catholics abstained from communion, except on rare occasions. The law was so absolute that even the accidental swallowing of a drop of water while brushing one's teeth was enough to bar one from communion. In explaining the law, it was pointed out that the Eucharistic fast could be broken by sucking a drop of blood from a pin-prick or a bleeding gum, but not by biting one's nails, because the latter were not edible, and could not be counted as food.

Pharisees not dead

Younger Catholics will not remember those days and may well be puzzled by it all, but the older generation can recall how scrupulously such laws were observed. They were intended to be helpful, but were enforced far beyond the point where help becomes a hindrance. Loyalty to the church may prompt one to point out the good intention of the legislators and the efforts of commentators to be helpful to people, but one can be forgiven for wondering if this is what religion is all about. The above examples are only a small sample of what was taken for granted as normal; one could easily quote a large number of others that are far more incredible. Law had become such an absolute in the church that the vast majority of the faithful, beginning with bishops and priests, were simply not aware of how faithfully we were following in the footsteps of the Pharisees excoriated by

Jesus. Internationally renowned scripture scholar Wilfrid Harrington OP claims that the clearer the words of Jesus in regard to Christian conduct, the more certainly have Christians done exactly the opposite. The absolutising of law led to excessive casuistry, misplaced priorities, over-emphasis on externals and increasing distance from the gospel message.

We are so accustomed to the bad press the Pharisees are given in the gospels that we forget that they were the religious establishment of the time. The scribes were the lawyers, moralists and theologians of the Jewish community to which Jesus belonged. They were the guides and teachers who spent their lives 'searching the scriptures'. The Pharisees were a middle-class religious party noted for their exact observance of the Mosaic law and of the 'traditions of the elders'. When the law of Moses forbade work on the Sabbath, 'work' had to be defined, so there were thirty-nine basic actions listed as forbidden, including carrying a burden, reaping, winnowing, threshing and preparing a meal. People wanted to know what constituted a 'burden', so it was decided that anything weighing the equivalent of two dried figs came under the ban. When the disciples of Jesus plucked the ears of corn on the Sabbath, they were guilty of several infringements of the Sabbath law (Mt 12). By plucking the corn they were guilty of reaping, rubbing it in their hands was threshing, separating grain and chaff was winnowing, and the whole process was preparing a meal. No wonder the Pharisees condemned them.

But why should we self-righteously applaud when we read of Jesus castigating the Pharisees, and fail to see that in many ways we are no different? The church loses credibility when we insist that of course there is a difference, even if it cannot be seen. A little humility and realism would be much more becoming to the Christian community. The command of Moses against setting up idols, and the words of Jesus about law being for people and not *vice versa*, are not simply for the Jews of the exodus or of first-century Palestine. They are for all God's people in every age, including our own. It would be unChristian arrogance to claim that we have no need of such warnings, that we are above temptation.

Confusion about law

Our reaction to the exaggerations of the past, however, should not be a rejection of law, but a better understanding of its true meaning and the purpose it serves in human living. But this is where the confusion starts, because we hear of God's law and human law, natural law and positive law, church law and civil law, and few of the faithful ever have an opportunity of getting clear answers to their questions: What is law all about? In what sense is it God's law? Is it really a sin to break a law?

First of all, we need to see the context from which law gets its meaning. We are social beings. We not only have a capacity for relating to other people, but we need them. People need people, nobody grows alone. We are what our relationships enable us to be. But if people are allowed to simply bump against each other in a group, pandemonium will follow and nobody will grow. If the physical, emotional, intellectual and spiritual needs of individuals are to be met even on a minimal level, there is need for community, for stability and predictability in the community, for role-definition, and for the recognition of certain rights and obligations. This is what laws are for. Any group of people, if they are to live and work together, soon discover the need for laws to regulate their relationships, so each community formulates the rules it needs.

Positive law

Individuals born in the community, and outsiders coming in, find an already established pattern of behaviour in the community, regulated by traditions and customs, and in modern society by written constitutions and laws. Thus, most people experience law as an imposition from without, something decided and established by an authority external to themselves, demanding obedience. This is commonly called 'positive law', a regulation of human behaviour positively formulated and enacted by the lawful authority for a particular community. Its purpose is to protect basic human rights and freedoms: the right to life, to bodily integrity, to property, freedom of movement, expression and association. It regulates conflicting interests, so that the common good of all will be served. It seems to limit freedom insofar, for example, as it imposes traffic regulations involving red lights and speed limits. But such limitation of freedom provides safety, which in the long run makes for greater freedom for all concerned. This element of limitation may reinforce people's feeling that law is imposed from without. But reflection will show that positive laws are not arbitrary, that most members of the community, if they had to reflect on the needs of the situation, would agree, not only to law as such, but also to the limitations on their freedom, in their own interest and in the interest of all. There is an element of arbitrariness insofar as it makes little difference to the smooth running of traffic whether people drive on the left or the right, but it is recognised that a decision must be made in favour of one or the other to avoid chaos. By having specific laws, carefully formulated and systematically enforced, people are freed from the necessity of deciding at every step what is the best thing to do.

Without such laws, each individual would have to discover individually the best course of action on every occasion, which would involve considerable time spent in collecting and assessing all the facts of the situation, calculating the short-term and long-term results on the individual and on the group of each possible decision. Not everybody would be in a position to know all the facts, or have the experience to evaluate them correctly, or foresee the possible consequences. Nor can we be sure that each one would be sufficiently free of selfishness to think of others and the common good. By formulating a law to be obeyed by all, the community frees the individual members from the burden of such decision-making in a variety of matters, thus freeing them for the ordinary business of living. To live in a law-abiding society where the laws are just, is to experience a high degree of freedom: freedom from the fear of bodily assault and the various forms of exploitation, freedom to travel safely, to possess property and provide for one's future and one's children, freedom to develop one's potential and to grow as a person.

Values before law
It is because people value freedom, order, stability, justice, bodily health, safety, community living, etc, that they enact and accept laws to promote, guarantee and protect these values. The laws themselves may be felt as an imposition and a burden, but the

values they enshrine or protect correspond to our basic needs as human beings. We may grumble at the tax laws, but we do really want the social services of health, education, etc. provided by our tax money. It is values, therefore, which are primary. Laws are secondary or derivative. The kind of laws needed for the safeguarding and promotion of a particular value will vary ac- MS cording to the culture and living conditions of the community. Laws governing taxation and traffic are an obvious example. But even more basic laws can change. For example, human life has always been regarded as a value with a high priority, but respect for life can give rise to very different laws. Thus, in primitive societies subject to frequent attack from enemies, the sick and elderly were put to death by relatives and members of their own tribe. This was not disrespect for life, but to save them from a worse fate at the hands of the enemy, and to save the healthy members from being slowed down in their flight and therefore killed by having to care for the weaker ones. Likewise, in some tribes, foreigners were considered enemies, potential attackers, so it was judged lawful to kill them, a kind of self-defence in anticipation. In our more settled conditions, however, we have laws against euthanasia, foreigners are not killed as enemies, and more and more the death penalty is seen as an inadequate response by the community to lawbreakers.

Besides, not only will respect for the same basic value give rise to different laws through time, but even the values themselves change. There are no values in the abstract. Values exist only in people's minds. They are what people consider worthwhile, what they are prepared to live for, to sacrifice their time, effort and money for, and at times even to die for. Human beings have changed considerably in the course of history, so people grow in their appreciation of basic values, and discover new ones. Thus, the notion of human freedom and dignity strikes a deeper chord in modern hearts than it did in earlier centuries. Slavery could be accepted without question by St Paul and even defended philosophically by St Thomas Aquinas, and the popes had slaves as late as 1800, whereas the very idea of slavery is abhorrent to people today. It was only at Vatican II that the church described the practice as odious, destructive, infamous, a scourge and a poison. It is obvious, therefore, that even values themselves have a history, that they are not static or absolute. It is only recently that people realised that respect for human dignity involves recognising sexual equality between women and men, though we still have considerable distance to go before this is reflected in all our laws.

God's law?

At this point, one might ask: what has all this got to do with sin? The theology text-book quoted at the beginning of this chapter defined sin as the free transgression of a divine law and went on to explain that all law derives from the law of God. Popular preaching often gave the impression that over and above 'human law', as described above, there is a special 'divine law' revealed by God, and that human law is unjust, not true law, not binding in conscience if it in any way contradicts God's law. There is indeed a sense in which this is true, as we shall see shortly. But the impression many people have is that there is a 'law of God' that can be consulted and read off in much the same way as one would look up a point of civil or ecclesiastical legislation. There is an idea of 'God's law' in the minds of some religious people which is at the root of so much confusion in discussions of morality and sin. It is argued that since God is eternal, immutable, all-wise, his law must likewise be eternal, unchanging, and perfect. It is frequently described as 'absolute', therefore binding in all circumstances and admitting of no exceptions.

There are a number of difficulties about such a view. First of all, there is no 'revealed law of God' in the sense of a specific, formulated law communicated directly and verbally by God to any individual or group. Older theology books used to present the Ten Commandments in this way as a revelation to Moses. Theologians explained that apart from the command to keep the Sabbath holy (a positive law of God), all the others were precepts of 'natural law', which could be discovered by unaided human reason. But since they could be discovered only with great difficulty, and yet are so necessary for people's moral life, it was said that God revealed them directly to the human race through Moses. This view rested on a very literal, fundamentalist interpretation of the Bible that cannot be accepted today. Not only do we know that much of the content of the Decalogue (Ten Commandments) in general pre-dates Moses by up to five hundred years, but we recall the many culturally conditioned, and to our modern mind rather barbaric practices, that were proclaimed in the Old Testament as the 'law of God' (e.g. the death penalty for a disobedient son or a wife found not to be a virgin on her wedding night). Nowhere in the Bible can we find a single specific law 'revealed' directly by God; much less can we look on the Old or New Testaments as a handbook or code of revealed morality. Jesus gave us a 'new law', that we love each other as he loves us, but he left it to us to discover what true love means in different situations, and what it demands of us in practice. His law of love is a principle of action, an ideal to inspire us, but not a law as such. Neither the 'law of Christ', nor the example of the life of Christ, nor any of the words of Christ will tell the conscientious doctor when to cease prolonging the life of an incurably ill patient, or show the scientist the precise limits to observe in his stem-cell research.

Official pronouncements of the church on moral matters frequently invoke the 'divine law', and state that certain things are against the 'law of God'. Most Catholics who got beyond the elementary stages of the catechism were told that the commandments of the church were ecclesiastical laws, therefore human laws. Human law was explained as an ordinance of human reason for the common good promulgated by the lawful authority: civil law for the civil society of the state, and ecclesiastical law for the religious society which is the church. But divine law is a higher law, a more basic law, the foundation on which both civil and church laws depend. It was recognised that ecclesiastical laws could change from time to time, that one could be given a dispensation from them, and that in certain circumstances they were not binding (e.g. the Sunday Mass obligation during illness). But the 'divine law' was unchangeable, absolute, allowing no exceptions, and could not be abrogated or dispensed from, even by the Vicar of Christ himself, since a vicar cannot overrule the will of his sovereign.

However, we have the same difficulty with the documents of the church as with the Bible itself. They contain no evidence of a specific, formulated law revealed by God to any authority in the church. They also have the other difficulty noticed in the biblical references to 'God's law', namely that in spite of the divine law being unchanging and absolute, there are so many doctrines officially taught for centuries by the highest authority in the church which were eventually, though quietly, given up as false. Up to the middle ages the church taught that marital intercourse during menstruation or pregnancy was a mortal sin. Intercourse with a sterile wife or by a man in old age was condemned. Pope Leo X, against Luther, declared that the burning of heretics was perfectly in accord with the will of the Holy Spirit. Slavery and the temporal power of the popes were defended for centuries as part of Catholic teaching. Pius VI rejected the 'abominable philosophy of human rights', and especially freedom of religion, of conscience, of the press and the equality of all human beings. Freedom of conscience was dismissed as 'sheer madness' by Gregory XVI and Pius IX, but solemnly proclaimed as a basic human right by Vatican II. For three hundred years *castrati* sang in the Sistine Chapel, spanning the reigns of thirty-two popes, but not one of them spoke out against the practice. In his encyclical *Pascendi Dominici Gregis* (*Feeding the Lord's Flock*, 1907) Pius X, a canonised saint, raged against '... that most pernicious doctrine which would make of the laity a factor of progress in the Church' (n 27).

Natural law

Does it follow, therefore, that there is no such thing as a 'law of God'? Yes, if we mean a set of specific laws already formulated, needing only to be read off as occasion requires. There are no such laws in the Bible, or in church documents. If we claim that they exist in God's mind, we have the problem of discovering them, because God's mind is in no way open to our inspection. Nevertheless, throughout the ages people have always appealed to a justice higher than law and against which all human law must be judged. It is spoken of as the unwritten law, the natural moral law, the law of God. St Paul says that the gentiles have this law written in their hearts (Rom 2:15). In a very real sense, therefore, there is a 'law of God'. Human beings are not a law unto themselves, the sole arbiters of right and wrong, but we are dependent on God, our creator. In the physical world, we discover a whole series of laws built into the very nature of things, the laws of physics, chemistry, biology, etc. Insofar as we formulate our discoveries into laws, they are simply a description of the internal structure of the universe which we can come to know more accurately with the progress of science, but which we have no power to change. These laws (e.g. gravity, aerodynamics, the laws of plant, animal or human reproduction) simply describe the nature of things, the way things are and behave. We ourselves are part of this created world, and we are subject to the same laws insofar as we are physical and living beings. These are simply the laws of nature, not a moral law.

But humans are a special kind of living being. We are capable not only of seeing how things are, but because of our powers of conceptual thought and free choice, we also know how things *might* be, and in some cases how things *ought* to be. When it comes to painting a house, for example, we can freely choose from a variety of colours. Our final choice may be a matter of personal taste and preference. But in our dealings with our fellow human beings, our choice of action will be influenced by an awareness of the fact that we ought not to deceive, exploit or murder them. This awareness will have come to us through the laws explicitly formulated by the community (e.g. the Ten Commandments). But to the extent that we have reached some degree of moral maturity, we will be convinced that behind the particular law there is a basic human value at stake, a value we must respect if we are to be true to our nature. We will have experienced some basic need in our own nature which must be met if we are to grow as human persons. There are physiological needs (food, warmth, etc), safety needs, the need to love and be loved, to belong, to have roots in a community, to be esteemed by our fellow human beings, to be self-determining and self-actualising. The meeting of these needs brings us satisfaction and fulfilment as persons, so down through the centuries society has formulated laws to ensure that they will be met. Since these laws are determined by the basic needs of human nature itself, and not the eccentricities of isolated individuals, they are referred to as the 'natural' moral law, the law governing human behaviour based on our very nature as human beings. Since we do not create our own nature, but discover it already shaped by God our creator, with its in-built needs and direction, the natural moral law is often described as 'God's law'. Since we cannot read God's mind directly to discover his law, we can find it reflected in his creation, in the same way that we can guess the blueprint in an inventor's mind by studying the machine he produced.

Blueprint theory

This 'blueprint' or 'maker's instructions' theory of natural law has given rise to misunderstanding and is responsible for much of the confusion in discussions of moral issues. Because 'human nature' can be studied and described in the same way as the nature of animals, plants or non-living things, the natural moral law is often compared to the laws of physics, chemistry, physiology, etc, clear, fixed, stable, needing only to be 'discovered' in human nature. But this is to leave out of account the most distinctive feature of human nature, namely our God-given creative human intelligence and free will. Though our basic needs remain the same, our nature is not something static and fixed for all time. The human person is a being of possibilities, and we develop and in a sense create our nature as we decide among these possibilities. Inwardly, we change each time we adopt a new image of ourselves or get a new understanding of ourselves. For example, our understanding of our body, of our sexuality, or of our relationship to the material universe is radically different from what it was in primitive times. Outwardly, we change insofar as we fashion instruments and technology that become as it were extensions of ourselves and we change the world we inhabit. Many of our inventions bring about a whole new civilisation, though it may not be realised at the time. Thus, printing was first thought to be merely a new way of reproducing books, and the motor-car just a faster means of travel, but both of these inventions transformed society, and in a sense our own human nature. Today's computer world and information technology is an even more striking example. Thus, change is an essential part of our unchanging nature. It is a mistake to imagine that God created an original human nature at the beginning of time, to which any subsequent development must be considered an addition, something almost artificial.

The fundamentalist understanding of human nature tends to give an exaggerated importance to our physical and biological nature in determining moral norms. The impression is given that we can best discover God's plan for human beings by studying our human functions in their natural state, prior to any intervention by us. Thus, speech is for communicating knowledge, eating for the conservation of health, and sex for reproduction and the continuation of the species. But this approach ignores the fact that all these activities are human, and have their full human meaning only in a human context, which includes intelligence, free will, human relationships and the whole world of culture and civilisation. The laws governing these activities insofar as they are physical are not moral laws, but merely physical or physiological laws. They tell us nothing about how these activities are to be used for responsible self-development and growth as persons, and this is what morality is all about. For most of its two thousand year history, the church claimed that the primary purpose of human sex was procreation, while the secondary purpose was the 'alleviation of concupiscence'. It is only since Vatican II that official teaching has rejected this subordination and recognised that the two purposes are equal since sexual intimacy and the quality of the relationship are as much at the heart of marriage as the physical production of offspring. In fact, in a very real sense the intimacy of 'two in one flesh' is far more important as the very essence of marriage (as taught by Genesis and Jesus) than procreation, which is only intermittent and indeed totally absent in many marriages.

What can be read directly in human physical or biological nature is nothing more than facts (like the laws of gravity, chemistry, or aerodynamics, etc.), namely how nature works spontaneously, without human interference. For example, nature, through the production of prolactin causes ovulation to be suspended during the early stages of lactation in a woman who has given birth, and the same effect is produced by taking contraceptive pills. Both of these are facts of nature. The fact that the latter involves human intelligence and skill to produce the appropriate chemicals in the laboratory does not make it less natural, since the ingredients of the pill combine in the laboratory according to the laws of chemistry and they function in the woman's body to inhibit ovulation according to the laws of physiology, and our human creative intelligence which discovers and applies these laws is itself part of our human nature. But 'nature' does not tell us whether it is morally better to make use of one rather than the other of these facts of nature. That one happens to be described as 'artificial' is not sufficient ground for moral condemnation, otherwise tranquillisers and most of the techniques of modern medicine would be immoral, not to mention cutting nails and dyeing hair. To decide what is morally good, we need to understand the meaning and importance of the particular activity or fact of nature in the totality of the human person as such. Thus, which method of birth control is morally right for a couple in the exercise of responsible parenthood will depend on a variety of factors, and not simply on whether or not it is 'artificial'. The encyclical *Humanae vitae* lamentably fails to understand this simple and basic fact.

A further indication of the weakness of this oversimplified approach to natural law can be found in the variety of practices condemned for centuries as unnatural, therefore against the natural law. Writers of the Eastern Church (Origen, Clement of Alexandria, Basil) prohibited third and fourth marriages as against natural law. Many of the earlier western writers forbade even killing in self-defence on the same grounds; it was left to Augustine to define the distinction between justifiable homicide and murder. Clement thought both ear-rings and nose-rings equally forbidden by the law of nature. Tertullian could not endure the actor's make-up, or the garland of flowers, because they were unnatural and, as he said, 'our God is a God of nature'.

It is easy to smile at these examples from history, but is there not a moral obligation to learn from history? Do we have to wait another century or more before asking whether many of the things condemned today as sins against the natural law are really such? At least 80% of Catholics are not convinced of the current teaching on artificial contraception and the thousands of committed married couples who were crucified in conscience by it and were refused absolution in confession are deeply angry at the injustice of their morally responsible decisions about marital intimacy being labelled as sinful where no sin can be proved.

Criticism of the 'blueprint' theory does not mean that there is

no such thing as natural law. It is simply to warn against expecting God to communicate his will through a particular channel
like the physical nature of human sexuality, expecting to be able
to read off specific precepts of moral law from an examination of
our biological, physiological, psychological or sexual make-up.
All that can be read like this in our human nature is the capacity
to ethicise, the power to make decisions about right and wrong
and to feel bound by them. What those decisions will be in specific areas will depend on a variety of factors, but they are not
determined in advance simply by the biological facts.

However, we can speak of a modified version of the 'maker's
instructions' theory insofar as we discover basic needs and potentialities in human nature that simply cannot be ignored, and
these give us some general insight into values like freedom, responsibility, sociability, love, etc. In striving to promote and pre-
serve these values, experience and reflection will enable us to
formulate some general principles like: treat others as you
would wish to be treated yourself, some arrangements should
be made for the preservation of life, for the regulation of the sex
instinct, for the organisation of the family and of society. These
principles may seem very vague, but they are the basis on which
we work out more detailed norms for moral behaviour. But the
further norms will vary according to changing historical circumstances, both because the same basic value may be served in different ways, and our understanding and appreciation of some
values may change. Thus, in a given set of historical circumstances (economic, social, cultural), polygamy might be the best
norm for family life, as it was for centuries in primitive societiès,
whereas nowadays we look on monogamy as best serving the
values of human dignity and family relations.

Absolute norms?
Does this mean that there are no absolute and unchanging moral
norms? In fact, it is not very helpful to speak of *absolute* norms.
The expression is confusing insofar as many of the precepts
commonly regarded as absolute actually do admit of exceptions.
Thus, in spite of the precept: Thou shalt not kill, we justify
killing in self-defence and we accept a theology of the just war.
Artificial contraception is said to be 'intrinsically evil', i.e. in all

circumstances and of its very nature immoral, and yet the Vatican allowed nuns threatened with rape in the Congo to take contraceptive precautions, and many hierarchies say that married couples may choose whatever method of birth control their conscience finds best, provided they avoid abortifacients and whatever would offend the human dignity of the partners. It was the constant teaching of theologians that a married couple are justified in interrupting intercourse if children come on the scene, but if all forms of contraception except abstinence during the fertile days are decreed to be 'intrinsically evil', then even this exception is 'against the natural law', and therefore forbidden by God. The very phrase 'intrinsically evil' attached to actions like lying and contraception is a reflection of the old blueprint theory of natural law, with its clear-cut, black-and-white, easily measured moral rules read off from the physical facts of nature. The phrase immediately conjures up the notion of an absolute norm, admitting of no exception. But it is extremely difficult to find such norms, at least understood in this sense, and this is the sense most people take to be intended.

Loyalty to the church does not require that we continue to use a phrase from a bygone age simply because it is consecrated by long usage. Loyalty to God and to his call that we serve God's people demands that we cease using terminology that confuses people. An action considered in total isolation from motive and circumstances is a mere abstraction, with no human meaning, and without its human meaning it can have no moral label. If phrases like 'intrinsic evil' need the involved reasoning of skilled theologians to explain that it does not really mean what it says, and at the same time that it nearly does, it were better dropped altogether. Perhaps it would be going too far to say that there are *no* absolute norms, but if there really are, they are extremely few. For example, it is impossible to envisage circumstances in which the torturing of innocent children would be justified. But is it really necessary to formulate absolute moral norms in order to bring home the absoluteness of the call to be morally good? Rather than speak of absolute moral norms and intrinsically evil actions, it is less confusing and more helpful to discover and develop the constants in human behaviour, the values which provide an overall direction and order in our human development.

Lust for certainty

The multiplication of absolute moral norms is part of the human lust for certainty. This lust for certainty is part of our human nature, but too often the tone and manner of church teaching pandered to it and encouraged it. Psychologist Erich Fromm warned that certainty can be a dangerous and dehumanising thing, and the quest or lust for certainty can block the search for true meaning. We Catholics can be more prone to it since we belong to a church that speaks with so much authority. We might learn a little more humility if we recall the views of saints and theologians that were taken as certain because they came from such authorities. A few examples: Clement of Alexandria: a woman should cover her head with shame at the thought that she is a woman. St John Chrysostom (died 407): woman is a necessary evil. St Jerome (died 420): women are the gate of hell. St Augustine (died 430): women are not made in the image of God. Pope St Gregory the Great (died 604): woman's use is two-fold: animal sex and motherhood. St John Damascene (died 750): woman is a sick she-ass ... a hideous tape-worm ... the advance-post of hell. It is easy to smile now at these prejudices, but the writers reallly believed these myths and proclaimed them with absolute certainty. Lest these facts be dismissed as 'water under the bridge,' best forgotten quietly, we should remember that Pius XI in *Casti Connubii* warned against trusting human reason alone to understand natural law in the area of marriage, 'where the inordinate desire for pleasure can attack frail human nature and lead it astray'. Pius XII in his address to Midwives (1956) explicitly denied the unitive meaning of intercourse. He said: 'The truth is that marriage is not ordered by the will of the Creator towards the personal perfection of the husband and wife as its primary end, but to the procreation and education of new life. The other ends of marriage, although part of nature's plan, are not of the same importance as the first, still less are they superior' (48). The attitude of these two popes is a far cry from the solemn official teaching of the church in the Second Vatican Council's document on *The Church in th Modern World.*

This lust for certainty is understandable as part of our moral concern, but not very helpful in striving for moral maturity. The attempt to formulate a long list of absolute norms would defeat their purpose by providing a false sense of security. It is true of course that many insights with regard to human conduct have a lasting value and will be passed on from generation to generation, so that we do not have to call everything into question on each occasion. But the norms we formulate are no more than general guidelines, reminders that an important value is at stake. They are not meant to bypass conscience or save us the trouble of thinking. We cannot be satisfied with prefabricated solutions from the past, especially as answers to questions which were never asked in the past. The basic moral call is to grow, to become actually what we are potentially. Insofar as we are continually changing and are faced with new questions, we are called to find new answers. On the basis of experience, inquiry and insight, we must discover which of the various possibilities that present themselves are right, reasonable, human, which of them enable us to grow as persons. It is a flight from personal responsibility to imagine that answers can be found ready-made in scripture, church documents or papal statements no matter how often repeated, although we can get valuable insights from these sources. The Second Vatican Council reminds us that the pastors of the Church do not always have solutions to every problem which arises, and admits that, in the complicated and rapidly changing world of today, the church needs special help from experts in various sciences in order to 'listen to and distinguish the many voices of our times, and to interpret them in the light of God's word' (*Church in the Modern World*, n 44). The weakness of *Humanae vitae* is that it totally ignored this sound advice. The world's bishops gathered in council were not allowed to discuss it because a papal commission had been established to study the matter. This commission, including cardinals, bishops, lay married people and various experts voted overwhelmingly that there could be no objection to artificial contraception. Even the four clerics of the minority opinion publicly admitted that they could find no proof for their position except to warn that changing the teaching would be a disaster for the church, implying that the church had been seriously in error in the past, and it was this fear that drove Paul VI to compose his text.

Natural moral law, therefore, is not an external law or set of precepts to be read off from human nature and absolutely obeyed. Rather it is an internal law, functional, dynamic, flexible, not a list of regulations and commands, but a basic thrust towards self-determination and fulfilment as a person. It can be called God's law insofar as he created our human nature with its fundamental needs, its irrepressible appetites of heart and mind: for self-preservation, for endless intellectual inquiry, for social living, for searching for God. But the best and most human ways in which these needs are to be met, and therefore the norms to guide us in meeting them, have not been spelled out directly and verbally by God in advance. They have to be discovered by us our own God-given, creative intelligence, from our collective experience, inquiry, reflection and decision, and this is an ongoing process. The moral call is to be faithful to the demands of each step in this process.

Continual discovery

It is clear from all this that neither in sacred scripture, nor in the official pronouncements of the church, nor in what is called natural moral law, can we point to a set of precepts and say: 'This is God's law' in the sense of a directly revealed code of morality. This simple fact ought to alert us to the danger of idolising law, allowing it to take the place of God himself. Our very concern for the sanctity of God and our respect for his will could well tempt us in that direction, as it did the Pharisees. Our lust for certainty can lure us along the same path; we would like to know where we stand before God, how far we can go before getting into the area of sin, etc. But this is not moral maturity.

There is a presumption in favour of law, that it is a good law, that it serves the purpose for which it was formulated and enacted. In general, we trust the legislators in both church and state, and we trust the wisdom and experience of previous generations, as we accept the laws handed down to us. But obedience to law can never be the whole of morality. To be morally mature is not simply to do what we are told, but to make our own the value which the particular law is intended to protect or promote, and to act from conviction. The real authority of any law, therefore, is not simply the will of the legislator, but the human value at stake (e.g. truthfulness, justice, order in the community, love for each other). Through passage of time and change of circumstances laws may cease to serve the value originally intended, in fact they may even come to defeat their purpose. This is true not only of positive civil law and ecclesiastical legislation, but even of norms claimed to be God's law as revealed in the natural moral law or in the Bible. Such laws lose their authority. Insistence on them creates a credibility gap for leaders. Blind obedience to them stunts moral growth in the individual. Failure to see this is sinful neglect on the part of the community, a refusal to read the signs of the times as an ongoing revelation of God's call.

Coping with change

A basic weakness in our church teaching is that it practically never admits failure in the past, but relies on reform by amnesia when the teaching changes, quietly and conveniently forgetting the many dreadful things solemnly taught in the past. For centuries married couples were told that it was a mortal sin to have intercourse during pregnancy or menstruation because until the discovery of the ovum in 1845 sperm was thought to contain the whole embryo (*homunculus*, little man), so that any waste of seed outside the vagina, even in wet dreams, was thought to be a kind of homicide. Pius XII in his Address to Midwives in 1951 dismissed the idea that sex fosters mutual love in marriage and implied, with St Augustine, that it came from the lust caused by original sin. These assertions were based on faulty physiology and psychology and make no sense in today's world. More recently Paul VI's *Humanae vitae* has no convincing proof that artificial contraception is immoral, but feared that admitting this would imply that the church was seriously mistaken in the past. The church would gain enormously in credibility if it had the humility to admit these sad but true facts of history.

It is true to say that sin is a transgression of the law of God in the sense that sin means a refusal to grow into what God wants us to be, a failure to grow into the fullness of the maturity of Christ. But it is an oversimplification to limit sin to the transgression of a law. In Paul's words, law can convict us of sin insofar as it points out to us the areas and sometimes even the ways in which we fail to live up to the Christian ideal. It can spell out the minimum requirements of what God expects of us. But God's call, to the individual and to the whole community, is an ongoing one that cannot be confined to a set of laws, any more than a love relationship between two people can be adequately described by a legal contract. To respond to that call is to grow, but the pattern of our response is something to be continually discovered in the changing circumstances of our lives. It is not enough to examine ourselves in the light of a set of laws and ask how we keep them. It is not enough to ask: what am I doing? We must also ask: what is the doing doing to me? What kind of person am I becoming as a result of what I am doing? Laws can help us to recognise God's call, they can educate our conscience by the insight they give us into human values, but they can never be the full measure of our response, and much less can they ever take the place of the God to whom we respond. In the light of the church's long history of insistence on law and obedience, and its frequent lapses into pharisaism and scribalism, it could do with a healthy dose of relativism in order to relativise some of our false absolutes. We can still joyfully sing the praises of God's law in psalm 119, provided we preface it and regularly intersperse within it the first of God's Commandments: 'I am the Lord your God ... worship no god but me' (Deut 5:6-7).

Obedience and law

In the Genesis myth of the first humans in paradise their original sin was disobedience, their refusal to obey God's law. Obedience to law is generally recognised as virtue, but in fact obedience as such is morally neutral, and there are situations where true virtue calls for disobedience. The recently beatified Austrian peasant Franz Jägerstätter is on the way to canonisation in spite of his refusal to obey his parish priest, his bishop and most of the German bishops, when he would not serve in Hitler's army, because of his conscientious belief that a Christian should not support evil. Church representatives told him that he had a duty to defend his country, and that the government was in a better position to decide what was good or evil in this situation. Because he believed he was doing God's will in following his conscience he was beheaded by the Nazis in 1943. His conscientious disobedience took tremendous courage because for centuries the church insisted on uncritical obedience to all its teaching. Its failure to encourage independence of mind among its members led to massive acquiescence in evils like the Nazi atrocities and the brutal dictatorships of Latin American. Historically, in fact, the church's reliance on total unquestioning obedience undermined authentic moral development among Catholics. Its unChristian treatment of theologians judged insufficiently obedient to 'church teaching' meant considerable loss of credibility for the Roman Church. Its insistence on absolute obedience led to a concern for power and centralisation which leaves little room for gospel humility. In spite of the wonderful vision of Vatican II, the church is more centralised and authoritarian than ever, with no facilities or structures for input from God's holy people who *are* the church. At the end of the seventeenth century the popes appointed bishops for only 24 dioceses around the world, but the pope now personally appoints bishops for 3000 dioceses in the world, so it is difficult to see how they can be representatives of the local churches. The exaggerated emphasis on total obedience in our church is not conducive to the development of moral maturity

It should be obvious by now that law is not the absolute that many Christians have taken it to be, though it will always have an essential place in civil society and in the Christian community of the church. What has been said so far should provide the beginnings of an answer to our last question: when is it a sin to break a law? A fuller answer may emerge when we discuss the question of measurement of sin and the ways in which the church should preach morality.

CHAPTER FOUR

How far can I go?

The first reaction of many traditional Catholics to the question: 'Is it a sin?' was to wonder: 'Is it allowed?' Not infrequently, this was followed with the query: 'How far can I go?' 'Law' played a dominant role in many people's understanding of morality. This is understandable insofar as laws are an attempt to spell out what the morally good response ought to be in various situations. But it is not easy to put a stop to the spelling out process. People want to know what a law means, to what extent it is binding. Religious authorities thus found themselves obliged to go into the measuring business, with the best intentions and full of pastoral concern, but with results that were often less than desirable.

In the Old Testament the simple precepts of the Decalogue were teased out until they became the six hundred and thirteen 613 prescriptions observed so punctiliously by the scribes and Pharisees. These explained, for example, how far one might walk on the Sabbath without infringing the commandment, and what circumstances might justify one in stretching it. Casuistry, or the art of applying general principles to individual cases, is necessary in order to make morality practicable, but it can also reach a point where it becomes a means for getting around the law. Thus, if the law allowed a journey of a thousand paces from home on the Sabbath, one could establish a temporary domicile by placing a pile of one's old clothing at that distance from home on the evening before, and one would then be able to cover twice the normally allowed distance and still observe the letter of the law. In the Catholic tradition, the Lenten fast allowed only one full meal and two collations or snacks in the day. The relative measure applied to the latter was that together they should be less than one full meal, so in order to get full value from them, one had only to increase the quantity of the main meal.

How much is a sin?

The Council of Trent imposed the serious obligation of confessing all mortal sins in detail, so the faithful needed to know exactly when a sin was mortal. For many people, the question: 'How far may I go before it is a sin?' was extended to include: 'How far may I go before it becomes mortal?' With the multiplication of church laws there was an increasing demand for theologians and pastors to mark out clearly the boundaries of sin and the dividing-line between mortal and venial. One doesn't have to be a centenarian to recall the casuistry about Sunday Mass, fasting, sexuality, to mention only a few areas. A venial sin was committed by voluntarily missing an unimportant part of the Mass, e.g. up to the gospel or after the communion. To miss both of these or the consecration alone would be mortal. With regard to the law of fasting, it was common teaching that it was permitted to interchange the noon and evening meals, and for a just reason one might also interchange breakfast and lunch. To interrupt the principal meal for more than half an hour without reason would be a venial sin, but should the interruption last more than an hour it would be mortal. For a proportionately good reason (e.g. to assist the dying, according to the textbook) one could interrupt dinner for several hours. As for the spirit and letter of the fasting law, it was held that if one had eaten two full meals on a fast day, either deliberately or by mistake, one could no longer observe the fast and, therefore, might eat as much as one wished afterwards.

A textbook reprinted in the nineteen sixties states categorically that 'kissing the private or semi-private parts of the human body is gravely sinful', without any distinction between married or unmarried people. The same manual teaches that it is seriously sinful to look at animals mating, though less serious if it is at a distance or it is a question of small birds. On this kind of logic David Attenborough's magnificently beautiful nature films would be serious occasions of sin, to be avoided. In the matter of justice, the 16th century Scottish theologian, John Major, taught that to steal up to five grains of corn from a rich man's harvest was no sin, from six to ten was a venial sin, and anything more than ten was mortal.

Once involved in the measuring business, it is hard to stop.

The original intention and concern were understandable; people need guidelines and directives. But the ultimate consequences in practice could be ridiculous. The idea of adding the tail-end of one Mass to the beginning of another in order to make up the amount specified in the Sunday obligation does not easily fit into our contemporary understanding of Eucharistic liturgy. It is not just today or yesterday that people found it hard to believe that a devout, good-living Catholic could be in hell for all eternity for missing one Sunday Mass or eating just one sausage on Friday. The teaching authorities in the church seemed quite happy to leave people with that impression. But today people will no longer accept that this is the case simply because the church says so. They may be confused in their groping for a more meaningful understanding of sin, but they are very conscious of the shortcomings of the older approach, and are particularly unhappy at the consequences of some of the older teaching.

Legalism and complacency
Over-emphasis on law and measurement can lead to legalism, minimalism, complacency and scrupulosity. We recall Jesus' condemnation of the scribes and Pharisees for their exaggerated reverence for the law and their minute measuring of it, and we know that the Christian community has not always escaped the same temptation. A new insight, a new discovery in Christian experience can be robbed of its vitality when legalism takes over, when it is frozen into a law and rigidly imposed. It has often been remarked that the worst thing that could happen to the documents of the Second Vatican Council would be to transform them into a new code of canon law. Minimalism is to be found in people who feel that there is no sin where a matter is not covered by law or cannot be easily measured. This explains why so many people confessed to missing part of Mass or eating meat on a day of abstinence, but seemed oblivious to the possibility of sin in their insensitivity to their married partner, their lack of concern for the underprivileged, or their share in the atmosphere of prejudice and discrimination in their community or work situation. Basic attitudes are not easily measured or legislated for, so they were frequently forgotten in an examination of

conscience. With so much emphasis on identifiable and measurable sins, less attention was paid to general sinfulness, either in the individual person or in the community as a whole.

Complacency and harsh judgement of others are always a danger for the law-abiding citizen and the conscientious Christian, but the danger is increased when fidelity is measured in terms of precise law, and morality is seen more in terms of quantity than quality. When morality is spelled out in so many laws, it is as though each law earned a certain number of marks, like questions in an examination, so that one's total of credits could be banked to one's account in heaven. With this attitude, it is easy to give the impression that one can score full marks, that one may go before God with an easy conscience and claim one's reward. Jesus had little time for this attitude, and in his story of the Pharisee and the publican he made it clear that quantity counts for little. Measuring one's own goodness by the yardstick of law, it is difficult to avoid the temptation to measure the failures of others by the same law and take comfort from the contrast. But the goodness preached by Jesus is not measurable in terms of quantity at all. What he looks for is the *quality* of our conduct, that it reproduce something of his own basic attitude – in Paul's words, that we 'have that mind which was in Christ Jesus'. This may be present in actions that, objectively speaking, hardly seem virtuous at all, as in the case of many neurotics, and be almost totally absent in the acts of politeness that are merely the result of good breeding and expensive education. Only God can judge where each one of us stands in his sight. Since he alone is good, and our own goodness is his gift to us, none of us can afford to be complacent or presume to judge our neighbours because they don't measure up to our standard.

Scrupulosity
If Jesus had little time for the complacent, he would surely be very sympathetic to the scrupulous. There are good, conscientious people afflicted with this psychological problem, and our multiplicity of laws and concern for measurement provides a fertile field for them to indulge their weakness and intensify their suffering. A Roman psychiatrist with an international clientele once remarked that of all his patients suffering from

this problem, only Roman Catholics had religious scruples. No matter how much advice and counselling they are given, they still agonise over whether a particular thought, word or deed was a sin, and whether it was mortal or venial. Added to the ordinary pain of indecision and compulsive worry, there is the awful fear of eternal punishment in the background. If such people did not have a religious upbringing which laid such emphasis on law and the precise measurement of sin, there is no guarantee that they would be free of the psychological disturbance of scruples, but at least their problem would not be aggravated. It would focus on other things, for example on checking and re-checking that a door is closed.

Emphasis on precise measurement in the assessment of sin came to some extent from the church's experience of the sacrament of penance. Not only did the faithful have the obligation to confess all serious sins according to number and kind, but the confessor was obliged to see that they did. The Roman Ritual, in its instructions on this sacrament, stressed the role of the confessor as physician and judge. The moral theologians spelled out more particularly the latter function. A textbook widely used in the sixties puts it: 'As judge, the confessor must pass judgement on the penitent before absolving him, and for this reason it is sometimes necessary to ask questions. In passing judgement the priest must consider both the sins and the disposition of the penitent. Sins are judged according to their quantity and quality. The duty to ask questions, to insure the integrity of the confession, is grave.' While most confessors were sympathetic and fatherly in dealing with penitents, some, through a scrupulous sense of responsibility or impelled by other subconscious motivation, applied a kind of third degree questioning that reinforced people's concern with measurement. For some, the sacrament was almost a court of law in which the priest was like a public attorney looking for an exact reconstruction of the crime, a judge trying to establish the precise degree of culpability, so that every last ounce of guilt could be accounted for. The new rites for this sacrament of reconciliation show a very different emphasis.

The 'sin-grid'

It would be unfair to paint a caricature, but if we are to be helped to a more mature understanding of morality and sin, it is necessary to acknowledge the weakness of the over-simplified older approach. It had the merit of being clear, easily taught, easily measured, easily supervised – at least in appearance. But a price had to be paid for this false clarity and unexamined security. Casuistry tended to isolate the individual sin from the overall behaviour of the penitent. Fidelity to God was split up into detailed, individual actions, taking attention away from the sinfulness of basic attitudes, trends and dispositions. The 'sin-grid' for examination of conscience established lists of sins individually registered and catalogued, with their varying degrees of seriousness: mortal and venial, sins of weakness and sins of malice. Not only was there an individualistic approach to sins in the life of an individual person, but this carried over into an individualistic approach to the individual sinner apart from the community. In spite of the doctrine of the Mystical Body of Christ, little attention was paid to the darker side of the coin, to our solidarity in sin, to the sinfulness of a whole community. In the area of confession, it was easy to think that we could pay our fine, make restitution, merit forgiveness, and forget that God's pardon is always pure gift, not a reward that can be earned. It would be a mistake of course, to conclude from all this that a Christian must be antinomian, that we can do without laws, that we have no need to spell out the meaning of sin, or that we can ignore the fact of degrees of seriousness in sin.

It is true that the law of Christ is a law of love, but it is an over-simplification leading to moral laxity to claim that love is our only criterion. St Paul could preach freedom from law, but at the same time felt it necessary to point to specific behaviour that contradicted the new life in the Spirit. He told the Galatians: 'If the Spirit leads you, then you are not subject to the law. What human nature does is quite plain. It shows itself in immoral, filthy, and indecent actions; in worship of idols and witchcraft. People become enemies and they fight; they become jealous, angry, and ambitious. They separate into parties and groups; they are envious, get drunk, have orgies, and do other things

70

like these. I warn you now as I have before: those who do these things will not possess the kingdom of God' (5:18-21).

Identifying sin

Both in Old and New Testaments, the people of God needed practical directives to identify sinful activities and were aware that there were degrees of gravity in sin. It was recognised that Israel's sins were more serious than those of others because of the special privilege and intimacy of their covenant relationship with God, and those of the Christian community were considered still more serious (Heb 10:26-31). The Old Testament has several catalogues of sins (Deut 27:15-26; Amos 2:4-8; 8:4-6; Hos 4:2; Ezek 18:5-20). Jesus himself gives an abbreviated version of the Decalogue list in answer to the rich young man's question about the conditions for receiving eternal life (Mk 10:18-19), and gives further examples of sinful behaviour in his description of the last judgement (Mt 25:41-46). There are several lists of vices and sins in the rest of the New Testament (1 Cor 6:9-10; Gal 5:19-21; Rom 1:24-32; 13:1-14; 1 Tim 1:4-11; 1 Pet 4:2-5; 2 Pet 2:12-22).

In the light of this experience, there can be no question of the Christian community at any stage dispensing with such practical guidelines, though we need to remember that some of the scripture lists are culturally conditioned and therefore require some care when applied to modern times. For example, when Paul spoke of homosexuals in Rom 1:26-27 or 1 Cor 6:9, he could not have been aware of the fact that a large percentage of the human race are not personally responsible for their homosexual orientation. Likewise, it would be an abuse of scripture to quote his lists as catalogues of mortal sins, and especially to claim that each and every act, on Paul's authority, is a mortal sin. Our notion of mortal sin, with the obligation of confession, was simply unknown to Paul. But Augustine held him to mean that one does not need to have all these vices to be excluded from the kingdom of heaven; any one alone would suffice, and each and every act of these vices is a mortal sin. He went on to teach that in lists like this we have God telling us precisely which sins are mortal. He admits that, without such revelation, we might be tempted to judge some of these sins much more lightly. He recalls that hell fire is threatened on the man who merely calls his brother a fool.

71

Augustine the bishop and pastor was concerned to make people aware of the seriousness of sin and the need for penance, but there seems to have been nobody in his congregation to ask him if he wasn't over-simplifying with his hard-sell.

The people of God have always been conscious of degrees of seriousness in sin, but the gradation was differently understood at different times. Our modern notion of mortal sin is not to be found as such in scripture or the early church, since it is so much conditioned by the church's legislation about confession, which is of much later origin. The clearest text to speak of degrees in sin is St John's first letter: 'If you see your brother commit a sin that does not lead to death, you should pray to God, who will give him life. This applies to those whose sins do not lead to death. But there is sin which leads to death, and I do not say that you should pray to God about that. All wrongdoing is sin, but there is sin which does not lead to death' (5:16-17). It is clear that, for John, not all sins are on the same level, that some are more serious than others. It is not clear what precisely is the sin that leads to death, or the 'deadly sin'. In the context, it probably refers to the 'sin against the Holy Spirit', final impenitence, the attitude of the person who simply refuses forgiveness and is impervious to the power of prayer (Mt 12:31-32; Mk 3:28-30; Lk 12:10).

Basic attitude

This reference to 'attitude' recalls an important element in the biblical notion of sin. Though it is clear in both Old and New Testaments that individual actions can be sinful, the emphasis is more on sin as a basic attitude, a state of sinfulness. In his various catalogues, Paul was not so much listing sins as describing the kind of people who exclude themselves from the kingdom of heaven by their way of life. He also speaks of the 'slavery of sin, which leads to death'(Rom 6:16). The sinful attitude, of course, is built up by individual actions, as James writes: 'A person is tempted when he is drawn away and trapped by his own evil desire. Then his evil desire conceives and gives birth to sin; and sin, when it is full-grown, gives birth to death' (1:14-15). John too speaks more of sin as a state than of individual sinful actions. To emphasise the seriousness of the sinful state he quotes Jesus at the Last Supper: 'Whoever hates me hates my Father also. They would not be guilty of sin if I had not done among them the things that no one else ever did; as it is, they have seen what I did, and they hate both me and my Father' (Jn 15:23-24). Sin is a continuing state of hatred of God, and contrasted with new life in the Spirit it is death. 'We know that we have left death and come over into life; we know it because we love our brothers. Whoever does not love is still under the power of death' (1 Jn 3:14). This is the origin of our notion of mortal sin or sinfulness, namely a state of mind and will, a way of life amounting to a total rejection of God, a condition of total selfishness. Nowhere in the New Testament do we get a list of individual mortal sins meriting the punishment of hell or needing confession and special absolution, but the various sin-lists are warnings and indications as to the kind of behaviour that can lead to the state of mortal sinfulness, spiritual death.

The early Christians soon discovered that in spite of their new life in Christ, they were still subject to temptation and sin, so there was need for repentance and continual conversion, hence the warnings of the sin-lists. But Paul was no believer in do-it-yourself sanctity. The community is a central theme in his theology, and he was particularly conscious of the harm that could be done to the community by the presence of an unrepentant sinner. We see the beginnings of the practice of excommunication in 1 Cor 5:3-11. Sinners were to be excluded from the community and shunned by their fellow-believers, both to shock them into repentance and to protect the community from the contagion of their sinfulness. This practice came to be systematised by later generations in the church, which imposed canonical penance as a condition for the re-admission of those excommunicated, and specified the sins which merited the penalty of excommunication. These were called 'crimes, grave sins, capital sins'. The main ones were idolatry, apostasy, murder, abortion and publicly known adulterous relationship. They were 'grave' not so much because of the degree of personal guilt, but rather because they caused scandal and serious injury to the church. For centuries the sinner could be re-admitted only once in a lifetime, but gradually re-admission became more frequent and the list of 'grave sins' became more extensive, including even internal sins. The Celtic missionaries, who were responsible for the development of frequent confession, drew up a sliding scale of penances for the various sins, and soon the church was fully involved in the measuring business. These tariffed penances were proportioned to the external act, without any reference to the degree of moral responsibility. The final phase came when the Council of Trent decreed that penitents were to confess all mortal sins according to number and kind.

Mortal and venial

The decree did not specify what constituted mortal sin, so it was left to moral theologians and canonists to answer the questions of the faithful on the point. Mortal sin came to be defined as the transgression of a divine law in a grievous matter with full knowledge and full consent. The textbooks distinguished: 1) Sins which according to their nature could never be venial, allowing of no lightness of matter (e.g. unbelief, lewd desires). Such sins could be venial only through imperfect attention or partial consent. 2) Sins whose matter is important in itself, but which in particular cases may be light; thus theft may be mortal or venial depending on the amount stolen. 3) Sins that always remain venial as long as no circumstance is superadded to change the nature of the sin, e.g. immoderation in sleep or laughter, although these may become mortal sins because of an erroneous conscience. Venial sin in general is when the matter is light or there is not full knowledge or consent. The textbooks also contained elaborate criteria for measuring not only the gravity, but also the number and kind of sins. Furthermore, since laws were binding in conscience, people wanted to know of individual laws whether they obliged under pain of mortal or venial sin, and for laws that could be quantitatively measured they wanted to know what quantity of time or matter was required for mortal sin. Hence the 'sin-grid' familiar to generations of Catholics, the long list of sins with their ascending or descending degrees of gravity, and their aggravating or extenuating circumstances.

Since the 'matter' of these sins was clearly categorised as mortal or venial, there was little room for discussion. The burden of the enquiry then shifted to the degree of awareness or the amount of consent in order to establish the gravity of the sin. This was the area in which the confessor sometimes asked: 'Did you take pleasure in it?' Since, in many cases, the examination was done long after the event, which may have been quite hazy in the first instance, it was not always possible to come up with a clear verdict, so for the sake of safety, the phrase 'insofar as God sees me guilty' was added to the confession of such sins.

Since mortal sin was considered to mean the rejection of God by the fully deliberate refusal to obey him in one of his commandments, it involved the loss of sanctifying grace, the divine life in the soul. This meant spiritual death, and a person dying in that state would be punished by an eternity in hell. It was a very serious affair, determining one's destiny in the after-life, and the fear it engendered often gave rise to considerable scrupulosity. On the other hand, a certain laxity developed towards sins which were dismissed as 'only venial'.

False clarity

It is true that this simple, clear-cut approach helped some people to examine their conscience truthfully and make sincere and fruitful confessions. The casuistry of moral theologians was a genuine pastoral concern to mix mercy and justice, to find a reasonable solution in the apparent conflict between inflexible principle and the intractable human situation. But the clarity and simplicity are only apparent. Today's Catholics no longer accept such a simple rule of thumb. Modern psychology has added several nuances to the notion of 'full knowledge and full consent', and we have come to realise that isolated actions, bits of behaviour, cannot be given moral labels unless understood in terms of their *human* meaning, and this is not possible except in the context of the total personality. The great theologians like Aquinas and Bonaventure were careful to explain that, in listing actions that were matter for mortal sin, they were simply providing an extrinsic criterion, a general indication of the kind of action that would normally involve a person's basic moral stance and require a choice that would be fundamentally for God or self. But the later tradition, concerned with measurement and control, came to attribute an independent and almost absolute value to the external action. In the minds of the vast majority of the faithful, to miss Sunday Mass deliberately with-out justification was a mortal sin and to die before repenting of it meant eternity in hell. Perhaps some of the clergy might have been able to explain that the position was never quite as harsh as that, but they seldom told the faithful.

Fundamental option

St Paul, the Old Testament prophets, and most of all Jesus him-self continually stressed that true religion was a matter of the heart, not simply as the symbolic seat of the emotions, but as the core of the whole personality. All of the commandments are simply expressions of the basic command to 'love God with all your heart, with all your soul, and with all your mind, and love your neighbour as yourself' (Mt 22:37-39). This involves first and foremost a basic choice about what is supremely important in life, a fundamental attitude or stance that will be expressed in our thoughts, words and deeds. Deep in our hearts we take a stand on the way we intend to live our life; for God and others, or totally for self, symbolised by Mammon or the idols of the world, such as money, power, ambition. God calls us to choose. We cannot live with a divided heart. As Jesus puts it: 'You can-not serve both God and money' (Mt 6:24). The explicit choice for God may be made in a peak moment of religious experience and further renewed in prayer and action, or it may simply take shape as the overall pattern of our lives built up by, and ex-pressed in, the individual decisions of daily living. On the other hand, mortal sin, in the biblical sense, is to choose self before God, to make something other than God the centre of one's life. This may be done in a single moment, when a clear decision is made involving one's subsequent life or, more frequently, it may be the result of a slow process of moral and spiritual de-cline.

Theologians today speak of this as our basic choice, or funda-mental option, our general life-direction, for or against God. This basic attitude of will flows from the core of our personality and determines the overall pattern of our lives. But not all our decisions and actions are central in the sense of coming from the centre of our person. Many of our actions are at the periphery and not at the centre. They come from instinctual drives, both positive and negative, such as the sexual urge, aggressiveness, fear, insecurity, all of which obscure our insight, or from routine, so that our full freedom is not involved. Such actions may be in line with our basic option, perhaps strengthening it, or they may be inconsistent with it and so weaken it, though not central enough to change it. It is clear that mortal sinfulness in the biblical sense of spiritual death is not present unless in the case of central acts coming from the core of our personality, acts which change our basic attitude away from God. The change need not be a dramatic one concentrated in a single act, but we can discover that we have arrived at such a state where God has been excluded from our lives. Human life, however, is seldom a clearcut, black-and-white picture, and the human heart has its own deviousness and perversity, so we cannot be certain where we stand in God's eyes. Only God himself knows. 'I, the Lord, search the minds and test the hearts of men. I treat each one according to the way he lives, according to what he does' (Jer 17:10). Thomas Aquinas reminds us that we can never have more than a moral certainty that we are in the state of grace. Hence, though we trust in the infinite love and mercy of God who is our Father, we work out our salvation in fear and trembling.

Living with uncertainty
Christian realism demands that we accept this uncertainty and learn to live with it. This applies not only to our basic option, but even to individual sin actions. Such is the basic imperfection of our human nature, the influence of subconscious factors, the weight of external pressures from the sinful world around us, and the gradual and groping development of our freedom and moral insight, that we can seldom be sure that a particular action is central, that it flows from the core of our personality and the depth of our conscience. Here too we must beware of the lust for certainty. It is far more helpful to keep our eyes firmly fixed on Jesus our model and the ideals he sets before us than to become preoccupied with self by trying to gauge the precise measure of our failure or virtue. It does not follow, however, that the external action is of little account, that we have nothing to learn from the sin lists of scripture or church documents. The community,

in the light of its experience of human nature, intends such lists to indicate that certain actions are so serious in their conse-quences that morally developed people performing them could normally presume that they came from the centre of their person and not from the periphery. People could well have a moral cert-ainty that such is the case, but no one else, lay person, priest, bishop or pope, is ever justified in pointing a finger at such peo-ple and judging that they are in mortal sin.

No matter how fickle or inconsistent people may be, however, there is a basic continuity in human living, so that one does not change one's fundamental option every second day. Psychologically, it simply does not make sense to think of peo-ple falling in and out of mortal sin every week. This ought to alert us to the inadequacy of our traditional mortal/venial divi-sion of sin. Mortal sin as presented in our traditional catechisms cannot be simply equated with the mortal sinfulness which is spiritual death described in the biblical texts. The Bible distin-guishes between sins that amount to a rejection of God, hence spiritual death, and lesser sins, the result of human weakness or inattention, the sins into which even the just person falls seven times a day. Modern psychology distinguishes between basic option and the actions that flow from the centre of the person, on the one hand, and peripheral actions on the other, actions that do not engage the totality of the person. But the traditional mortal/venial distinction of the catechism owes its origin to the church's discipline for the sacrament of confession. Mortal sins, in this tradition, are those for which sacramental confession is required before communion. Because they obviously included the biblical kind of mortal sinfulness, and the same name 'mortal' was used, all sins subsequently listed as 'mortal' were understood in the biblical sense, and confusion followed.

Threefold division
Theologians today prefer a threefold division: 1) mortal sinful-ness, 2) serious or grave sin, and 3) less serious or venial sin, in general the daily faults of the earnest good person. The term 'mortal sinfulness' is used in the biblical sense explained above. Some of the 'mortal sins' of the catechism tradition could well come within this category, if they involve a change of basic

option. Others would not. For example, the decision to omit Sunday Mass, for one person, might well be the final step and the external expression of a state of mind that had already become alienated from God. The same decision, for another person, might be nothing more than laziness or a bout of depression, leaving intact the basic orientation towards God. The new category 'serious or grave sin' would straddle the old mortal/venial division, insofar as some sins once considered 'mortal' do not involve total alienation from God (and so do not merit the title 'mortal sinfulness'), and on the other hand, some of those formerly considered 'venial' cannot be simply dismissed as 'only venial'.

The older tradition, at least in its popular understanding, had a clear boundary-line for mortal sin, and everything short of that was considered venial. But there is a world of difference between the ordinary daily sins of weakness, the occasional delays, halts and even minor detours of the person sincerely trying to walk in the path of the Lord, and the creeping paralysis, the emptiness of those who only pay lip-service to God, who do not really care, who blind themselves to their growing alienation from God with the rationalisation that their sins are 'only venial'. In the light of what we have said about central and peripheral acts, good people sincerely doing their best need not worry even if they experience serious faults. Their 'heart' is in the right place. They know that they cannot rely on their own strength, but all their trust is in the Lord, and they make their conversion a daily-renewed life-commitment.

Perhaps at this point the old lust for certainty will again make its appearance. People will accept this new threefold division, but immediately ask for a list of sins for each category. It would be a mistaken kindness on the part of theologians or pastors to meet the request. There is real need for a catechesis of sin, but a new 'sin-grid' to replace the old would be disastrous. Surely the time has come to trust people to grow up, to take the emphasis off measurement and control. The old sin-lists can still be referred to, even developed to encompass new problems and situations, but without the mortal-venial labels that encourage a quantitative approach to morality, with all its dangers of legalism, minimalism, complacency and scrupulosity. A later chapter will deal with the problem of 'teaching morality', for parents, teachers, pastors, in fact for all the teaching authorities in the church, but a few points may be appropriate in the present context. The real challenge is to enable people to internalise and make their own the basic Christian values, to evaluate their daily living in the light of these values, and to go on forming their conscience in an ever-growing sensitivity to what God expects. Morality cannot simply be decreed. People need to be persuaded and convinced, so it is not enough to label something a 'sin' or a 'mortal sin' and leave it at that.

Objective sin?

To describe something as 'objectively sinful', implying that it is sinful in itself, without any reference to motive or circumstances is nonsense. There are no 'objective sins'. Sin is present only where people freely choose something which they personally know to be evil. Their action may be bad or wrong or evil in the sense that it is harmful to others or to oneself, and so may be described objectively as 'wrongdoing', but it is not a moral evil, not a 'sin', unless people themselves judge it to be so and yet go ahead and do it. However, even though an individual may not be subjectively guilty of sin in a particular action, he or she is responsible for the consequences of it, and so may be bound to make 'restitution' for the harm caused.

The word 'sin' cannot be applied to a physical activity as such, but only to the total action in its human meaning, therefore including motive and circumstances. In fact, the same physical activity can have several human meanings. Thus, killing may be murder, self-defence or carrying out a legally-decreed death-sentence. Speaking a falsehood may be lying or preserving a secret to save a life. An act of human intercourse might be an expression of married love, rape (even within marriage), hatred of women, etc. These are essentially different human actions, not the same action plus different motives or circumstances. It is only the total act, with its full human meaning for the person doing it that can be described as 'sin'. This does not mean that the physical component does not enter into the moral assessment of a particular action. Normally, the physical action is an expression of the doer's attitude of will, so that, for example, it is generally presumed that one who deliberately burns down a neighbour's house has more hatred than one who merely calls the neighbour names. But the physical act alone, without motive and circumstances, cannot decide the sinfulness of the action.

Intrinsic evil?

If one should speak of 'objective wrongdoing' rather than 'objective sin', the same caution applies to the use of the word 'evil' and particularly the phrase 'intrinsically evil'. An evil is a disvalue, something harmful to people, like poverty, suffering, disease, injury, death. Whatever good consequences they may occasionally have, these are bad or evil in themselves. We have a moral obligation to fight them as far as possible. But they are not sins, not moral evils, whether they are caused by chance, by natural causes or by human action. Even when caused by human action, in themselves they still remain non-moral or pre-moral evils. The word 'moral' attaches only to free human behaviour. These pre-moral evils do not become moral evils until they are willed for their own sake, without proportionate reason. In this case, they still remain pre-moral evils in themselves, bad things to happen, but they are moral evils, immoral actions, sins, only for the persons bringing them about, e.g. inflicting injury or death without proportionate reason. Thus, to kill a person with no justifying reason is a sin, a moral as well as a pre-moral or non-moral evil. Killing a person in self-defence is still evil, a pre-moral evil, a bad thing to happen, something to regret and to be done only with great reluctance, but it is not morally evil or sinful; it is part of the morally good act of self-defence. Too often in the past we marched off to battle and killed with gusto because we reasoned that the war was just. It was too easily forgotten that the killing was still evil, a bad thing to have to do, even though it might not be counted as sin.

To say that something is 'intrinsically evil' means that it is evil of its very nature, and the impression is given that nothing would ever justify it. We can say of non-moral or pre-moral evils like death, injury, sickness, etc, that they are evil in themselves, and in that sense intrinsically evil. But it does not follow that there are never situations in which they are necessary and therefore justified. It serves no purpose to use the phrase 'intrinsically evil' of pre-moral evils, especially since it gives rise to such confusion.

It makes even less sense to apply it to moral evils or sins, since these are always individual human actions each with its own motive and circumstances. The same physical action, e.g. using contraceptives, for one person may be an exercise in responsible married love and parenthood, and for another an act of selfishness and exploitation. To say that artificial methods of contraception are intrinsically evil is to give the impression that in no circumstances could they be morally justified. But this is not the case. Our Catholic Church claims that they are immoral as a means of responsible parenthood, yet the Vatican allowed nuns threatened with rape in the Congo to take contraceptive precautions, and it is accepted that contraceptive pills may be taken for therapeutic reasons (to regularise the cycle, etc). All these cases involve the same pills, working in precisely the same way according to God's chemical and physiological laws. Since the main difference is the intention or motive, it cannot be the 'artificial contraception' which is evil, but the whole human action involving motive and circumstances, in which case 'intrinsically evil' makes no sense whatever.

Most theologians nowadays admit that the phrase 'intrinsically evil' as applied to moral evil serves no purpose. Perhaps out of reverence for traditional usage, some try to justify it on the basis of pastoral concern for formulating practical norms. It is claimed that if questioning were allowed in some cases, exceptions would multiply, hence the need for a simple direct prohibition. This seems a short-sighted pastoral policy. The church may be concerned about psychological and sociological as well as logical factors when formulating moral norms, but pastors who ignore logic too blatantly are insulting the God-given intelligence of the faithful and putting a premium on a kind of unquestioning simplicity and obedience which does not help moral maturity or responsibility. That the phrase could profitably be dropped is shown by the fact that the Holy See's *Declaration on Abortion* (1974) makes no use of it whatever and yet presents a very convincing moral argument, whereas its *Declaration on Sexual Ethics* (1975) uses it freely with reference to masturbation and homosexuality and signally fails to prove its

point. If homosexual people are considered intrinsically or objectively disordered (the more recent expression to avoid a
harsher word) because they have an inbuilt natural inclination
towards morally evil acts, the church ought to be able to explain
why God created so many millions of them.

Under pain of sin?

Another phrase that might well be dropped in the church is that
certain laws are binding 'under pain of mortal sin'. From all that
has been said above, it should be clear that the transgression of
no law can automatically be described as mortal sin, meriting
hell for all eternity. Neither the authority making the law nor a
lawyer commentator nor a moral theologian can specify the precise moral obligation of a particular law. This will depend on the
individual, the situation, and particularly the value the particular law has in promoting the welfare of the individual or the
community. A law that is arbitrary simply cannot bind in conscience. The individual needs to be aware of his or her own
limitations and bias, and realise the wisdom of the old saying
that no one is a judge in their own case, but a law will appeal to
conscience only to the extent that the person is convinced of its
necessity or usefulness. It is true that canon law decrees that
'laws made to counter a common danger impose an obligation
even though this danger does not exist in the particular case',
but a much older tradition left more to conscience by the principle that a law founded on presumption of common danger loses
its binding force when the presumption is not verified. In principle all laws are binding in conscience, but the extent of the obligation is not something that can be precisely measured and expressed in a blanket phrase applicable to all.

Most clearly of all, no lawgiver has the power to impose the
sanction of mortal sin, and certainly not eternal punishment. To
decree that 'dancing after midnight or attendance at non-
Catholic schools is a mortal sin' is simply nonsense. If the situation demands it, a legal sanction may be applied (e.g. the law-
breaker may be excommunicated or denied certain privileges),
but the legal order should not be confused with the moral. The
two orders simply do not coincide. People who have been excommunicated lose their standing in the community, but it does

not necessarily follow that they have lost their standing with God. No human authority can deprive us of divine grace or interfere with our relationship with God. If the relationship is strained or broken, we alone are responsible, because God is the ever-faithful, infinite lover who never goes back on his word. The church ignores the agony of conscience suffered for years by thousands of faithful Catholics because of 'church teaching' which in fact was simply the declaration of a single pope, *Humanae vitae*.

Divine paradox

The question: 'How far can I go before it is a mortal sin?' is too much like the attitude of a husband who would ask his wife: 'How much can I play around before you consider me definitely unfaithful?' or: 'How far can I stretch our relationship before it breaks?' A more Christian attitude is 'How much can I give? How much can I love? How do I show my love?' Our conversion and commitment to the Lord must be continually renewed, and from time to time we need to look into our hearts and take stock of our position. But in evaluating our response to God, whether positive or negative, we should not look for more clarity and security than is possible. A relationship cannot be measured in quantitative terms. It is the quality that counts. Of course, the quality is shown in action, as Jesus makes clear in his description of the final judgement (Mt 25:31-46), but the quality itself is not subject to material measurement. We need to beware of false security and the lust for certainty. The spiritual tension we experience can be a healthy safeguard against the dangers that flow from over-concern with measurement, and it is something we must learn to live with. It should certainly warn us against judging by appearances and measurable results. The divine quality that God expects to see reflected in our action may be present even at very low levels of achievement. The neurotic or psychologically crippled person may be very close to God although the expression of that person's love is hindered and blocked by disabilities for which he or she is not responsible. On the other hand, the divine quality flowing from 'that mind which was in Christ Jesus' is never fully present even in the activity of the saint, because only God himself is totally good.

There must be millions of saints far higher in heaven than the ones we have been able to measure and canonise. God's ways are not our ways, and Jesus himself warns against the dangers of measurement with his paradox about the first being last, the last being first, and the weak confounding the strong.

CHAPTER FIVE

How Sinful is Sex?

One of the reasons for confusion about the notion of sin today is our preoccupation with sexuality. The saddest commentary on the church's moral teaching is that when a person is described as immoral, most people think of sexual sin. The individual may be selfish, greedy, spiteful, cruel, jealous, unjust, brutal, violent, unscrupulous, arrogant, but such a person will not be thought immoral unless he or she is involved in sexual sin. Not only did traditional moral teaching seem to pay more attention to the sixth and ninth commandments than to the others, but also its understanding of sex was predominantly negative. There seemed little in the sexual sphere that was not sinful. Any positive treatment of the subject spiritualised it to the extent of almost losing contact with the world of reality. The bulk of the teaching was concerned with the danger of sex, and the textbooks were even hesitant about what was 'permitted' to engaged couples and married people. It is not sufficiently realised how much of this attitude is owed to non-Christian influences in the early centuries and failure to benefit from the insights and discoveries of the human sciences. Sin is as much a reality in the sexual area as in any other, but if we are to get a balanced understanding of it we need to look critically at the factors that influenced our tradition and see how we can make the Christian view of sex meaningful in today's world.

Sexual wilderness
A reaction against the over-emphasis and negative treatment of the past is the tendency among many priests and teachers to soft-pedal it now, to take it for granted that the subject has too many grey areas to allow us to speak clearly of sin. There is a real risk in this, insofar as a generation of teenagers are growing up without any norms or guidelines in this most difficult area of

their development, and what we are witnessing is not so much a sexual revolution as simply a sexual wilderness. This in turn provokes a reaction from those who complain bitterly about the 'permissiveness' of the age and want pastors to preach the old black-and-white rules, conveniently forgetting that many of those who swing along with the so-called permissiveness were themselves brought up on such rules.

It is sad to see such polarisation in the church. But in reacting against these two extremes and searching for a positive and meaningful view of sex in the context of Christian faith, we need to beware of a certain 'mystique' of sex, the kind of glorification of sexual activity embodied in the view that 'bad sex is better than no sex'. It is no exaggeration to say that our western culture is obsessed with sex, and we need to be reminded that obsession with sexuality is every bit as inhuman as suppression of it. Our concern for a new and more meaningful understanding of it should be seen, not as a last-minute rush to catch up with the 'modern world', but rather in the context of our attempt to understand the sexual dimension of our human nature in the service of love.

That the sexual dimension is no minor matter is recognised in the opening paragraph of the Holy See's *Declaration on Sexual Ethics* (1975), which says: 'The human person, present-day scientists maintain, is so profoundly affected by sexuality that it must be considered one of the principal formative influences on the life of a man or woman. In fact, sex is the source of the biological, psychological and spiritual characteristics which make a person male or female and which thus considerably influence each individual's progress towards maturity and membership of society.' This simple statement has implications for Christian morality that were seldom recognised in the older tradition. But the older tradition has so moulded, not only our thinking, but more so our feeling and gut-level reactions, that it is difficult for many people to adjust to the new insights. As in the previous chapters, it is necessary to take a critical look at the older tradition and explicitly recognise its shortcomings in order to exorcise the ghosts that haunt our imagination. Again it could be objected that it is not fair to criticise the past, and it is so easy to paint a caricature. But the fact remains that much of our thinking is still subconsciously affected by factors seldom explicitly adverted to. To face these explicitly and recognise their influence will help to clarify our thinking.

The positive strand

It would be totally untrue to say that the older tradition had no positive and healthy teaching on sexuality and Christian chastity. One can find the basis for such teaching in the Bible itself, beginning with Genesis. The Bible 'demythologised' sex, took it out of the realm of the gods, with its fertility rites and temple prostitution, and made it something basically human, good and beautiful. The creation narrative is quite explicit: 'God made human beings, male and female ... and God was pleased with what he saw. The man and woman were both naked, but they were not embarrassed' (Gen 1-2). The Song of Songs describes the physical beauty and erotic love of two young people, a relationship that is sensuous, passionate, and fully human. The prophets, and later St Paul, were not ashamed to use the marital relationship as a metaphor for God's love for his people. The gospels make no mention of Jesus ever giving genital expression to his sexuality, but Hebrews tells us that he was like us in all things but sin. He was a sexual being, and the affective dimension of his personality is clear from the picture we have of him as a compassionate, gentle, loving, tender and warm person who touched people physically, psychologically and spiritually. Far from the cerebral, abstract language of Vatican documents, he described the essence of marriage in the words of Genesis, that husband and wife become 'two-in-one-flesh'.

The positive strand in our tradition was never lost down through the centuries, and in every age there were people whose common sense, emotional balance and secure family background enabled them to appreciate and live it. They were not unduly perturbed by the more negative strands in the tradition, and they are the people who today are best able to understand and appropriate the new insights from the human sciences, because they have already been discovering them implicitly in their own experience. This fact needs not merely to be tacitly admitted, but in the interests of truth and justice to be loudly proclaimed. Any new sexual ethic must be in continuity with the best of the past, although the deeper continuity may sometimes involve a radical discontinuity at certain points. But the best of the past was far from being the whole of the past. Even a slight acquaintance with marriage counselling, confessional practice and the history of moral theology should make it clear that for large numbers of people the positive strand was a remote ideal, only hazily glimpsed through a dark fog of emotional hang-ups, religious scruples and crippling guilt. Knowledge alone is not virtue, but a sober look at some of the ingredients in that fog may help to clear away the mist from people's minds and enable them not merely to cope with their sexuality, but to rejoice in it as God's gift.

A fact that can easily be overlooked is that 'church teaching' on sexuality is to be found in papal encyclicals which are never seen by over 99.9% of Catholics. Those who do read them find them heavy going, with very little of the joy and hope that is a feature of the documents of Vatican II. Each one was promulgated by just one man (Pius XI, Pius XII, Paul VI), a male celibate cleric steeped in the clerical culture of the Vatican civil service, possibly with the help of some theologians, but with no indication of input from other bishops or from the experience of happily married intelligent women. The writings of Dr Jack Dominion (over 30 books), a happily married layman, world-renowned therapist and lecturer, are far more theological, spiritual and inspiring than all of the official documents on the Christian meaning of relationships, sexuality and marriage. Too many fundamentalist Catholics think that Vatican documents are to be accepted in faith and obeyed in blind obedience, and whatever suffering they may cause is to be accepted as a share in the sufferings of Christ. This comes close to blasphemy.

Benedictine Abbot Christopher Butler, one of the most outstanding members of the Second Vatican Council, explained that our Christian faith and belief are limited to a few essentials: the existence of one God, of two natures in Christ, of Three Persons in the Blessed Trinity, of Jesus in the Eucharist. Divine faith does not include every statement of every pope. Church teaching about morality is human reason interpreting the eternal law and this human reason is fallible, open to change, development and refinement as we grow in understanding. This is the church's teaching function or Magisterium. As human and fallible it can get things right, but also horribly wrong, and when this happens it sadly relies on reform by amnesia, conveniently forgetting the dreadful things it mistakenly taught for centuries. Unfortunately it seldom has the humility to admit its failures.

Moralism

One of the reasons for today's confusion is moralism, the temptation on the part of pastors, parents and teachers to teach morality by decree. When society was less democratic and there was more unquestioning acceptance of authority, preachment and prescription served well enough. But from their first years in school, children are now taught to question and discover things for themselves, and they cannot understand why religion should be an exception. As young adults they find that their questions about the Christian meaning of sexuality are not getting convincing answers. Some of the answers remind them of the preacher's sermon notes with the red-pencilled directive in the margin: 'Argument weak here, shout like hell!' It is false loyalty to the church to pretend that our argument was never weak, that we were never ignorant of the facts, that we never overstated the case.

History is there to show how much the church's teaching has changed through the centuries. A narrow view of the church's teaching role has given the impression that the changes were only minor details, and that on all major points there is an unbroken line of tradition going back to scripture itself or to the early Christian communities. This is simply not the case. It is too easily forgotten that it was the constant teaching for centuries that intercourse had to be for the purpose of procreation in order to be free of sin, that intercourse during menstruation or pregnancy was a mortal sin, and that any other position apart from the so-called 'natural' one (husband on top) was at least a venial sin. St Augustine taught that intercourse during pregnancy is gravely sinful, indeed a greater sin than fornication, adultery or even incest, if these are done with the intention of producing a baby. He set up flawed standards of sexual behaviour which no-one could possibly live out without crippling emotional damage producing failure, shame and guilt. Ascetic church men became prurient voyeurs, searching out sexual temptations from even the most innocent of women. This weird nonsense was based on the ignorance of physiology, which at that time believed that the male seed contained the *homunculus,* or little man which needed the female seed-ground in which to be planted, but no farmer would ever sow twice where seed has already been planted.

Cultural conditioning
These simple facts exemplify what has already been explained in an earlier chapter about the cultural conditioning of moral norms. The Bible is not a code of revealed morality with ready-made answers to moral questions, so when it came to formulating specific rules of practical morality, the people of God in both Old and New Testaments and the church ever since had to fall back on the wisdom of the time, which, in the very nature of things also reflected the ignorance and superstitions of the particular stage of civilisation. The negative elements of various stages may have been dropped intellectually by later generations, but in many instances their influence continued in the form of basic attitudes that still distort people's understanding of sexuality.

Paul and the early Christians accepted the Stoic philosophy of the time, which exalted nature, reason and decorum, and downgraded the emotions and feelings. This tradition was continued and intensified by Christian writers all through the history of the church, until it reached a kind of rationalism in the neo-scholastic period up to the Second Vatican Council. A consequence of this was the almost morbid distrust of venereal pleasure that is so marked a feature of theological writing on sexuality down to recent times. Another element that entered in was the Manichean downgrading of matter as evil. This came particularly through St Augustine, one of the most distinguished theologians in the history of the church. His writings are six times as voluminous as the whole corpus of Cicero, and his theological views were at the heart of the subject for over a thousand years and are still quoted. At the age of eighteen, when he took an African concubine, he joined the Manichees, a sect which renounced most of the ordinary pleasures of life associated with eating, drinking and sexual expression. When his companion left him after fifteen years to return to Africa, he took another concubine, and then was converted and baptised at the age of thirty-three. In spite of the grace of conversion he carried much of the Manichean influence in his thinking for the rest of his life. He had no real understanding of marriage but only his own guilt-ridden experience of long years of sinful fornication. John Noonan describes him as holding that there was nothing rational, spiritual or sacramental in the act of intercourse. He saw it as intimately linked to original sin, a distortion that has blighted Catholic theology until the present day, believing that innocent babies are born with original sin needing exorcism in baptism and their mothers needing to be 'churched' to purify them after childbirth. This teaching crucified millions of devout Catholic mothers who suffered up to ten or more still-births and still worry today about the fate of their unborn children. Until very recent times the church's guess-work in theology has given them no consolation.

The essence of marriage

Augustine's theology of original sin, which was bequeathed to the whole Catholic Church of the West, was unknown in the East. Genesis and Jesus describe the essence of marriage as the 'two becoming one flesh', whereas Augustine blasphemously changed those words of Jesus into: 'in intercourse a man becomes all flesh' (Sermons, 62, 2). One tragic result of this is that those beautiful words of Jesus describing the essence of marriage as 'two-in-one-flesh', the intimacy which is the very heart of their relationship, have never been used in official church teaching down to the present time. That sexuality in marriage was marred forever by original sin is clearly stated in the modern *Catechism of the Catholic Church*: 'As a break with God, the first sin had for its consequence the rupture of the original communion between man and woman. Their relations were distorted by mutual recriminations, their mutual attraction, the Creator's own gift, changed into a relationship of domination and lust, and the beautiful vocation of man and woman to be fruitful, multiply and subdue the earth was burdened by the pain of childbirth and the toil of work.' (n 1607). Is this in fact what people feel as they make their marriage vows to each other in the presence of God and of the Christian community?

This may well have described Augustine's relationship to his slave woman, but it is an affront to the millions of happy holy marriages down through human history. In fact, it is individual actual sin which causes damage to individual marriages. What is perhaps yet more shocking is that Genesis 3:16 is used as a quotation to support that assertion of the presence of domination and lust. God said to the woman: 'Your desire shall be for your husband and he will have dominion over you.' Firstly, would God, the most loving of fathers, make the relationship at the centre of human life a hideous sin-trap fraught with instincts against which the couple must fight throughout their whole lives together? Sadly this seems to be an idea still present in some clerical thinking and writing. Could we transpose those words to another plane saying: 'My desire is for the Lord and he has dominion over me' and that the love of wife for husband and his gentle authority should be a mirror image of this divine love?

Augustine went even further in his declaration: 'I feel nothing more turns the mind of man from the heights than female blandishments and that contact of bodies without which a wife may not be had' (Soliloquies 1, 10). Augustine legitimised the split between love and sex so that sexual intercourse is depersonalised. He wrote that carnal concupiscence, namely sexual desire that is not motivated by the desire for children, is never acceptable even in marriage, because it is an evil which is the accident of original sin. For him, sex is always corrupting if it is enjoyed, so that a man who loves his wife with passion is an adulterer with his own wife.

Over sixteen centuries later we find that negative thinking repeated by John Paul II in his *Theology of the Body*: 'This shame induces man and woman to hide from each other their bodies and especially their sexual differentiation. Their shame confirms that the original capacity of communicating themselves to each other had been shattered' (p 117). It is sad that Augustine is still being quoted on sexuality and marriage as though he were part of divine revelation. In fact the official writings of Pius XI, Pius XII, Paul VI and John Paul II bear the mark of his negative influence and his Manichean background. The Second Vatican Council has made amends by defining marriage as a covenant rather than a contract and making it clear that its primary purpose is the ongoing personal and loving union of the couple which in God's plan is only occasionally procreative. As a sincere and gifted theologian, Augustine, if he were alive today, might well be the first to acknowledge the new knowledge we now have from physiology and the human sciences, and admit the regrettable errors of the past.

Anti-feminism

All through the centuries of tradition, reaching back into the Old Testament and beyond, there is a negative attitude to women and all things feminine. In spite of the Genesis account of the complementarity of the sexes, and the personal roles played by many women in the Old Testament, women were considered the property of men, with a utilitarian value. In its original context, the sixth commandment of the Decalogue was not concerned about sexual morality as much as with the injustice done to husband or father by the man who has unlawful relations with a girl. Jewish rabbis feared women as a distraction and temptation. In the Jewish tradition, women were generally considered greedy, curious, lazy, and jealous. Christian writers took over Aristotle's notion of the female as a half-baked man, a male manqué. Over a thousand years later, St Thomas Aquinas found no reason to differ from this view or even question it; he accepted it as a fact of nature. With all the arrogance and simplicity of the male, he discussed whether women should have been created at all, and with colossal ignorance (natural enough for the time) he proclaimed that the female is something defective and manqué. He explained that the active power in the seed of the male tends to produce something like itself, perfect in masculinity; but the procreation of a female is the result either of a weakness in the seed, of some unsuitability of the material, or of some change brought about by external influences such as the south wind. Often quoted by church authorities as an oracle on natural law, he maintained that even before original sin, women by nature would have been governed by men for their own good, because the power of rational discernment is by nature stronger in men.

Pessimistic bias

St Paul could compare marriage to the union between Christ and the church and *vice versa*. But no matter how well the glories of Christian marriage were later sung by the great doctors of the church, their pessimism came through. According to Augustine, only procreation could justify marriage, sex, or even women. Pope St Gregory the Great affirmed that it was as impossible to have intercourse without sin as it was to fall into a fire and not burn. Clement of Alexandria compared marital intercourse to 'an incurable disease, a minor epilepsy'. The great St Jerome held that virginity was the norm in paradise, that marriage came about as a result of sin, and that the only good in marriage is that it can give birth to virgins. In the fifteenth century St Bernardine of Siena claimed that of 1000 marriages, 999 are of the devil's making. One wonders how he did the survey. This was in the 'age of faith', when most of the known world was Christian. The same saint, the greatest preacher in Europe in his day, maintained that it was a piggish irreverence and a mortal sin if husband and wife do not abstain from intercourse for several days before receiving holy communion. During the Middle Ages, a woman who died in childbirth was often buried in a special corner of the cemetery and without the usual honours, though some theologians permitted such a woman's burial in consecrated ground if the baby had first been cut out of the womb.

St Augustine of Canterbury felt it necessary to write to Pope Gregory the Great to ask if it were permissible to baptise women when pregnant or during their monthly periods, and whether they could enter churches and receive communion at such times. The pope told him it was no sin, but in spite of this, Archbishop Theodore shortly afterwards forbade nuns and lay women to enter a church or take communion during their periods. The penalty for breaking the law was three days fasting on bread and water. The prohibition remained part of the general law of the church until the sixteenth century. This notion of ritual impurity infiltrated Christian thinking from pagan superstition, according to which terrible things were believed to happen when women touched anything during their periods: crops would dry up, fruit rot on the trees and iron would turn rusty. No one would claim that this kind of thinking is still at work in the church, but it is hard to avoid the impression that something of the basic negative attitude lurks behind even the idealistic language of modern church documents on the role of women, especially since it is taking us so long to give practical recognition to the equality of the sexes. It is said that when Pope Paul VI wrote an encyclical on women, holding up the Blessed Virgin as their model, the Vatican refused to accept a third secretary of the German embassy to the Holy See simply because she was a woman.

This negative attitude to women was reflected in the constitutions of many religious congregations of men. On the subject of chastity, monks were told that little need be said of this 'angelic' virtue, but they were advised to flee the company of women. If it was necessary or really useful to speak to them, conversation should be as brief as possible. They were told that since the Blessed Virgin was troubled and afraid at the approach of the angel, how much more they themselves, weak and shaking reeds, had reason to fear. However much they may have outgrown it, this was the kind of writing that the majority of the world's male religious were brought up on.

Literal repetition

The more recent documents of the church show some advance on previous teaching insofar as, since Paul VI, they go beyond the harsh dichotomy between sex primarily for procreation and sex merely for pleasure. The fundamental importance of the sexual dimension of human personality is explicitly recognised, but once the realm of general principles is left behind, confusion returns. Official statements often repeat the old black-and-white prescriptions of sexual morality, with little reference not only to the discoveries of the human sciences of physiology and psychology, but even to developments in scripture studies, dogmatic and moral theology. It is taken for granted that Augustine, Aquinas and other theologians were justified in laying down norms for Christian life on the basis of the contemporary outlook on sexuality, seriously defective though it was, but today's theologians seem to be denied this right and duty.

Much of official teaching simply repeats statements from the past as though they could be valid for all time, independently of

historical and cultural developments and differences. It is frequently asserted quite simply that the 'constant teaching of the
church' has condemned contraception, with no reference to the
fact that the problem could not possibly have been understood
in today's terms until the facts of human reproduction had been
discovered, within the last century. The so-called 'safe period'
was 'permitted' only with the greatest reluctance by Pius XII in
his Address to Midwives (1951), whereas now some preachers
present it almost as one of the glories of natural law, God's gift
to women. St Jerome justified the prohibition of intercourse during menstruation for the good of the foetus. He argued that 'if a
man copulates with a woman at that time, the foetuses conceived are said to carry the vice of the seed, so that lepers and giants
are born from this conception, and the corrupted menses make
the foul bodies of either sex too small or too big.' This is a fair example of the guesswork that took the place of knowledge, but it
was often on the basis of such defective knowledge of the facts
of nature that moral norms were formulated in the church.
Perhaps the ignorance seldom went to the extreme of the Roman
emperor who claimed that homosexuality was the cause of
earthquakes, but there are enough bizarre examples in the history
of the church to alert us to the need for critical reflection.

Physicalism
Following the method of Aristotle, the scholastic theologians of
the Middle Ages used philosophical principles to reach truths
that we now know can be reached only through empirical obser-
vation. They maintained that the stars must be perfect spheres,
whereas our telescopes reveal that they are not. They believed
that the male seed was a human being in miniature and they
knew nothing of the contribution of the female apart from her
function as receptacle; modern physiology tells us a different
story. Reverence for the 'little man' contained in the semen
meant that any form of contraception was thought of in terms of
murder rather than an exercise in responsible parenthood. That
same reverence for the seed as bearer of life led to a continual
concern about 'loss of seed' or 'waste of seed' which created
endless scruples and dominated so much confessional practice
in this area, whereas modern science shows that nature's own

97

'wastage' has truly astronomical proportions. For fifty-five years I have heard the confessions of bishops, priests, male and female religious and thousands of laity, married and single in twelve different countries. The most frequently confessed 'sin' was 'impurity' meaning 'self-abuse'. Husbands would accuse themselves of having 'lost seed' and their wives would confess to making their husbands lose seed. If this wastage is a sin, then God himself is the greatest waster of all, since we now know as scientific fact that more than 250 million sperm are produced every day by men, which in fact are wasted through urination and wet dreams. Of the millions released into a woman's body during intercourse, only a few hundred survive the journey to find an egg. How many trillions are lost to produce the average family of two or three children in a lifetime?

The contrast between the massive sperm loss of the male with that of the female could not be more dramatic: she produces a single ovum a month, or possibly two, or very rarely three. It is to this tiny pin-point object that all sperms race. Yet women usually have as strong and continuous a sexual urge as men on a more emotional level, for comfort, affirmation, fulfilment. To realise that this is a life-long urge independent of ovulation is to see that the unitive, emotional side of intercourse needs moral assessment independently of fertility, and this raises the question: how is anything like justice to be achieved in discussions of marital morality? Are we not embarrassed that all through church history the rules of sexual morality were all thought up by men?

We face the specific problem in later marriage of impotence in the male, or medical indications in the female which rule out intercourse. Is self-relief or mutual masturbation acceptable and excusable in these circumstances? 'Traditional' morality would condemn such activity as mortal sin because it is not procreative in form. To fight it, however, is simply to increase the tension until it becomes unbearable and sleep becomes impossible. For the wife to satisfy herself can in fact increase her sense of well-being, enabling her to love and care all the more for her husband and family. Why should God condemn her for doing what is natural, using his gifts for her comfort and well-being? In fact, it can be said in general that where there are medical or other marital problems which make intercourse inadvisable or impossible, 'self-service' can be a natural release for sexual tension for both partners. Might the same not be said for those who have no spouse?

Not much of the church's outmoded 'science' is preserved in its more recent pronouncements, but the physicalism of their approach seems to indicate that they have not progressed far beyond it. Much of current teaching deals exclusively with the finality of the physical act of intercourse itself, in spite of the fact that the Vatican Council insisted that sexual morality is based on the nature of the person. The sexual act is discussed in isolation, with little or no reference to the psychological, personal, relational and spiritual aspects of it, or to sexual maturity as a goal to be striven for over a period of time. It is said, for example, that both the Magisterium of the church and the moral sense of the faithful have declared that masturbation is an intrinsically and seriously disordered act. The Magisterium in this case is a letter of Pope Leo IX in 1054, a decree of the Holy Office in 1679, and speeches of Pope Pius XII in 1953 and 1956, none of which have an in-depth study of the problem or could take any account of today's insights into the nature and meaning of sexuality. Nowhere is it made clear how the 'moral sense of the faithful' is measured, since it is never consulted, in spite of the fact that God's holy people *are* the church. Good-living people are shocked today to hear sexual self-gratification decreed to be intrinsically disordered without any convincing explanation and to be labelled as 'mortal sin' meriting eternal damnation. Many feel that this 'teaching' cannot be substantiated. If the Holy Spirit is invoked it should be explained why that same Holy Spirit cannot enlighten the minds of the faithful who are God's holy people, or enable the 'teachers' to provide reasons that convince. The experience of vast numbers of the faithful is that the traditional teaching made their lives miserable for years on end and often made confession a torture instead of a sacrament of healing and peace.

If a text of the Magisterium is to have such binding force, how are we to react to a decree of the Holy Office in 1666 (never revoked) which condemned a proposition saying that a kiss given for the pleasure of it is probably not a mortal sin but only a venial sin? Is it necessary to wait for another decree to tell us what most sensible Christians already know, namely that it is no sin at all, or at least that one cannot discuss the morality of it until the actual meaning of the particular kiss is known? There is no need to get upset about decrees like this, but they need to be seen in their cultural and theological context and interpreted accordingly. This does not mean that everything is relative, but only that we need to relativise some of our mistaken absolutes. The moral law is discovered and explained by human reason, which is fallible and can make mistakes.

No consultation

A major weakness in the church's moral teaching, particularly in the area of sexuality, is that it is abstract and deductive, logically drawn from a theory of nature now seriously questioned and in many cases simply abandoned. It seems to take little account of what ought to be a central element in the discussion, namely how the faithful actually experience their sexuality. Celibate male theologians are in no position to dictate to them what they experience or how they should feel. People are now trusting their own experience and discovering that the new insights on the meaning of sexuality in terms of relationship, love and growth can give their Christian living a new depth. They are disturbed that theologians and church authorities can go on analysing concepts and dogmatising about sex with all the arrogance of ignorance without consulting Christian married people.

Barely two hundred years ago, the influential theologian Billuart insisted that only procreative purpose could make intercourse lawful, that married people had to want children each time unless the act of intercourse was to be a sin. To the objection that the church allowed the old and sterile to marry, he replied that they could marry provided 'they intend to live chastely or use marriage by only returning but not demanding the debt'. Since these persons might commit greater sins if they were not married, he taught that it was better to 'dissimulate' the truth that they will probably commit sin in marriage anyway. He went on to say that 'even their confessors' must practice this dissimulation. To the objection that his position made marriage for anyone a continual occasion of sin, which seemed 'hard, odious, and in some fashion absurd', Billuart replied, 'I know this is true, not indeed precisely by reason of the state of matrimony, but from the corruption of men.' This is simply arrogant nonsense, but it was accepted in pastoral practice for far too long.

The ivory tower mentality of some moral theologians is not restricted to those who have been dead for centuries. A random selection from manuals still on the shelves of the clergy would frighten the laity. A volume dealing with the sixth and ninth commandments has three pages on the virtue of chastity, one of which is taken up with describing how virginity is lost, and almost fifty pages listing in detail all the possibilities of sexual sin, with their degrees of mortal and venial. Without a blush of hesitation it says that 'Company keeping with the intention of early marriage may be looked upon as a necessary occasion of sin, and as far as sexual liberties are concerned, engaged persons are forbidden to do anything which is not permitted to other single people.' Is this how good Christian couples view their relationship? Should they feel guilty if they fail to share this attitude? Today's Catholics feel ashamed of such 'teaching'.

Humanae vitae
The publication of *Humanae vitae* in 1968 brought world attention to Catholic sexual morality, although forty years later it is generally recognised that 80% of Catholics, including bishops and cardinals, are not convinced by it. Thirty years ago it was the most frequently confessed 'sin', whereas nowadays it is hardly ever mentioned in confession. For the average Catholic, the encyclical condemns artificial contraception, and church leaders have been repeating the condemnation ever since, often in the same breath as abortion and divorce. Any debate on the subject quickly moves on to the question of authority and obedience. Acceptance of the teaching is often seen as a test of loyalty to the church, a necessary condition for promotion. Sadly, responsible parenthood itself gets lost in the process. Conscience, moral discernment and responsibility often seem to be bypassed, even in official statements by church leaders. *Humanae vitae* was certainly a watershed for the church. Some would see the fall-out from the encyclical as a disaster, while others maintain that in spite of the deep suffering it has caused to so many

devout Catholics, the overall effect has been positive in helping people towards a more mature understanding of conscience. It follows the Second Vatican Council in stressing the importance of the unitive purpose of marriage. This contradicts the teaching of both Pius XI and Pius XII, who saw it strictly in terms of the primacy of procreation. As will be quoted later (p 116), Pius XII actually denies that intercourse has a unitive meaning.

Most of the encyclical is a positive treatment of married love as human, total, faithful, exclusive and fruitful. But it completely fails to prove its central point that artificial contraception is immoral, while so-called natural family planning is permitted as God's will. The distinction between artificial and natural has no probative value, since when the Pope is seriously ill and needs an anaesthetic he will not ask for a 'natural' one, but he will insist on the most efficient method available which, like most of what we use in our daily lives, is artificial.

Likewise when a married couple find themselves morally bound to avoid conception they will naturally want the most effective contraceptive available. But church teaching allows only so-called natural family planning (NFP), which means restricting intercourse to the infertile times of a wife's monthly rhythm. This can mean that the couple may behave as honeymooners for the few safe days, but must live as single people or brother and sister for most of the month. For enthusiasts of this method to say that the long periods of abstinence can unite them with the sufferings of Jesus on the Cross is not a healthy spirituality. Elizabeth Price once remarked that timing intercourse round menstruation is as idiotic as trying to time one's mealtimes round our bowel movements. Intercourse in its unitive sense is above all a form of communication between the couple, a bodily expression of their love, to be used in the context of when such communication is appropriate. Another simile for NFP might be a certain Cistercian monk suggesting that because *silence* is at the core of his spirituality, everone else's inner life would improve by forced silence at certain fixed hours (the fertile period). Members of religious teaching orders would rightly complain that they need freedom to use their faculty of speech at all appropriate times to fulfill their vocation. Celibate clerics seem to force abstinence at times of ovulation upon the married as a means of spiritual betterment, not realising that in fact they are removing a faculty God himself has given them to be 'no longer two but one flesh', which is the very essence of marriage, whereas contraception makes this faculty freely available to those who should not conceive at that time.

Most people find the onerous routine of calendars, thermometers, mucus testing, etc, totally unnatural and artificial, not to mention trying to do the testing while looking after a family, and coping with colds and various health problems, plus worries about mortgages and job security. But the biggest objection of all is the prolonged, unnatural, imposed celibacy that destroys the very essence of the marriage itself, namely the beautiful mystery of 'two-in-one-flesh,' especially when the couple most need the intimacy, togetherness, affirmation and consolation that enable them to cope with the problems of life.

The encyclical offers no scriptural argument for its teaching, and its use of natural law is limited to biological factors with little awareness of the theological richness of this concept and its modern development. The core of the official teaching is the inseparable bond between the procreative and unitive aspects of intercourse. It is claimed that, as natural law, this is God's will. But in fact these two purposes are inseparable only in the male. The female is quite different. She ovulates once a month and for the rest of the time is sterile. She is also sterile during lactation, when nature produces prolactin to avoid fertilisation, and she becomes totally sterile after the menopause when she is too old for safe child-bearing. Nature itself, therefore God, has arranged that for most of her life the unitive and procreative purposes of intercourse are totally separated. Not only did Pope Paul VI declare that the bond between the two is inseparable, but he was also the first pope to admit that intercourse has a unitive meaning, as declared by Vatican II. Pope Pius XII in his Address to Midwives (43) actually denied that intercourse had a unitive meaning, as did Pius XI before him.

God's plan for marriage

The beautiful mythological story of the first humans in the garden of paradise should be the starting point of any discussion on sexuality and marriage. The Genesis text is very clear: it tells us that God created humankind in his own image, male and female and they were naked and were not ashamed. God said: 'Therefore a man leaves his father and his mother and clings to his wife, and they became one flesh.' Jesus refers to this same beautiful teaching on marriage when he says: 'They are no longer two, therefore, but one body. So then, what God has united, man must not divide' (Mt 19:6). In other words, what Jesus is teaching is that intercourse and marriage are inseparable. The consummation of the marriage changes the relationship of the couple so that they are no longer two separate people, but one flesh. This is what marriage is all about. If they are lucky they may also be blessed with children. The fact that for some couples frequency of intercourse becomes less important with time in no way diminishes its central importance in the relationship, as most married couples readily admit.

Theologians explain that the Christian sacraments are rooted in primordial human experiences that arise at crucial moments in life, namely fertility, birth, the transition to adulthood, to marriage, the assumption of leadership, and finally death. But Elizabeth Price would vehemently object to this sequence with the statement: 'No, the human life cycle starts with marriage (as in Genesis 2:24 and Matthew 19:5) and it is the fusion of the two-in-one which is the initial stage of life. Marriage (two-in-one-flesh) is the primnordial sacrament. Without that protection we have the awfulness of bastardy. The church has sacralised fertility, but unfortunately not the essential fusion of man and wife which ought to lead up to it, protect it and enhance it. Augustine, John Paul II and the *Catechism* refer too easily to the influence of lust (from original sin) for what is the natural and essential servicing of their "oneness" and togetherness, the security which protects the life, health and growth of their relationship and the welfare of their children.'

Imposing so-called Natural Family Planning (NFP) as God's way of spacing or avoiding conception when this is a moral obligation can hardly be God's will when it is a denial of the very essence of marriage itself. It is precisely when a couple are morally forced in conscience to avoid conception that they most need the consolation of marital intimacy, making them no longer two but one flesh. This intimacy, togetherness and union is what marriage is all about, bringing them an incarnation of God's love. The awful demand that they restrict intercourse to the infertile periods removes the possibility of their being one when they may most need it and lengthens the period of enforced abstinence when the husband's work involves periods away from home.

There is no convincing proof that periodic abstinence is God's law for married couples. NFP enthusiasts cannot answer the simple question: if human beings as we know them have been on this earth for about 40,000 years, why did Almighty God wait until the 1930s to reveal NFP to us, and then wait for Pius XII to give permission to use it in the 1950s? We often have recourse to 'authority' in moral argument: the authority of God, of the Bible, of the church, but too often we ignore the most basic authority of all: the authority of the facts. There can be no worthwhile discussion of contraception without serious knowledge of the facts. The facts about the subject are to be found in the magisterial study of Professor John T. Noonan Jr, *Contraception*.[1] Few Catholics are aware of the absolutely weird things that were accepted as 'church teaching' for centuries. Professor Noonan was special advisor to the papal birth control commission of experts in Rome before the publication of *Humanae vitae*.

The contrast between NFP and contraception is quite radical. When a couple decide in conscience that it would be immoral for them to risk a pregnancy, they have two possibilities: either by changing the act of intercourse to render it infertile (contraception) or by changing the marital relationship itself by removing the sexual intimacy which is its very essence. Responsible married women faced with this choice, who know what marriage means in God's mind, in the words of Jesus and in their own personal Christian experience, believe that no authority on earth has the right to demand that they sacrifice the intimacy which is the very essence of their marriage for an abstract rule for which there is no convincing foundation. The beautiful words of Genesis, repeated by Jesus, to describe the essential meaning of

---

1. John T. Noonan Jr, *Contraception, how the Catholic Church has viewed birth control from the earliest times to the present day*, Harvard University Press, Cambridge, Mass, 1967.

marriage is what they see as God's will, much clearer and more beautiful than man-made rules.

The voice of experience
If the church is first and foremost the People of God, before there is any reference to how it is organised and governed, the lived experience of God's holy people must be a central source of inspiration and enlightenment for any 'teaching' proclaimed by a pope. *Humanae vitae* seems to leave little room for conscience. Paul VI chose to ignore the witness of thousands of devout married people who had to decide on how best to regulate their fertility for the good of their marriage and the welfare of their family. These people of faith had received the sacramental grace of matrimony and were Eucharistic people of prayer. The Holy Father found himself in an agonising situation, concerned that a change in teaching might cause a schism in the church, so he accepted the view of the four clerics who disagreed with the Commission's report. These clerics had no experience of the actual God-given graces available from the sacrament of Christian marriage, because they never had need of them. Succeeding popes have been repeating that worn-out misguided theory of Augustine that married men are driven to exploit their wives rather than 'observe their rhythms' as though the ovulation cycle, only discovered in 1933, is the most important thing about women, whereas it is in fact their need to sustain the 'two-in-one-flesh' ideal, which is the very essence of marriage. This instinctive and God-given grace of insight is part of their lived experience, which is prior to and more important than any academic training in 'theology'. Celibate clerics have never been given this grace (since they never had to make personal decisions in this area of life). Instead of dictating Augustine's flawed theology to laity, they should have had the humility to listen to and learn from God's holy people who have daily experience of the presence of God in their sacrament of matrimony.

A final argument against so-called NFP is from natural law itself. When women are breast-feeding, nature renders them sterile by the production of the hormone prolactin, so that they can have intercourse with their husbands whenever they like without the risk of an imprudent pregnancy. Their sexual intimacy brings them closer together so that they fulfill the purpose of marriage by becoming two-in-one-flesh, creating the warm, healthy community of love their children need so that they in turn will experience God's love incarnate in their home. When scientists use their God-given creative intelligence and follow the God-given laws of chemistry to create a pill which produces the same sterility for the good of responsible parenthood, are they not obeying the natural law, God's law of nature? Where is the sin in this?

Scientifically, lactation is by far the most reliable contraceptive, but to be fully successful the natural rhythms must be respected. If the mother can breast-feed her baby for at least ten minutes six times in every 24 hours she is totally infertile all through the lactation time. A mother, now a grand-mother, who had five children while following this regime had only three periods in ten years, and the one 'surprise' or unplanned baby came because she missed a few feeds! For mothers who cannot be as disciplined or organised as this, why should God condemn them for getting help from chemicals which provide the same infertile periods, just as their health is protected and enhanced by the thousands of other chemicals produced in the laboratory according to God's laws of nature?

Loss of credibility

It is no exaggeration to say that during the past forty years *Humanae vitae* has done enormous damage to the credibility of the Catholic Church. The painful experience of thousands of married couples is reflected in the words of Angela Hanley: 'As a woman and a mother I always found the music of *Humanae vitae* to be distinctly off key. I thank God that I had an instinctive understanding of the sanctuary of conscience, and therefore was spared the agonies of scruples trying to live an unworkable, and in many cases emotionally damaging, directive. As a woman and mother who, in recent times, has delved more deeply into the background of the same encyclical, I can truly say that it has become a "hideous cacophany".' To read about what amounts to the subversion of the truth certainly does not add lustre to the teaching authority of the church. We need now, as never before, the 'loyal dissent' of able theologians to keep the church on track and keep it true to its mission of being a sign of God in the world. In the words of Bernard Häring, one of the greatest moral theologians of recent history: 'It is part of our task and our service to the church as moral theologians to take the variety of moral norms that have been or are taught and submit them to scholarly (not necessarily existential) doubt. We must ask whether they were once appropriate and whether they still are appropriate today. This is not challenging for the sake of challenging, but a reverential testing in absolute love for truth and goodness.'[2] Häring further warns that the church is now learning what not being listened to means – people who themselves do not listen are ultimately not listened to. Obedience and responsibility, if they are authentic, are designed for reciprocity. Häring, who knew what it meant to love the church and suffer for it, also said: 'I am convinced that the desire of the laity for free and frank exchange of opinion in the church and the world is a prominent sign of the changeover to a new church. If the church's leadership were to close itself to this "sign of the time", it would lose a good deal of authority, credibility and attractiveness.'[3]

When it comes to the experience of marriage a truly prophetic voice is that of Dr Jack Dominian, probably the most qualified and experienced writer and counsellor in the English-speaking world. In his autobiography he writes: 'What has gradually emerged in my life is a shift of understanding of sexuality from biology to love – an evolution of the theology of marriage from its legalistic and canonical roots seen primarily as a contract to understanding it as a relationship of love, first described in my book *Christian Marriage* in 1967, and the Vatican Council confirmed this interpretation. Second, I came to see sexual intercourse as a recurrent act of prayer, giving life to the couple every time, and occasionally new life; and importantly I came to see marriage expressed as a community of love whose inner life is the daily liturgical living prayer of the overwhelming majority of Christians which together with the Eucharist provides their

---

2. Bernard Häring , *My Hope for the Church*, Hampshire, Redemptorist Publications 1999, p 85.
3. Ibid, p 104.

sanctification in this world, preparing them for their union with the love of the Trinity in the next.'[4]

Church teaching

The above arguments treat of the nature of contraception itself. But an equally strong argument against the encyclical is its claim that it is 'church teaching' when in fact it is the personal view of one pope, Paul VI. It is sad that although he will certainly go down in history as one of the truly great popes of modern times, he seriously misjudged two burning issues in the church: contraception and priestly celibacy. He did not allow the bishops gathered in the Second Vatican Council to discuss them, but reserved them to himself and wrote an encyclical on each. If it is true that, as the Second Vatican Council solemnly declared, the church is the People of God, how can God's holy people accept as God's will the statement of a celibate pope which has no scientific basis and flies in the face of their own life-long experience of Christian sacramental marriage? Many of them feel that *Humanae vitae* can be compared to a decision made by a human brain cut off from its blood supply and the myriads of nerves continually sending their messages to inform and guide it. It is well known that the world's bishops gathered in the Second Vatican Council were not allowed to discuss the question, because a papal commission had been established to study the matter. This commission, enlarged to 72 members, voted that there could be no objection to artificial contraception, that it could not be proved to be 'intrinsically evil'. Even the four clerics who voted against this conclusion admitted that they could find no proof for their contrary position except to warn that changing the teaching would imply that Pius XI, Pius XII and a great part of the Catholic hierarchy 'had condemned most imprudently, under pain of eternal punishment, thousands upon thousands of human acts which are now approved'. Seemingly it was this fear of having to admit that past teaching was so terribly wrong, that drove Paul VI to compose his text. He paid no attention to the thousands of written testimonies submitted from committed Catholic couples around the world that have still not

4. Jack Dominian: *Being Jack Dominian, Reflections on Marriage, Sex and Love*, SPCK, London, 2007

been published. He failed to see the injustice of continuing to condemn people for sin where no sin can be proved.

In concluding his encyclical, Pope Paul invited bishops to uphold this teaching of the church, exhorted priests to give an example of obedience by preaching it, assured married couples that the grace of the sacrament would help them to follow it in spite of its difficulty, and he appealed to doctors and scientists to show that there can be no contradiction between God's law concerning human reproduction and the fostering of married love. The factual position in today's church makes one wonder if all of these appeals fell on deaf ears. Many episcopal conferences (surely a recognised part of the teaching church) issued pastoral statements to help people understand the encyclical and they considerably softened the declaration of paragraph 14 condemning all artificial means of contraception. It is an open secret that many cardinals and bishops today (like most of those on the papal commission) are not convinced of the teaching on this point, but out of loyalty to the church or fear of offending the Holy Father will not admit this publicly. Cardinal König, the recently deceased archbishop of Vienna, is an exception. In a debate with Cardinal Ratzinger in 1992 he dismissed the 'irritating distinction between artificial and natural contraception,' and declared that on the question of birth control we have ended up with a bottleneck mostly because of this distinction, almost as if the morally important thing is the 'trick' of cheating nature.

Retired Jesuit Cardinal Martini, a favoured candidate for the papacy had it not been for his failing health, is very strongly of the same view. In his recently published *Jerusalem Nightly Conversations*[5] (not yet translated) he calls on Vatican authorities to have courage in facing up to the need for reform, especially in the whole area of sexuality, where they have lost so much credibility. He says: 'Unfortunately the encyclical *Humanae vitae* had negative results. Paul VI deliberately avoided consulting the Council in session, and took sole personal responsibility for condemning contraceptives, and this purely personal stance was not a positive premise on which to discuss matters of sexuality and family life.' The sad truth is that after forty years science has

5. Cardinal Carlo Maria Martini, *Jerusalem Nachtgespräche*, Herder, 2008.

not produced a single fact to support NFP and the encyclical. Statistics suggest that 80% of Catholics agree with the majority finding of the Pontifical Commission that there is no convincing argument that contraception is sinful, so they continue to use it without scruple. Some also believe that the church's ban on contraception undermines its credibility among other Christian groups as well as in the secular world, which lessens the power of its voice against abortion or other moral questions.

Comparison with judicial procedure in the secular world can be embarrassing for Pope Paul's encyclical. If the Pontifical Commission established to advise the pope were a jury in a court case where no one, not even the four dissenting clerics, could state wherein the guilt of contraception lay, the Pope in continuing to maintain that contraception was a sin would be overlooking the most fundamental tenet of justice, namely 'innocent until proven guilty' by accusing couples of sin when no guilt for their action can be proved. If an appeal judge who refused to accept fresh evidence refused the appeal on the grounds that changing the previous judgement would undermine the credibility of the judiciary and people would no longer trust the legal system, he would be struck off for malpractice.

A very balanced judgement of *Humanae vitae* is that of Fr Raphael Gallagher CSsR, a highly respected Roman professor of moral theology: '*Humanae vitae* presumed a worldview and type of church which no longer exist. Its failure is a precise but important one: it formally promulgated a law on contraception which has not been received in practice by the faithful of the church. Forty years is a decent span of time to judge whether a law has been effective. On other points *Humanae vitae* is still valid, though we need courage to face today's new sexual challenges with a different philosophical analysis and a more collegially responsible church than was the case when Pope Paul, after two years of personal anguish, finally published *Humanae vitae* 40 years ago.'[6]

Baggage from the past
The lesson to be learned from this sad experience is that church

6. Raphael Gallagher CSsR, 'Forty Years after Humanae Vitae', in *Reality*, Dublin, July-August, 2008.

teaching needs to free itself from unnecessary baggage from the past. Church documents too often repeat the phrase 'as the church has constantly taught' with the implication that repeating something ten or a hundred times makes it more true, when in fact developments in human knowledge and experience can alert us to the appalling views repeated for centuries by some of the greatest Christian minds, including popes (see chapter 3 above). We can now see that the source of all the problems in the theology of sexuality and marriage is the warped view of Augustine, one of the greatest theologians in the history of the church. Influenced by his experience in the Manichean sect and his guilt-ridden years of fornication, plus the culture of Roman society with regard to the place of wives, he had no experience of the beautiful ideal of married couples delighting in their union of mind, soul and body, living out the biblical picture of being naked and not ashamed, of 'two-becoming-one-flesh' in their marital relationship. In his classical book *On Marriage and Concupiscence*, chapter 7, he claims that it was because original sin struck us in our genital organs that Adam and Eve covered their genitals with fig leaves, and that people do not copulate in public. He writes that the members which were created for the procreation of children 'will not obey the direction of the will, but lust has to be waited for to set these members in motion, as if it had a legal right over them, and sometimes it refuses to act when the mind wills, while often it acts against its will! Must this not bring a blush of shame over the freedom of the human will, that by its contempt of God, its own Commander, it has lost all proper command for itself over its own members?'

All of Augustine's theology of sex and marriage is saturated and dominated by this view of the unruly phallus, and warped by his conviction that original sin (by Adam and Eve in the garden) is intrinsically bound up with intercourse. Nowhere in his writings is he aware of the centrality of the genitals in the emotional and spiritual effects of the marital relationship, making the couple 'two-in-one-flesh'. For Augustine, intercourse occurs in marriage simply because the couple are overcome by lust resulting from original sin in the Fall. To avoid moral blame they must have the explicit intention of procreation. His theology could never describe intercourse as 'making love'.

Augustine's legacy

With our 21st century understanding of human nature and the human sciences, it is easy to smile at this other-worldly negative nonsense, but this basic attitude is at the root of papal statements on the subject right up to our own times. John Paul II does not quote Augustine explicitly in his homilies published as *Theology of the Body*, but parts of Augustine's teaching are faithfully reproduced therein. He sees the unsolicited erection not as an autonomic nervous system reaction to sexual stimuli preparing the body for action, as does adrenalin in the 'fight or flight' situation, but as the effect of original sin, making men lustfully seek sex far in excess of procreative need. Instead of seeing the important words of Jesus in Mt 19:4-5 as revelation about the emotional and spiritual aspect of intercourse making the couple one, he stresses that the words 'In the beginning' are Christ calling the married couple to go back to Augustine's pre-Fall notion of marriage where, although there was physical pleasure in intercourse, this would be experienced only in a completely disciplined manner, namely when procreation was intended. Furthermore he uses the Sermon on the Mount stricture on 'adultery in the heart' to suggest that a man who looks at his wife with sexual desire is committing adultery with her within marriage. This accords with Augustine's idea found in the *Catechism of the Catholic Church* quoted above. Furthermore, in his book *Love and Responsibility*, John Paul echoes the teaching of Augustine that 'What food is to the health of the individual, intercourse is to the good of the race' (*The Good of Marriage*, 18, CSEL 41:210), implying that the physical pleasure in each is given to ensure the survival of individuals and of the race. In that same book John Paul II compares the attitude of the Creator with regard to contraception with that of a father who gives his child a piece of bread and jam, and sees him eating the jam and throwing away the bread. Elizabeth Price is much closer to the truth when she says that the relationship itself is in fact the bread of marriage, while the children are the occasional jam, if the parents are lucky.[7]

---

7. An excellent, well-researched discussion of the birth control controversy is the booklet by Elizabeth Price, *Seeing Sin where None Is*, published for Catholics for a Changing Church by Blackfriars Publications, 13 Laneside Close, Chapel-en-le-Frith, High Peak, SK23 OTS, 2000.

The four clerics who disagreed with the recommendation for change presented by the Pontifical Commission questioned the integrity of the married people who were members of it. Their view is as unreal as anything from Augustine. They wrote: 'Conjugal love is above all spiritual (if the love is genuine) and it requires no specific carnal gesture, much less its repetition in some determined frequency. Consequently the affirmed sense of generosity and the absence of hedonism are suspect when we find the intimate love of the whole person between a father and a daughter, a brother and a sister without the need of carnal gestures.' One wonders if these male celibate clerics ever had a meaningful discussion with their parents. Sadly there is no official church statement to point out that this unnatural and unChristian nonsense has no foundation in our Catholic faith or in human experience. Their public statement brings shame on our church.

One can sympathise with the agony of Paul VI struggling with his burden of responsibility for the good of the church and concerned about the danger of schism. But it is hard to understand how he could ignore the verdict of the special Papal Commission, reporting after five sessions of meetings between 1963 and 1966 that contraception was not intrinsically evil and pay more attention to the four clerics opposing that decision. Their attachment to a theory of sexuality untested in real life is absolutely incredible. It is sad that Pope Paul seemed not to notice their outlandish view that married love is above all 'spiritual', needing no carnal expression, much less at specific intervals. Their suggestion that married couples during their imposed celibacy times should be inspired by parental/sibling love may be the result of their own experience of imposed celibacy as male celibate clerics. They seem to have had no understanding of the unitive function of marriage, which is its very essence. They could not see that it is in the marriage act of bodily love that the union of heart and soul of the couple finds fullest expression. Nor could they recognise the healing value of marital intimacy when the relationship is under strain for one reason or another. These celibate clerics seem to have had little understanding of the theology of marriage as a sacrament and covenant rather than a mere canonical contract. The new *Catechism* explains sacraments as 'perceptible signs (words and actions) accessible to our human nature, which by the action of Christ and the power of the Holy Spirit make present efficaciously the grace that they signify' (1084). Sexual intercourse is intrinsic to the relationship of marriage. The words of Genesis and of Jesus (Mt 19:4-6) suggest that it is the outward sign of the inward grace of being 'no longer two but one', that is, forming the strong, stable and permanent background in which God intended humans to rear their children. As the duty to sustain that union is continuous, so also access to sexual intercourse as needed to be 'two-in-one-flesh' should be continuous, whereas the duty to procreate is intermittent (and spaced by God in lactation). The imposition of abstinence preached by NFP requires that the innate language that expresses the total reciprocal self-giving of husband and wife is blocked by an external interference of the Magisterium denying to the couple the possibility of giving themselves to each other, which is the very essence of marriage. Both those who use NFP and those who use contraception withhold *their fertility* from each other, but in NFP they have to withhold *themselves* from each other as husband and wife, whereas contraception allows the others the freedom to give themselves to each other in love at times when conception should not occur.

John Noonan has a beautiful quotation from Professor Herbert Doms OSB on the sacramental meaning of intercourse in marriage. Whereas Augustine and much papal teaching presented sexual pleasure like bait and the spouse seeking intercourse like an animal lured by the bait to procreate, Doms stressed that sexuality involves the whole human person and not simply the genital organs. He developed the parallel with the Eucharist. The physical union in marriage completes the moral participation in the life of the other spouse just as physical union with Christ in the Eucharist completes the believer's moral union with Christ.[8] To impose intermittent abstinence on a couple with the suggestion that this will improve their marriage is as crazy as saying that abstaining from the Eucharist will improve one's closeness to Christ. The discussion is not about abstinence or frequency of intercourse, but rather the very essence of marriage itself as 'two in one flesh' so beautifully ex-

8. John T. Noonan, *Contraception*, 1965 edition, p 498.

pressed in Genesis and repeated by Jesus, where intercourse is the fervent expression of love, a peak moment in the sacramental sign of marriage. If intercourse is not this in marriage, then it is a travesty of what God intended it to be. Children ought to be the fruit of such love, so that a child born of rape is the ultimate insult to what God willed parenthood to be.

The Second Vatican Council resolutely dropped the traditional teaching that the primary purpose of marriage is procreation, and stressed that the procreative and unitive purposes are on the same level, of equal importance. Pope Paul was the first pope in history to state that explicitly. Pope Pius XII in his Address to Midwives (1951) summarily dismissed the view that the bodily union of intercourse is the expression and actuation of the personal and affective union. He said: 'The truth is that marriage as a natural institution is not ordered by the will of the Creator towards the personal perfection of the husband and wife as its primary end, but to the procreation and education of new life. The other ends of marriage, although part of nature's plan, are not of the same importance as the first, still less are they superior' (47). Reflecting Augustine's outlook, he castigates contraception users for the selfish use of pleasure given for the good of the human race, and happily teaches total abstinence to married couples, saying that God will provide for such heroism (41, 42). Before him, Pius XI held the same view, and criticised the Anglican bishops at their Lambeth meeting with a tirade in which he quoted Augustine 13 times and declared: 'This criminal abuse (contraception) is claimed as a right by some on the ground that they cannot endure children but want to satisfy their carnal desire without incurring any responsibility' (*Casti Connubii*, 53).

Older women have sad memories of the prurient, third-degree interrogation they were subjected to for years in the confessional by male, celibate, clerical confessors who had no experience of intimate love. They were advised not to lose hope, but to have recourse to the sacrament of penance for God's forgiveness. Since the circumstances of their marriage required contraception they could not make a 'purpose of amendment' not to sin again, so they felt that the sacrament was reduced to a mere guilt-shedding process that did nothing for their spiritual lives, instead of the sacrament of reconciliation and peace which it is meant to be.

Married Catholics during the past forty years have felt a deep sense of injustice that the official church should accuse them of sinful behaviour in using contraceptives when in fact it cannot convincingly be shown that they are 'in sin'. Male celibate clerics can have interesting intellectual discussions about the morality of artificial contraception, but it is not really a matter of conscience for them. None of them ever stand at the crossroad of decision faced by married couples who have to decide how to be responsible parents in the regulation of their family. Such couples will be guided by church teaching and helped by competent advice, but the final decision is theirs alone before God. Intellectual discussion is a matter of reasonable debate searching for truth, but conscience as a decision is a very personal matter. For the married couple conscience is central and they are only too well aware of their responsibilities in forming, informing and following it. The 'official teaching' in this area totally ignored the world's bishops assembled in Council, the overwhelming decision of the Papal Commision established to study the matter, and the thousands of written testimonies from committed Catholics around the world.

In brief

The past forty years have been a crucifying experience for conscientious married Catholics throughout the world and they have caused a huge loss of credibility to our beloved church. It serves no purpose to insist on the 'constant teaching of the church' when in fact it was far from constant. Pius XI and Pius XII (within living memory) ignored, indeed vehemently denied, the unitive purpose of marital intercourse, whereas the Second Vatican Council (the highest, latest and most official organ of 'church teaching') solemnly proclaimed it on a par with the procreative purpose, an integral part of the very essence of marriage. Instead of trying to guess God's will from biology and natural law in the animal kingdom, should we not begin with God's beautiful words in Genesis 2:24-25, repeated by Jesus himself who is the incarnation of God's love (Mt 19:4-6)? These words make quite clear that the sexual instinct in humans is not merely about procreation, but is an essential element in creating and nourishing the ongoing environment needed for new life to grow and develop. This instinct guides young people to leave the parental home, find a spouse with whom they set up a life-long loving relationship, so that their intercourse changes them from two separate people into a 'two-in-one-flesh' couple, trans-forming them into a God-made duality 'which no man should put asunder'. The emotional welfare of the couple, of their children and of the whole of society rests on the constancy of that union.

It may help to clarify this truth if we replace the words 'unitive and procreative' with the more exact and meaningful words 'marital and parental' to describe the experience of intercourse in marriage. Marital intercourse refers to the physical expression, augmentation and celebration of a lifelong continuous commitment of the spouses to each other in love, whereas parental intercourse describes the occasional isolated act resulting in the conception of a child. This distinction gives the couple the freedom of continuous access to the marital function of inter-course at times appropriate to the well-being of marital unity, whereas if they obey the church's prohibition of contraceptives they must either go without the marital function of intercourse or risk the very conception that responsible parenthood demands that they must avoid. 'Church teaching' in this case forbids them to become 'two-in-one-flesh', which amounts to 'putting asunder what God has joined together'. If so-called Natural Family Planning is used, then intercourse is limited to that time in the ovulation cycle when the marital and parental functions can be separated and intercourse happen without conception resulting. But this means that calling NFP 'being open to life' is semantic nonsense. As mentioned above, if NFP enthusiasts accuse contraception of being artificial, surely tying marital intercourse to the reading on a thermometer and/or chart, and/or the results of a somewhat squalid mucus examination or urine test, is far more artificial?

Homosexuality

The Second Vatican Council had no hesitation in reminding us that, to be faithful to the gospel, the church itself is always in need of purification. It is a real disloyalty to the church, to truth and to God to pretend otherwise. An area crying out for attention with regard to the sacredness and truth of language is the church's current attitude to God's holy people who happen to be homosexual. In its concern for justice and respect for human dignity, the church has recently warned against the harassment and persecution of homosexuals, but fails to see the contradiction between this and its continued 'teaching' that our sisters and brothers who happen to be homosexually orientated have a condition that is 'intrinsically disordered', naturally inclined towards immoral acts that are selfish and depraved. This is not divine revelation or a message from the gospel, but a 'teaching' that was culturally conditioned and repeated mechanically for centuries, without any input from the lived experience of homosexuals themselves, who are temples of the Holy Spirit and as close to God as the writers of church documents.

The Catechism of the Catholic Church (2357) refers to homosexual acts as acts of grave depravity, condemned by sacred scripture (Gen 19:1-29, Rom 1:26-27, 1 Cor 6:9, 1 Tim 1:10). But the church has never convincingly shown why these few texts have to be interpreted literally, whereas other clear commands of scripture are not binding in conscience, e.g. the death penalty for a disobedient son (Deut 21:18-21), or the stoning to death of a wife found not to be a virgin (Deut 22:30-21). The Bible condemns intercourse during menstruation, and marriage with non-Israelites, but permits behaviours that today we condemn as immoral: prostitution, polygamy, concubinage, sex with slaves, and treating women as property. Old Testament writers and even St Paul saw homosexuals simply as perverts (as indeed some of them were, just like many heterosexuals in their abuse of God's gift of sexuality), but they were totally ignorant of the fact that the homosexual condition is no more personally chosen by individuals than heterosexuality. Both are facts of nature, and in Christian theology God is the author of nature. The question is: What is God's will in this area? Does the church have a convincing answer? If it is so clear and convinced in its 'teaching', why not answer the simple question so often asked by Dr Jack Dominian: Why did God create so many millions of homosexual people? Nobody chooses to be homosexual.

The church has never even tried to explain, but it could be a little more humble in looking at the facts. It is a fact that at least 5% and possibly 10% of men throughout the world are homo-sexual, with a lower percentage for women. It is now recognised that it is genetic in origin and recent post-mortem studies have shown a significant brain-difference between homo- and hetero-sexuals. It is also a fact that for some people their sexual identity is not clear until teenage or even later. Another mystery is that a person may have all the physical characteristics of one sex (even to being married and having children) and later discover that psychologically and emotionally they belong to the other sex. Another fact of nature is that some people are bi-sexual. One has to beware of sweeping generalisations. Also a distinction needs to be made between homosexual people and the homosexual culture. One can drift into and out of the latter, but one's sexual orientation is a matter of nature, of human make-up.

New knowledge
Truth cannot simply be decreed from on high and imposed by sanctions. Truth can only be discovered and shared, by God's holy people listening to each other and learning from each other, and nobody has a monopoly of truth. There is a vast amount of knowledge now available on this subject from anthropology, sociology, psychology and sexuality, and we should remember the wise words of the Second Vatican Council: 'By the very cir-cumstances of their being created, all things are endowed with their own stability, truth, goodness, proper laws and order. We need to respect these ... for earthly matters and the concerns of faith derive from the same God.' (*Church in the Modern World*, n 36).

Another fact is that human beings have a basic need to love and be loved. Nobody grows alone. People need people. We are what our relationships enable us to be. This is true of both homo- and heterosexual people. These orientations are simply different ways of being human sexual persons, not two separate sexes. Both were created by God. The moral obligation for all of us is responsiblility, to be responsible in our loving and in our relationships, respecting each other in our human dignity, in our commitments (vows of marriage or religious life), in all the circumstances of our lives. Many gay and lesbian couples have 30-40 years' experience of committed love relationships which compare with the best of marriages, but this in no way threatens or lessens the special dignity of marriage. Over thirty years ago, Dr Jack Dominian wrote: 'The Christian community needs to summon every ounce of care and compassion towards one of the largest minorities that is still considered deviant without any reason, for exclusive homosexuals are no more responsible for their state than heterosexuals.' What a pity the church continues to pay so little attention to that call.

Signs of the times

It may seem that we have delayed too long with the negative elements in our tradition, but it is necessary to bring them into the open and recognise them publicly. The confusing details may have been familiar to historians, but the faithful can be helped by recognising them. The confusion would be unsettling enough if it were merely an intellectual muddle, but it is much more serious when it involves an agony of conscience compounded by emotional hang-ups and guilt-complexes. To realise how much of the traditional teaching in the area of sexuality is coloured by influences that have nothing to do with the gospel, and so need to be re-evaluated today, is already a liberating experience. While learning from the valid insights and experience of history, we should never become imprisoned by the past. Neither the Bible, church pronouncements or natural law provide a code of morality to be read to the faithful by experts who alone know how to read them. Jesus promised his followers that the Holy Spirit would lead them into all truth, so the whole church is a learning and pilgrim church. It is the whole Christian community, God's holy people, men and women, together in dialogue and prayer, who have to discover the meaning of sexuality today and formulate the principles that will guide them in its responsible use. An extremely valuable contribution to that enterprise is retired Australian Bishop Geoffrey Robinson's book *Confronting Power and Sex in the Catholic Church: reclaiming the spirit of Jesus*. It has been well described as 'a local encyclical addressed to the world'. It has no Vatican stamp, but it is a prophetic voice with the ring of truth and deserves the widest possible readership, particularly by church leaders.[9]

Sex is not the whole of life, but the sexual dimension of our human nature touches the deepest levels of our being, so it is understandable that it be a moral concern, not only for the teaching authorities in the church, but for Christians who want to love God and grow in his love as whole persons, as men and women. If they are to be helped, we need to explicitly disown the negative and pessimistic elements in our tradition, honestly admit the weakness of many of our positions in the past, and face up to the challenge of making the Christian view of sexuality meaningful in today's world. From what has been said in previous chapters about the Bible and the various types of law in our understanding of morality, it should be clear that a literal quotation of the past will not do. The problems of human life cannot simply be brushed aside by triumphantly brandishing a text from scripture or an ecclesiastical decree.

The Second Vatican Council speaks of reading the signs of the times in the light of the gospel as a continuing sign of God's will. We are not doing this if we dogmatise about sexual morality without any reference to our contemporary understanding and experience of sex. Quite radical developments have taken place in the last few decades. The equality and complementarity of the sexes, the personal dimensions of the sexual relationship, our growing control over fertilisation, the changing patterns of family life, and the greater awareness of what marriage can do in terms of deep personal fulfilment, are all factors that must be taken into account before we can even begin to talk about sexual morality. Our starting point should be the central truth of our Christian faith, namely the incarnation of God's love in the person of Jesus of Nazareth. God's love took flesh in Jesus who became one of ourselves, but that same love becomes incarnate, takes flesh in people who touch our lives with love. The ability to love is one of God's greatest gifts to us, and it is differently experienced and expressed by different people and different cultures. The challenge is to accept and live the great gift of intimate loving, to recognise and reverence it wherever we find it.

9. Geoffrey Robinson: *Confronting Power and Sex in the Catholic Church: reclaiming the spirit of Jesus*, Columba Press, Dublin, 2008.

New Challenges

The new focus on person-centred morality and the interpersonal relationship symbolised by the two-in-one-flesh as the heart of marriage is a healthy development. But there is no 'happy ever after' ideal marriage to solve all the problems. Our world has changed dramatically in just one generation and most developed countries have similar experiences. The ideal of marriage for life has diminished. Civil marriages, cohabitation, divorce and serial marriage are now commonplace. Extended families are a thing of the past. The new focus on the personal relationship as the prime value can lessen appreciation of its social dimensions. Pre-nuptial agreements imply that the marriage is expected to fail, whereas the social aspects of the traditional contract can give stability and security. The alarming increase of suicide among young males is not unrelated to confusion about sexual identity and roles. A narrow focus on the ideal Christian marriage may prevent us from coping with new and unusual relationships. A striking example was a 2004 BBC television documentary showing a gay Anglican priest who described his 'family': he lived with his partner of twenty-five years, his elderly and disabled mother and a foster child with learning difficulties. Explaining his situation, he made clear that his Christian orientation was of more importance to him than his sexual orientation, recalling the words of Paul to the Galatians (3:27): 'There is no longer Jew or Greek, there is no longer slave or free, there is no longer male or female, for you are all one in Christ Jesus.' He saw his situation as a model extended family. I believe Jesus would understand and accept him. But I feel that the same infinite love of Jesus would not be happy with the way our Catholic Church harshly treats its members whose marriage has broken down irretrievably and find themselves in a new relationship where they experience God's love to the full, but are refused a place at the table of the Lord which is the heart of every Christian community. Current practice and canon law have changed the Eucharist, which theologically is for the forgiveness of sins, into a reward for good behaviour. There is very little of the joy and hope of Vatican II in today's church. But it is interesting to recall that our present Pope, writing as Professor Ratzinger in 1972 with regard to divorced and remarried

Catholics who thought that they should be allowed to receive holy communion, said that 'Communion can be given to someone living in a second marriage, without the suspension of the second marriage (in other words, without having to live as brother and sister); this in confidence in God's mercy ... It seems that the granting of full communion ... is nothing less than just, and is fully in harmony with our ecclesiastical traditions.'

Person-centred morality

To drop the negative and pessimistic 'do's and don'ts' of the older approach is not to cut loose from all norms and principles. It means to get away from the old physicalism and the fragmented approach to human actions, and to begin with the more basic question of what sexuality is all about, what it means to be a man or a woman, indeed what it means to be human. The Second Vatican Council reminds us that sexual morality is based on the nature of the human person, so it can only be understood in human and personal terms. It is true that we do have a certain nature that sets limits on us and defines our possibilities. But it is not a ready-made nature, already fully defined, but one of beings who must fashion their own potentialities into a harmonious whole. We must freely become what we are potentially, so human sexuality involves freedom and development.

It is men and women themselves who give meaning and shape to their sexual drive. Norms of sexual behaviour cannot, therefore, be established simply on the basis of biological facts, but will be shaped in accordance with our growing understanding of ourselves and in the light of our human experience. Once again, the historical dimension of morality enters in, because our self-understanding is growing, and our experience is changing. Vatican II quietly dropped the time-worn and misleading distinction between primary and secondary ends of marriage in its document on the *Church in the Modern World*, and produced a chapter on responsible parenthood and the relational aspect of sexuality that would have been condemned by the Holy Office less than forty years earlier. For Aquinas, 'primary' originally meant generic, what was common to both animal and human reproduction, while 'secondary' meant what was specific to humans, but the later tradition turned this upside down and took primary to mean more important, and secondary less important. The new approach will not be trapped into making long lists of laws covering every conceivable situation and describing the precise boundaries of the different degrees of sin. More searching questions will need to be asked about the human meaning of particular kinds of behaviour, rather than simply the biological function of certain acts.

Sex as language

Morality is about becoming a person, and nobody grows alone. People need people. It is only through relating to others that we grow in maturity and develop as persons. Our relationship is expressed and grows through communication: by speech, gesture, touch, and working with and for others. Sexuality is part of this language of communication, a very deep and powerful part. Through it we can enter into varying degrees of intimate relationship with, and commitment to, other people. The personalist approach to sexual morality advocated by Vatican II means understanding sexuality as language, a form of communication. Thus, the moral evaluation of any sexual expression will depend on its truthfulness, whether or not it faithfully expresses the truth of the person and the particular relationship in a given situation. Since relationship is a growing, developing thing, from the casual acquaintance to the total commitment of marriage, with its openness to, and responsibility for, new life, there is a whole sliding scale of what is appropriate or inappropriate, truthful or deceitful, in the expressions of that relationship, both sexual and other.

The moral challenge in our use of sex is to keep it meaningful, not to falsify or trivialise it. It is said to be the easiest language to speak, but the most difficult to make meaningful and to keep meaningful. The full human meaning of intercourse is the whole person saying with all their being, body, soul, mind and heart, 'I love you, you only, and you always.' Someone who says this without being in a position to follow through in commitment is saying more than he or she means. This impoverishes the sexual language to the point where people can no longer say all that they mean when they really want to and are in a position to. On a deeper level, such people will have so scattered their personal being in isolated acts without meaning, that they will no longer be capable of the total self-giving that is the essence of sexual relations at their highest point of intensity and fulfilment. It might be feared that this new approach leads to individualism, that individuals can give any meaning they wish to their actions. This can in fact happen. Sex can be for breeding, for fun, for revenge, for exploration or exploitation, for escape or for a variety of other purposes. But just as we are not free to create our own language (unless we wish to talk only to ourselves) but we learn the language of our community, so the community will already have established the essential meaning of sexual activity on the basis of its experience of human nature and its needs. It will have discovered that certain forms of sexual activity do not lead to growth in maturity and fulfilment, and so are considered cul-de-sacs, dead-ends. Others are part of the groping, experimental growing-up process, to be overcome and integrated into the mature personality. It will have discovered the emptiness and meaninglessness of sex isolated from its human context, the sadness of pornography, and the banalisation of sex that comes from a sex-obsessed culture.

Many of today's young people see sexual activity as an experience in closeness and intimacy, a protection and refuge against the loneliness of much of modern living. But deeper reflection will show that this is simply one more 'use' of sex. It can only banish the loneliness and isolation of the moment. It cannot of itself link past, present and future into the harmonious whole that is human life. The universal experience of people is that sex does not create friendship and intimacy, but that it needs the constancy, stability and commitment of real friendship in order to retain its power of true expression, to be the language of closeness, intimacy and love. Experience has also shown that in general the institution of marriage provides the best possibility for the protection and growth of such a relationship. This is not a popular truth in today's world of casual encounter, experimental sex, throwaway friends and disposable relationships, but it is one that the Christian community needs to proclaim from the housetops, not merely in words, but in the living sermon and quiet example of its married couples and other really committed relationships.

Wholeness and growth

It will be found that the 'new sexual ethic' already taking shape in the church, though not fully developed in official teaching, largely agrees with the traditional view on the essentials of sexual morality. It condemns pre-marital and extra-marital sex, and warns of the dangers of exploitation of persons in the use of sex, both within and outside of marriage. But it avoids the listing of physical actions as mortal or venial sins. While not ignoring the physical facts of nature and the laws of biology, it assesses the morality of sexual behaviour in the context of its appropriateness to persons in their wholeness and in their relationships. But this newer approach in no way ignores the basic values of Christian morality. It is very much aware of the tragic consequences for society of the sexual promiscuity of today's world, where so many children have no idea who their father is, and where sexually transmitted diseases have increased fivefold in a few years.

The concepts of wholeness and growth are central to the new approach. The moral call is to grow into the fullness of the maturity of Christ by responding to those around us. Not all will be able to respond to the same degree, and we must beware of equating holiness with psychological wholeness. God's grace and love are available to all who open to him, though not all may be able to show it in their lives because of obstacles beyond their control. But within the limits of our ability we are expected to strive for whatever degree of wholeness is possible, and help others do the same by our response to them. This is what it means to love God 'with all our heart, with all our soul and with all our mind' and to love our neighbour as ourselves. Wholeness refers to the totality of the human person, including the spiritual, intellectual, emotional and physical dimensions, in oneself and in others. To grow as a person is to develop all these harmoniously. To concentrate on any one of them (physical, intellectual or sexual), at the expense of the others, is dehumanising, depersonalising, and this is sinful. It could even be said that some of the arguments of traditional moralists are seriously at fault here, since they allow biological processes to take precedence over personal and spiritual values.

The notion of growth is important because the individual is a developing being, and sexuality shares in this development. People move through various sexual stages, not only physically, but emotionally, psychologically, socially and spiritually. We are all called to use our sexuality in the service of love. Love makes people whole. The precise nature of that love is immaterial, but the complete acceptance of oneself with all that is good and admirable and equally all that is weak and less than admirable, by another person is necessary for our completion as human beings. When we can love in that way in return, we are complete. What characterises this relationship and contributes most to its stability is friendship, so that lovers are each other's best friend.

It is beyond our purpose here to give a complete theology of sexuality, but it should be clear that if people are to be helped to integrate their sexuality into their growth as Christians, much of the older theology needs to be discarded. It is sad, though understandable, that so much of the church's energy in the past forty years has been wasted on the question of contraception, and sadder still that so much of the controversy centred more on 'authority' than on the moral issue itself. Though it was agonising for large numbers of married couples, it is not the most important question in Christian morality, or even in sexual morality. The same may be said of pre-marital sex. We need to re-focus our moral vision so that we are not hypnotised by sex. We must realise that in spite of all the talk about the permissive society and the sexual revolution, for most people their sexual sins constitute only a very small proportion of their general burden of sinfulness. There are no easy answers.

We have already seen that if we could take the emphasis off law and precise measurement, people might have a more balanced and responsible approach to morality. This is particularly the case in the area of sexuality. There would be less confusion, fear and scruple about sin. Some would need to learn to live with a degree of uncertainty, but the experience of some spiritual tension would bring a touch of realism and seriousness to their moral striving. It would be a disservice to them to introduce a new legalism by listing specific acts as mortal and venial sins, and outlining what is now 'permitted' in the various zones of the body. Instead, we have the far more difficult task of explaining the Christian meaning of sex, providing them with the know-how of the decision-making process, and trusting them to use their conscience as they make their personal choices. We can invite them to reflect, and give them pointers for their reflection.

There may still be simple people who prefer just to be 'told' what is right and wrong, but it is an abdication of authority and spiritual leadership to look on them as the ideal and to wish that all were like them. The church is a community in which people should grow and be helped to grow. Part of that helping is to provide them with the facts about the meaning of scripture, the nature, extent and limits of the church's teaching authority, the purpose and limitations of law, the historical development of moral norms, and the discoveries of the human sciences. Knowledge like this may free them from pseudo-sins (like sexual thoughts being automatically bad thoughts), and alert them to the more serious questions they should be asking themselves, questions to which there may be no easy, black-and-white answers.

CHAPTER SIX

My Conscience or the Law?

There are large numbers of Catholics to whom it comes as a profound and disturbing shock to be told that there are moral questions for which there are no black-and-white answers. Believing in the one true church, with its divinely revealed deposit of faith, they were given the impression that there is a Catholic position on everything from bus driving to bee keeping, and a Catholic solution to every moral and social problem. Of course, they believed in conscience, and were aware that they had an obligation to follow it. But the obligation applied only to an *informed* conscience, and the information would be supplied by the church, which provided the objective moral norms. The function of conscience was to know the moral principles, the rules of right and wrong, judge which ones applied to the particular case, and then decide how they were to be obeyed according to the circumstances of the situation.

For many such people, the controversies of recent years were confusing and upsetting, particularly the contraception debate. They suddenly discovered that the information they were given was no longer as clear as they would like, and that it was being variously interpreted, not only by laity but by priests, bishops and indeed whole hierarchies. Quoting Vatican II, many priests told them they should 'follow their conscience'. But this was not particularly helpful since they had always believed that following one's conscience meant accepting the teaching of the church, and to do otherwise would be simply disobedience, a sin, using the excuse of conscience to do your own thing, to please yourself. This attitude is not restricted to the simple faithful, but seems to be still shared by some priests and bishops. It is generally accepted that Vatican II admitted the principle of freedom of conscience, indeed proclaimed it as a basic human right. But there is still a huge gap between the notional assent people give to this on the surface of their minds, and the real assent it calls for in personal conviction and practical acceptance of all its consequences. Unfortunately there are clergy who in practice still reduce 'following one's conscience' to 'doing what the church commands'. It is sad, though understandable, that decades after the Council it should still be necessary to spell out the role of conscience in the moral life.

Loyalty or confrontation

That there could be any conflict between conscience and authority in the church seemed unthinkable until fairly recently, apart from extreme cases, and even there authority was always presumed to have been in the right. One recalls the exhortations to loyalty by preachers in the period immediately before *Humanae vitae*, telling people to accept the decision of the Holy Father whenever it came, whatever it might be. Such preaching was well-intentioned, concerned with the common good of the church, but reflected a theology of conscience, authority and indeed morality that falls far short of Vatican II principles. It was taken for granted that right and wrong can simply be decreed and must be blindly accepted. During that same period busy pastors and confessors were heard to complain impatiently about the contraception debate: 'Why can't those people in Rome tell us what's right and stop all the nonsense?'

Another aspect of the tension between conscience and authority, and of the inadequate theology of conscience so common in the church, became obvious in the years immediately following *Humanae vitae*. Confrontation between individual bishops and their priests, and between priests and laity, ended in head-on collisions in which people were deeply wounded and some were scarred for life. It brought shame on the church. For the traditionally-minded, these sad episodes were simply cases of normal authority dealing with disobedience. But developmental psychologists tell us that the earliest and most elementary response to authority tends to be blind and automatic, and since we all carry within us the child we once were, in situations of stress we revert to childish levels. Both civil and religious leaders tend to rely on this primitive form of response and insist on it when under attack, rather than exercise true leadership by promoting autonomous moral decision. Perhaps this is an over-simplified and one-sided reading of these sad incidents, but people are confused when they are given the impression that on moral grounds they can say No to a civil regime, but a situation can never arise where they may have to say a personal, conscientious No to an ecclesiastical authority. That there can be dissent, and indeed loyal dissent, not only in, but for the church, is not easily understood.

Confusion about conscience

That Vatican II's notion of conscience should be one of the least appreciated of the Council's insights is understandable. The very objectively orientated theology that dominated the church's thinking for centuries made it difficult for people to think of conscience except in terms of obedience. If 'reality' was simply 'out there' to be accepted, studied, and contemplated, the laws of reality and morality were likewise already there, only to be read off and obeyed. The human being, the subject, the person, tended to be seen as an object among the other objects of creation, rather than as a self-determining person sharing in God's own freedom and creativity. The emphasis on law and measurement that was so large a feature of the church's practice gave the impression of absolute clarity and certainty, so that difficulties could only arise from subjective elements. The ideal was to overcome these and bring one's thought and action into line with 'the church'. This is simply a statement of fact, of how things were.

However, a more general reason why there is so much confusion about the meaning of conscience, and difficulty in accepting Vatican II's principles, is that the vast majority of people, irrespective of whether they are Christians or not, have not progressed beyond Kohlberg's 'fourth stage' of moral development. Some spend their whole lives doing what they are told by authority simply out of fear. This is stage one, where we all begin as children, fearing punishment. Others obey because it brings them pleasure; this is stage two. Others are at stage three, where they obey because the group expects it, and they enjoy the esteem of their peers and are loyal to them. Stage four is that of most people, who obey simply because it is the law. They obey even when there is no pleasure in it and even when others ridicule them and disobey. The law is seen as good, because it is society's law, for the common good. At this stage, the ideal conscience is that of the law-abiding person. But some move beyond this stage to see the values the law is intended to promote and protect, and realise that mature conscience is not simply a matter of internalising the law itself, but of being committed to a personal belief in the values behind it.

Levels of conscience

Of course, the word 'conscience' can be used in different senses, but all of them involve two basic elements: knowledge and obligation. We know that certain actions are right or wrong and we feel an obligation to act in accordance with this knowledge. When we do what we believe to be the right thing, we experience peace and satisfaction. When we go against our 'better judgement' we feel guilt and remorse. In ordinary experience, conscience is felt as a judgement in a concrete situation. I can continue working on this chapter or I can go and watch TV, but I know that I should continue working if I am to keep my promise to send it to the editor by the end of the week. Not only do I know that to continue is the right thing to do just now, but I also know that I *ought* to do so, no matter how much my tiredness or laziness tempts me away. In this sense, and on this level, conscience is always concerned with the concrete decision about what is to be done here and now.

But there is a deeper level presupposed by this particular judgement. Even before I arrive at the decision that to continue working is the right thing for me to do just now, I know that as a general principle it is a good thing to keep promises, that promises ought to be kept. Society depends to a large extent on people being faithful to their commitments, keeping their word. This level of conscience is our general knowledge of moral principles of right and wrong, good and bad. Depending on the individual, it can be more or less extensive. It includes the basic principles: do good rather than evil, treat others as you would wish to be treated yourself, and can extend to the Ten Commandments and specific developments of them. But it is more than neutral, speculative knowledge. It calls to something deep within our nature, stirs us with the conviction that we must obey it if we are to be true to ourselves. In this sense, conscience extends to a much deeper level than intellect and will, knowledge and consent. On this deepest of all levels, conscience is the core of our being as free persons. Here it can be said that 'conscience *is* the person'. It is on this level that the 'basic option' or 'fundamental attitude' spoken of in chapter 4 finds its context.

The human person is not a finished article, possessing a ready-made nature, but a being of possibilities with a built-in call to grow in wholeness, to become *actually* what we are *potentially*. This forward and upward thrust is part of our God-given nature. The possibilities for good that we see before us summon us as the voice of conscience. Part of us reaches out ahead of the rest as we discern the good we ought to do, so we experience a certain stretching and tension, the tension of being challenged to grow. Good choices and right decisions in concrete situations enable the rest of our being to catch up, so to speak, with the part that reaches forward, so the tension is relieved, we are 'at one' with ourselves, and we experience not only growth, but peace and wholeness. This is the experience of a 'good conscience'.

When we ignore or refuse to do what we know we should, the tension remains, so we lose our basic oneness, we are torn within ourselves; we experience alienation and guilt. This is sin. It is a basic inconsistency between our knowing and our doing, and so we become divided within. We may make excuses for ourselves, rationalise our failure, but the very attempt to 'rationalise', to give 'reasons' for something which is really against reason, only makes more explicit our alienation and loss of oneness. Since we are not self-sufficient atoms, but relational beings, the sin and lack of oneness within ourselves spills over into our relationships. Whatever the occasion or the area of our sin, it cannot be confined or contained. Not only are we not at peace within ourselves, but on a deep level we become alienated from our fellow human beings, and from God. Even the material world that God meant to be our home and garden becomes a hostile environment to aggravate our inner lack of harmony. This is the 'bad conscience' that follows sin.

Self-awareness

On the deepest level of our personality, then, conscience is a special kind of self-awareness. It is a consciousness, not only of what we are doing, but of what we are and of what we are becoming. It tells us the kind of person we are, but at the same time it also tells us the kind of person we ought to be. It discloses the gap between the two. In this sense, it is not only a mirror or indicator, but also an invitation and a summons, commanding us to become and to be what we are meant to be. Since God is the author of our nature, it is God himself who calls us through the basic thrust of that nature, through the irrepressible appetites of mind, heart and body, recognised in the experience of conscience.

It is to this level of conscience that Jeremiah referred when he spoke in God's name: 'I will put my law within them, and write it on their hearts' (31:33), and the same message came through Ezekiel: 'I will give them a new heart and a new mind' (11:39). That God's call is not restricted to a particular religious group, but is addressed to all people in their very nature through the voice of conscience, is made clear by Paul, when he says that the conduct of the Gentiles shows that 'What the law commands is written in their hearts. Their consciences also show that this is true, since their thoughts sometimes accuse them and sometimes defend them' (Rom 2:15). Since the Gentiles knew nothing of the Jewish law, Paul is referring to something much deeper, to the experience of conscience itself. This insight of Paul is echoed by the Second Vatican Council, speaking of the salvation of non-Christians in its *Dogmatic Constitution on the Church*: 'Those who, through no fault of their own, do not know the gospel of Christ or his Church, but who nevertheless seek God with a sincere heart, and, moved by grace, try in their actions to do his will as they know it through the dictates of their conscience – they too may achieve eternal salvation' (n 16).

Vatican II

The Council uses the word 'conscience' no less than seventy two times in eleven of its seventeen documents. Thirty-eight of these occur in the pastoral constitution on *The Church in the Modern World*, and thirteen in the declaration on *Religious Freedom*.

This is not the place to analyse all these passages, but the essentials may be seen in one or two quotations. The first chapter of *The Church in the Modern World* gives a beautiful picture of the human being created in the image of God, though spoiled by sin, and speaks of the essential unity of our human nature, of the dignity of the intellect, of truth, and of wisdom, of the dignity of the moral conscience, and of the excellence of freedom. This is the context in which the Council presents its understanding of conscience. 'Deep within their consciences men and women discover a law which they have not laid upon themselves, but which they must obey. Its voice, ever calling them to love and to do what is good and to avoid evil, tells them inwardly at the right moment: do this, shun that. For they have in their hearts a law inscribed by God. Their dignity lies in observing this law, and by it they will be judged. Their conscience is their most secret core, and their sanctuary. There they are alone with God, whose voice echoes in their depths' (n I6). This text echoes many of the points we have already made. It makes clear that conscience is knowledge, awareness of a special kind, namely the consciousness of being obliged by a law not of our own making, yet within ourselves. That law is the innate thrust of our nature to love the good and avoid evil. This directive of our nature is permanent, ongoing, but not specified in detail as to what precisely is good or evil. But from time to time, 'at the right moment', the obligation becomes specific to do this or avoid that. The text says nothing about how we discover and decide in the concrete what is right or wrong. That the law 'written in our heart' is simply a metaphor should be clear from chapter 3 above. What this metaphor refers to is our unrestricted desire to know and the urge to make our activity consistent with our knowing. This urge is the inclination towards wholeness, 'at-oneness' with ourselves, peace and harmony within ourselves.

Conscience a sanctuary

The 'law in our heart' is written there by God in so far as God is the author of our nature. Our dignity lies in observing this law; that is to say that we are only true to ourselves when we act in accordance with what our conscience tells us is right. That we will be judged on the basis of our fidelity to conscience is a reminder that morality is part of religion. The text says quite clearly that we will be judged, not according to rules learned by heart, or the views of our parents, or ecclesiastical documents, or laws from the Bible, or even some law in God's mind if it could be read, but according to our own personal conscience; not according to whether we did the right thing, but basically according to whether we did what we saw and understood as the right thing to do. Our actions are judged for the light they throw on our mind and heart, insofar as they show the kind of person we are. But it is really we ourselves who are judged. Our conscience is thus said to be our secret core, our innermost being. It is an area so intimate that only God can penetrate it, God who alone can read our hearts. It is our sanctuary, a sacred place not to be violated, a place where we can take refuge from all but ourselves and God.

For all people
The voice of God that is heard there is not a detailed code, a dictated law, but rather the consciousness that morality is not simply convenience, efficiency or utility, but a demand of God himself as to what he wants us to be. For Christians, this is explicit in our belief that in Jesus, God our Father/Mother calls us to be his children, and expects us to live 'with that mind which was in Christ Jesus'. It is explicit insofar as what we see to be the right thing to do is understood explicitly as what God wants us to do. For non-believers, God's voice is implicit insofar as their moral consciousness is tinged with religious consciousness as they discover the absoluteness of the moral call through conscience, and find themselves grasped by an ultimate concern, without any explicit reference to God.

The Council makes clear that conscience is not the exclusive prerogative of Christians, and that Christians have no monopoly of wisdom when it comes to knowing right and wrong, though our faith can provide us with a new context and motivation for our moral striving. The text continues: 'Through loyalty to conscience, Christians are joined to others in the search for truth and for the right solution to many moral problems which arise both in the life of individuals and from social relationships' (n 16). The voice of conscience, therefore, does not answer our questions or solve our problems in advance. There still remains the demanding task of discovering the right thing to do. Though utterly personal, conscience is not meant to function in isolation from others. The search for what is right is a continuing process in which we share with others, with all people of good will. That it is a process rather than a static possession is clear from the following sentence: 'The more a correct conscience prevails, the more do persons and groups turn aside from blind choice and try to be guided by the objective standards of moral conduct' (n 16). Correct conscience is not instantly established by being told the right thing to do. Rather it is gradually attained insofar as people move away from blind choice and are guided by objective standards; and on the other hand, to the extent that people try to be guided by objective standards, their choices will not be blind, but governed by reason.

Objective norms

The reference to 'objective standards of moral conduct' or 'objective moral norms' could give the impression that correct conscience means simply acceptance of, and obedience to, a law laid down by some authority. This is not the case. It means rather that the reasons for claiming that a particular action is the right one must be good convincing reasons, not mere whim, that in one's search for the right thing to do, one will be faithful to the laws of reason, be conscious of the dangers of prejudice, bias, selfishness, be aware of one's obligations and commitments, of the possible consequences of one's action, of the effect it may have on other people, etc. These are all objective norms, in the light of which one discovers the right thing to do in a concrete situation. The guidelines provided by laws are an important factor in our deliberation, and in most cases we need little discussion to realise that obedience to the law is the responsible and right thing to do. But there are vast areas of life not covered by any law apart from the most general principles that we should not exploit others, that we should treat them as we would wish to be treated ourselves. In those areas where there is a specific law, there may be occasions when conscience will dictate that we disobey it in the name of a higher law, in the name of justice and in the name of God. It would be a misuse of this text of the

Council to claim that people in this situation are simply pleasing themselves, deciding for themselves apart from the 'objective moral norm'.

The text speaks of right conscience knowing the objective norms, but it is clear that knowledge is not virtue. It is not enough simply to know what principles apply. One must 'try to be guided' by them, the implication being that this is not always easy. Effort is needed to put them into practice in trying to discover what is right, and further effort is required to decide to do what conscience dictates. Doing what conscience dictates as the right thing to do is virtuous action. Acting against conscience is moral wrong-doing, moral evil, or in religious terms 'sin'.

Mistaken conscience
The Council acknowledges that one may be mistaken as to what is really the right thing to be done, that what one decides in all good faith may in reality turn out to be a bad thing. But even in this case, one is still obliged to be consistent with oneself, to act in accordance with one's honest conviction. Even in error, the sanctity of conscience remains intact. But there is an obligation to do one's best to keep conscience alive and healthy, delicately sensitive to objective norms and to the true good of the human person. The paragraph concludes: 'Yet it often happens that conscience goes astray through ignorance which it is unable to avoid, without thereby losing its dignity. This cannot be said of the person who takes little trouble to find out what is true and good, or when conscience is by degrees almost blinded through the habit of committing sin' (n 16).

The sanctity of conscience is further emphasised in the following paragraph, under the heading: the excellence of freedom. 'It is, however, only in freedom that people can turn themselves towards what is good. The people of our time prize freedom very highly and strive eagerly for it. In this they are right ... But genuine freedom is an exceptional sign of the image of God in humanity. For God willed that men and women should 'be left free to make their own decisions so that they might of their own accord seek their creator and freely attain their full and blessed perfection by cleaving to him. Their dignity therefore requires them to act out of conscious and free choice, as moved and drawn in a personal way from within, and not by their own blind impulses or by external constraint. We gain such dignity when, ridding ourselves of all slavery to the passions, we press forward towards our goal by freely choosing what is good, and, by our diligence and skill, effectively secure for ourselves the means suited to this end' (n 17). That freedom is essential to the exercise of conscience is stressed in the declaration on *Religious Freedom*: All 'are bound to follow their conscience faithfully in every sphere of activity so that they may come to God, who is their last end. Therefore the individual must not be forced to act against conscience nor be prevented from acting according to conscience, especially in religious matters' (n 3).

This applies even to the erroneous conscience. Quoting the example of the apostles and the early church, who steadfastly preached the gospel but did not impose it by coercion, the Council says that: 'At the same time, however, they showed respect for the weak even though they were in error, and in this way made it clear how "each of us shall give account of ourselves to God" (Rom 14:12) and for that reason we are all bound to obey our conscience' (n 11).

Sanctity of conscience

This emphasis on the sanctity and freedom of conscience was heady stuff for a number of people who, with only a superficial acquaintance with the Council documents, began invoking conscience almost daily to justify their eccentricities. The Council itself was well aware of this danger, and indeed adverted to it explicitly in its declaration on *Religious Freedom*. But notwithstanding the possibility of misunderstanding and abuse, it did not water down its basic teaching on the dignity, rights and obligations of conscience. It is clear from its text that the morally mature person is not the obsequious 'yes-man' beloved by some authorities, but people who can form their own judgements in the light of truth and objective reality. 'People today are subjected to a variety of pressures and they run the risk of being prevented from following their own free judgement. On the other hand, there are many who, under the pretext of freedom, seem inclined to reject all submission to authority and make light of the duty of obedience. For this reason this Vatican

Council urges everyone, especially those responsible for educating others, to try to form people who will respect the moral order, obey lawful authority and be lovers of true freedom – people, that is, who will form their own judgement in the light of truth, direct their activities with a sense of responsibility, and strive for what is true and just in willing co-operation with others' (n 8).

A basic right

These statements are not true simply because the Vatican Council decreed them to be so. The Council itself acknowledges that freedom of conscience and of honest conviction is one of the most basic human rights, that it is rooted in the very dignity of the person, 'the demands of which have become more fully known to human reason through centuries of experience' (*Religious Freedom*, n 9) It is a right to be respected by all people, but 'Christians are bound to respect it all the more conscientiously' (ibid).

The Council caught most people unprepared for the new insights, and in the confusion of the post-conciliar period it is understandable that many should come to think of conscience and authority as being necessarily opposed. In fact, they are complementary aspects of the same basic search for the human good. Whether in the church or in civil society, authority is simply the voice of the community deciding what is right, what is the best thing for all concerned. The morally mature and responsible person will admit that there is a presumption in favour of authority and law, that even though it may not be the absolute best, it is still good, and normally should be obeyed. The body of laws constitutes a kind of traditional wisdom or conventional morality that grew out of the conscience and experience of the community. But it can also happen that they reflect the narrow-mindedness and prejudice of a particular community, as in the case of racist and discriminatory laws. Unless individuals could challenge the commonly accepted moral standards of their society and refuse to be mere conformists, there would never be any moral progress; we would still be in the jungle. If society today is more sensitive to and concerned about the dignity of the human person and the equality of all people, it is only because there were prophetic voices down through history to protest against exploitation and discrimination, and to rebel against even lawful authority.

It would be a mistake to imagine that this holds true only with regard to civil laws, and that conscience could not clash with ecclesiastical authority. History proves the contrary. The laws of the church are not divinely-revealed absolutes, but human ordinances for the religious good of the community of believers. As such, they reflect not only the wisdom of the church at a given time, but also the cultural and theological outlook of a particular period, with all its limitations and defects. It is instructive to read a list of the propositions that the faithful were expected to hold down through the centuries. A few of the more bizarre ones have been quoted in an earlier chapter. Even those decreed within the present century make one wonder. Most of them were never officially withdrawn, so in theory they are still the 'official position' of the church. It was decreed that the gospels were written in the same sequence in which we enumerate them today, that the Pentateuch was written entirely by Moses, that most of the psalms were composed by David, that the epistle to the Hebrews was written by Paul. Not one of these statements is accepted as true today. One would have been called a 'modernist', and therefore condemned, for suggesting that the *Index of Forbidden Books* be abolished. Created in 1557 during the Counter-Reformation, it was in fact abolished in 1966, with its 492-page list of over 4000 condemned books.

A service to the church
Does it follow that one is not free to dissent from any of these positions until they are withdrawn? Such an attitude would do violence to reason itself. Respect for authority demands that its laws be accepted with reverence, that its teaching be received with docility, but one is still bound by the dictates of conscience guided by objective norms. No church authority can order members of the faithful to close their minds, so anyone convinced of the falsity of a particular doctrinal decree has the right to hold this conviction and to explain the reasons for holding it. Had nobody ever done this, the church would have suffered serious loss in the course of its history. There is no shortage of examples

to choose from, even apart from the Galileo fiasco. To speak of collegiality in the church was tantamount to heresy for years. Had everybody accepted this position without question, it would not have been possible for the Vatican Council to produce the *Dogmatic Constitution on The Church* as it did. Sadly, in spite of Council teaching on this point, there are still no structures in place to make collegiality a reality in today's church. Had French and German monks not broken liturgical laws in the nineteen forties and fifties, it is unlikely that the liturgical renewal launched by the Council would ever have taken place. It was the constant teaching of the church for over fourteen hundred years that slavery was not intrinsically evil. This was not officially changed until Vatican II, but it would never have changed had not conscientious people spoken out against it. An acquaintance with history and a more nuanced understanding of the teaching authority of the church might have cooled the contraception debate considerably. The 'teaching' of *Humanae vitae* has failed to convince most people, and to give the impression that it can be imposed under obedience does serious harm to the church's teaching authority. Cardinal Léon-Joseph Suenens, one of the most respected members of the Second Vatican Council, argued that the encyclical would have had much more authority had it been a collegial production instead of the lonely decision of Pope VI. When John Paul II was elected pope in 1978 he set about strengthening the rule of the church from Rome. John Wilkins, former editor of the London *Tablet*, claims that he did this by redefining collegiality to empty it of any real meaning.[1]

The debate about its 'obligation in conscience' is a perfect example of a 'category mistake'. The words 'teaching' and 'obedience' do not belong together. When it was presented to the public it was clearly stated that it was not 'infallible'. Later it was rumoured that Pope John Paul II wished to declare it infallible but was persuaded not to. Why do church authorities expect it to be 'obeyed'? When I work hard and conscientiously to prepare a lecture and deliver it to students, I would never ask: 'Do

---

1. John Wilkins, 'Bishops, not Altar Boys', in *Commonweal*, New York, June 6, 2008.

you obey my teaching?' I would be interested to know if they found it convincing and were persuaded by the truth of it. The word 'obedience' has no meaning in this context. But if I were president of the institute and made an order within the limits of my authority, I would certainly expect 'obedience'. But truth cannot simply be 'declared' and imposed under obedience. Truth can only be discovered and shared. Truth shines by its own light. When the phrase 'church teaching' is used, it would be far more convincing if it were used with the Vatican II understanding of the primary meaning of church as the People of God. A major weakness in our Catholic Church is that popes and bishops for far too long have behaved as absolute monarchs instead of leaders of a Christian community. 'Church teaching' is seriously impoverished when they do not recognise the conscience of God's holy people who are the church as a divine resource, together with scripture, tradition, reason, etc, in our search for truth. Church leaders seem to be afraid of the sacred conscience of church members as a threat to their authority. Have they forgotten that in the family of God that we call church, authority is service, not power?

A major element in the credibility of church teaching is body language. Jesus taught by word and deed, but discussion of church teaching can focus almost exclusively on words and documents. If the church in practice were living up to the ideals it preaches, its most effective teaching would be the silent sermon of its example. Outsiders do not read our documents, but what they see in church action can sometimes reinforce their prejudices, and some see the church as an ideological power-structure in the hands of repressive authorities. Its political concerns can often blur its gospel image, for example when it sides with dictators and military regimes. Its record in Haiti was a scandal. Moreover, when clerical sex scandals reached world headlines, the automatic response of church leaders, even in Rome, was one of damage control, to cover up and protect the church's image. Only later was it realised that this reaction did even more damage to the church's image. It took considerable time before compassion and justice for the innocent victims became a concern, which would seem to indicate that the gospel response of mercy is not a spontaneous reaction of the church.

Authoritarianism

What puts many people off the Catholic Church is not its authority, but its authoritarianism, its way of exercising authority. It presents a most unattractive picture when it publicly humiliates or disparages saints, prophets and pastors loved by millions of believers, people like Bishop Helder Cámara, Cardinal Arns, Archbishop Romero, and it censures respected theologians like Rahner, Schillebeeckx, Häring, Boff, Curran and others. It can seem more interested in power than spiritual insight or pastoral concern. At times the church's central authority is not only at variance with the normal procedures of justice and fairness now commonplace in the civilised world, but even contradicts its own official teaching. For example, when it condemns a theologian for his views, there is no real dialogue. He is called to Rome to be lectured, and the same authority carries out the investigation, produces the evidence and pronounces the condemnation, while the accused is not even told who his accusers are, and the whole procedure is kept secret, allegedly to protect the accused, but in fact so that the prosecutors are saved the embarrassment of being called to account. Already in 1215 the Fourth Lateran Council decreed that: 'He who is the object of an inquiry should be present at the process, and should have the various headings of the inquiry explained to him, so as to allow him the possibility of defending himself; as well, he is to be informed not only of what the various witnesses have accused him, but also of the names of those witnesses.' The harrowing experiences of Frs Häring, Curran, Boff and so many others at the hands of the Congregation for the Doctrine of the Faith in recent times would have been condemned as unjust by the church itself in the thirteenth century.

Just a few years ago, an archbishop from one of the Vatican congregations publicly declared that the church had nothing to be ashamed of in the Inquisition, that it was quite justified. A sobering thought is that so many of the documents from Roman congregations will be lying unread in church archives except as material for students seeking doctoral dissertations, whereas the writings of Rahner, Schillebeeckx, Häring, Küng, Gutierrez, Boff and Curran have already entered into the church's bloodstream to enrich its intellectual, spiritual, and pastoral life.

Theological censorship was exercised in such a way in the church for the past four hundred years that there was a real lack of freedom of theological expression. Books were placed on the Index *en bloc*, with no discussion of their contents. Because of the severity of the censorship, moral theology as expounded in textbooks for generations was largely thoughtless conformism. That the climate in today's church is different is due to the fact that there were conscientious non-conformists to ask questions and look for reasons. To be faithful to conscience, therefore, is not simply to go one's own way in spite of the church, but to be faithful to the reality of the church, which is Christ, to contribute to the welfare of the People of God who are the church. It is not merely the exercise of a personal right to question and speak out, but a vital contribution to the very life and health of the church itself.

Conscience not infallible
But Vatican II's insistence on the sacredness of the individual conscience should not allow us to forget that conscience is not infallible, that it can be blunted by sin, and that even good people can be guilty of self-deception. There is wisdom in the old saying that no one is a judge in their own case. But the solution is not that people should therefore abdicate their moral responsibility and let someone else take the place of their conscience. Rather, when people find themselves perplexed or in conflict with authority, they should look to their fellow-believers for counsel, seek guidance from the Bible and church teaching, and turn to God in prayer. All of these may enlighten us to our own ignorance or self-deception, and we must always remain open to this possibility. But should we find that, having done everything possible, we are still convinced that we cannot accept the ruling of authority, this is the conviction we are bound to follow. Should this mean losing our reputation, our standing in the community, or even our life, our conscience is still the voice we must obey. No church, no authority, no superior can take its place.

Theologian Joseph Ratzinger, now Pope, summed up perfectly the teaching of the Catholic Church in the words: 'Over the pope as the expression of the binding claim of ecclesiastical authority, there still stands one's own conscience, which must be obeyed before all else, even if necessary against the require-ment of ecclesiastical authority. This emphasis on the individual, whose conscience confronts him with a supreme and ultimate tri-bunal, and one which in the last resort is beyond the claim of ex-ternal social groups, even of the official church, also establishes a principle in opposition to increasing totalitarianism.'[2]

Because the individual conscience is so open to distortion and self-deception and therefore may often be in error, and be-cause there is normally a presumption in favour of authority, it is sometimes taken for granted that authority is automatically right, that dissent is simply disloyalty, and disobedience there-fore sinful. But there is no principle in the Bible or church teach-ing to the effect that authority is always right, or that the conser-vative side must always win. In fact, the language of winning or losing is totally out of place here, especially in the Christian community of the church. Since both authority and conscience are complementary elements in community living, it is not sur-prising that people should experience a tension between them. But this tension is something we must learn to live with. It can become almost unbearable for either side at times, and there is a natural inclination to get rid of it by bulldozer tactics. Authority may rigidly insist on conformity, or individuals may reject all dialogue and make their decisions in isolation.

Situations like this can involve sin, on the part of either or both sides. If non-conforming individuals are sometimes intemperate or violent in their relations with authority, it may simply be the reaction of their sinful, but very hurt, human nature to the violence originally done to their conscience and human dignity by the authority. Violence breeds violence, and there are more kinds than physical assault. No one has a monopoly of sin any more than any one side has a monopoly of grace or inspir-ation. The church which is not only an institution with its neces-sary organisation, but also a fellowship of brothers and sisters in the Lord, needs to discover ways and means of resolving con-flicts, and exercise the ministry of reconciliation rather than the strategy of unconditional surrender.

---

2. Joseph Ratzinger in Herbert Vorgrimler, ed, *Commentary on the Documents of Vatican II*, vol V, p 134.

CHAPTER SEVEN

Am I really guilty?

Conscience, sin, guilt – these three terms are inevitably linked in any discussion of morality. The simple catechism presentation of them made their meaning quite clear. Conscience judges when an action is right or wrong, in accordance with God's law or not. To act against this judgement knowingly and deliberately, is sin. The awareness of having sinned is the voice of conscience telling us we are guilty, and this spills over into the emotions to create the feeling of guilt, though of course guilt itself is simply the other side of moral consciousness. This, in fact, is the experience of the normal person trying to live a good life. But for many people today, the terms are no longer as clear and simple as they used to be.

Brainwashing?
There are those who claim that there would be no experience of sin and guilt were it not for the indoctrination and brainwashing of children by the conventions and taboos of society. It is said that conscience is no more than Freud's super-ego, with its litany of do's and don'ts to tyrannise over us and make us feel guilty. It is simply the finger-wagging parent, no longer supervising potty training, but now internalised to hound us even in our secret thoughts and hidden desires. The all-seeing eye of an avenging God is simply the religious extension of this.

Psychiatrists can tell of the high percentage of their patients who are crippled by a burden of neurotic guilt that has little to do with real sin and moral conscience. On the other hand, so much is now known of the limitations of human freedom that come from our physical make-up, psychological blocks, subtle social pressures and even the material environment in which we live, that people ask if we are really free in any meaningful sense of the word. If we are not free, we cannot be held responsible, so there is little room for sin or guilt. If sin is to be made meaningful in today's world, some of the confusion must be removed from the related areas of conscience, guilt, freedom and responsibility.

Real guilt and feelings

The word 'guilt' is used in a variety of senses. In general, it means the state of having committed a specified or implied offence. A distinction is sometimes made between subjective and objective guilt, depending on whether the person concerned subjectively feels guilty, or it is imputed to him by others. If a law has been broken, we speak of legal guilt, admitted or proved. When the wrongdoing is considered a moral evil or sin, we speak of moral guilt. But in the strict sense moral guilt can never be merely objective, or imputed by others, since the moral meaning and evaluation of a particular action necessarily involves the acting person's intention and freedom. Society can say that murder, adultery, lying, etc, are wrong, and condemn them as such, but it cannot point to an individual and say that he or she is in sin. Only God, or the individual, can make this judgement. Subjective guilt, on the other hand, is the personal awareness of having done wrong, or the belief (possibly mistaken) that one has done wrong. This awareness is not simply a cold, clinical knowledge, but usually involves feelings of uneasiness and remorse. Subjective guilt may be normal, rational, based on the knowledge of real wrongdoing for which one was responsible, or that morbid, neurotic state of emotional disturbance unrelated to any wrongdoing, or out of all proportion to the wrong done.

Another way of looking at the distinction between subjective and objective is to consider the inner element and the social element in guilt. The social element is to be found in legal or juridical guilt, and involves paying compensation or being subject to a penalty for the wrong done. If the moral guilt has been repented and forgiven, for example in confession, the legal guilt remains until compensation or a fine has been paid. The inner element is the psychological state of the person experiencing guilt, and this may be real moral guilt, as explained above, or simply neurotic feelings of guilt.

The distinction between healthy and morbid, normal and abnormal, is clear enough in principle, but can be confusing in practice. One of the reasons for this may be that not many people reach a high degree of moral maturity, and even when they do, they still carry within themselves the infant and adolescent they once were, and can be troubled by ghosts from the past. Guilt feelings thus become a prominent feature of the moral life. Another reason may be a certain imbalance in the church's teaching and preaching, relying too much on fear and threat of punishment. This causes anxiety, which is fertile soil for guilt feelings. The emphasis on law and the concern with precise measurement aggravates the tendency to scrupulosity, which is also a great source of exaggerated guilt feelings. Furthermore, the sexual dimension of life is already a difficult area to navigate in, but when it becomes the central concern of morality, as it is for many people, and as it is often preached, it adds its own turbulent and mysterious force to the experience of guilt. All of these can reinforce the notion of a taskmaster God easily vexed and quick to punish, and so we get a spiralling vicious circle of fear and guilt.

Super-ego and conscience
It would be wrong to assume, however, that the morally mature person is above all this, that conscience is simply a matter of intellectual judgement above and apart from the rest of the person. This latter notion is more akin to Freud's super-ego. The discoverer of psychoanalysis arrived at the concept of the superego by noticing that psychotic patients often had the delusion of being watched. They believed that people were waiting for them to do something forbidden so that they could be punished. From this, Freud formed the idea of a self above the normal self, a superego judging the self as an object. In early life this superego is formed by internalising the attitudes and rules of parents, and as time goes on the young person accepts these personally, along with the conventions of society, and gradually the superego takes on all the functions of early authority figures: observing, accusing, punishing or rewarding.

There is enough truth in this for some psychiatrists to identify super-ego and conscience. Indeed the childish, immature conscience of many people has all the characteristics of Freud's super-ego, but the notion of conscience outlined in the previous chapter is different. The super-ego contains unconscious as well as conscious elements, but though mature conscience may feel the influence of unconscious factors, it is not determined by them. It makes its judgement in the light of consciously recognised and rationally evaluated circumstances. When it judges that wrong has been done, sin committed, the person feels guilt and remorse, realises that it needn't have been so, and accepts responsibility for the sin. People in this situation experience inner alienation, lack of one-ness and general disharmony within themselves. But such people do not punish themselves inordinately or torment themselves with irrational fears. They know they can repent, be forgiven, repair the damage, recover their peace of mind, and continue to grow. As Christians they know that they are still loved by God, that they don't have to earn that love, but simply respond to it, and that the appropriate response in sin is repentance and the acceptance of God's gift of forgiveness.

Normal and abnormal

The super-ego is quite normal and natural in the child. Indeed, it is the basis on which conscience will later develop. The mature conscience outgrows it, but many people never fully leave it behind. It begins with the child's first experience of itself and its relation to its parents. This first experience is of the human being's most basic need, the need to be loved, to be accepted, to get approval. Side by side with this, there is the fear of rejection. This can cause such terror that it is felt as a threat to life itself. So powerful is this fear that it conditions the child's learning process. The child quickly learns what behaviour brings approval, acceptance and love, and which actions earn disapproval and cause feelings of rejection. This 'learning' extends all the way from toilet training to table manners and the moral principles of right and wrong. The latter are accepted without being fully understood, simply in order to retain the approval and love of the parents. When the child disobeys, it experiences guilt feelings, not because of any appreciation of the wrongness of the action, but because of the fear of rejection.

This conditioning is so successful that the child gradually internalises the rules laid down by parents, so that even when the parents are no longer present, disobedience brings on the feeling of not being loved or loveable, a feeling of badness. This feeling is hard to bear, so the individual resorts to a variety of ways to earn approval, to win back the lost love or at least escape from the bad feeling. We can confess and look for reconciliation, or simply punish ourselves internally with guilt feelings. The guilt is often compounded by feelings of anger, at ourselves for our failure, at others in general, or at authorities for burdening us with the super-ego. Another escape from the pain of guilt is to project onto others the fault or evil we discover in ourselves. Hatred of self quickly leads to hatred of others.

Psychiatrists are familiar with even more extreme forms and manifestations of guilt feelings. But from all of this it does not follow that conscience is simply a matter of conditioning. Neurotic guilt feelings can be traced to a variety of factors. They are more likely to be found in certain types of people, among introverts more than extroverts, and especially in people who experienced an insecure childhood, who lacked a sense of basic trust, whose parents were themselves insecure, rigid, overbearing, or perfectionist. Such people are predisposed to inordinate and often neurotic guilt feelings, and the guilt is further compounded when their experience of religion is one of rigid conformity to rules, and God is pictured in terms of threat and punishment. It can be said that such suffering is the result of conditioning. But not all conditioning is bad.

Healthy conditioning
Education involves a certain amount of conditioning, and the formation of conscience is no exception. The young child learns patterns of behaviour on the basis of reward and punishment. 'Good' behaviour brings approval and love; 'bad' behaviour brings feelings of badness, guilt, rejection. Children conform on the basis of fear or pleasure. This is the pre-moral level of conscience. But gradually we move beyond this to the stage of conventional role-conformity, where we try to please others and be accepted by them. Here we are considering others, but our motive is still self-centred, in order to win their approval.

A further stage is reached when we act out of respect for authority. At this stage moral obligation is equated with duty to social and religious authorities. Psychologists claim that most people operate at this level of conscience all through life, which explains their preoccupation with law and obedience. A higher level is reached by those who act on the basis of self-accepted moral principles, people who can be obedient to law and respect authority, but who are more concerned with the values behind the law.

This sequence of stages in the development of conscience is now generally accepted. But it would be a mistake to imagine them as watertight compartments with a sharp transition from one to the next. In fact, the earlier ones are integrated into the later ones, and in a sense provide the underpinning for them. The felt emotional states inculcated in childhood and early adolescence are quite healthy in themselves and prevent us from doing many anti-social acts. It is because of this kind of healthy psychological conditioning that we are freed from all kinds of irrational impulses. Because we don't have to battle with them and wonder on each occasion whether they are morally good or bad, we obey them naturally, almost spontaneously, so that we are free to devote our attention to more serious matters. Likewise, our conditioning in the area of conformity to law is a help insofar as we realise that there is simply not enough time in one lifetime to puzzle everything out for ourselves, so we take a lot of answers on the authority of others whom we trust. But in the case of the morally mature person, this conditioning is not uncritically accepted. The conditioning which limits us in some areas of freedom is accepted for the sake of the greater freedom it provides in the more important matters of life. It frees us from irrational impulses, endless discussion and worry, and so frees us for the ordinary business of living.

The whole person

That morally good people do not go around deceiving, assaulting or murdering people, however, is not simply the result of conditioning from without. Up to a point, the conditioning is a help, but the real reason is that such people have grown into a certain pattern of behaviour, and have become a certain kind of people. It is because they have adopted a certain basic attitude of life that their lives have an overall pattern or orientation because they have accepted certain principles and a set of values like respect for others, for truth, for sincerity, for love of God. When such people consciously and freely act against these values and principles, they experiences guilt, sin. Guilt for such people is the consciousness of having acted against their conscience, and in religious terms, of having sinned. The inconsistency between knowing and doing is felt as a break in their inner harmony. Since it is not just an abstract 'conscience' that makes this judgement, but the whole person of mind, will, body and emotions, the consciousness includes feelings of shame, remorse, guilt. Though this feeling may be heightened by echoes from the past, it is still normal and healthy, part of our human nature. It is morbid, unhealthy, irrational only when it is out of all proportion to the wrong done, or is unrelated to any real wrongdoing.

But, of course, few things in life are simply black or white, all or nothing, particularly in human affairs. Few people are at the top of the scale of moral maturity, whatever about the number who may be at the other end. Most people are at various points in between, and even within the same individual there can be varying mixtures of healthy and morbid, mature and childish. But it is important to be aware of the difference between the two, not to confuse neurotic guilt feelings with real moral guilt, or to confuse the super-ego with moral conscience.

Mature and immature
The super-ego is at work in people who see morality largely in terms of obedience to law or authority, who feel that they constantly need 'permission' for things, and cannot act on their own initiative and responsibility. Such people analyse their moral behaviour in isolated acts, with particular reference to the physical component, the quantifiable and easily measurable part. They are also very much concerned with the past, continually worrying about where they stand before God, afraid that God will tax them with some forgotten sin. They are particularly anxious in the area of sexuality, and are frequently plagued by scruples. They often feel the need to be punished for their sins, and they punish themselves even if only with their neurotic guilt feelings. The punishment can often come out in disguised form. For example, a circus performer used to end his nightly act by putting

his head into the gaping jaws of a lion. The audience saw it as an act of daring, but he confessed to a friend that it terrified him to do it, but he did it each time as a punishment for a sin of his youth. The burden of guilt, imaginary and yet very real, can have almost cosmic proportions. A particularly sad case was that of the poor lady who was convinced that she was the cause of the Second World War because she concealed a minor sin in her confession prior to confirmation. People whose lives are dominated by the super-ego are often governed by rigid rules to which they feel bound. They seldom experience a sense of freedom and they show little evidence of moral growth. Such people have moments of elation after confession, but quite easily slip into deep depression.

The super-ego may also be felt by morally mature people, but they are not dominated by it. Mature people recognise its presence, but they have it under control. Such people can respect law and authority, but their lives are governed more by freely chosen values than specific commands. Theirs is a morality of responsibility rather than of permissions. They see God as a loving Father and Mother interested in their growth and happiness, rather than as a hard taskmaster chasing after every last ounce of guilt. They are more concerned about their basic attitudes and the overall pattern of their life than about isolated bits of behaviour, though they are not careless about individual actions. They can accept responsibility for their failures and sins, but they do not torment themselves about them. They can forgive themselves and feel loved and worthwhile, because they know that God forgives them. They believe that God loves them in spite of their sin, loves them for their own sake and not simply because they have earned such love by their good behaviour. In repentance and trust, they can leave the past to God, live fully in the present and look confidently to the future.

Knowing their own limitations and weakness, they are constantly open to new information, new insights, and they want to grow in sensitivity and willingness to do good. They are ready to dialogue with others and be corrected by them. Their life is not tied to a rigid set of laws, but they are flexible, aware that growth is a slow process, that things take time. Though conscious of the danger of mediocrity and complacency, they do not get into a panic over the occasional lapse as long as they are doing their best. They know that God listens to sentences rather than to isolated syllables.

From our discussion of the influence of the super-ego as distinct from mature conscience it would seem to follow that some things considered as sins belong more in the category of moral disease, that many of the evil actions of everyday life, obsessive thoughts, aggressiveness, etc, come more from psychological complexes than from basic moral stance. The mature conscience will not be complacent about or indifferent to occasional lapses, but at the same time it will not react with the panic of the super-ego. Morally mature people have a calm approach to the problems of life, and whatever the storms that trouble the surface of mind or emotion, they can experience in the depth of their conscience the peace that only God can give.

Felt-experience needed

The fact that the super-ego can wreak havoc in people's consciousness, that it can cripple them with its burden of neurotic guilt, should make it clear that there can be no instant cure. Merely telling people new facts may produce the illusion of an informed conscience, but it will not develop a healthily formed conscience. The formation of conscience is a lifelong process involving the whole person, the feelings and emotions and not merely the mind. People operating with a childish, immature conscience, still under the influence of the super-ego, certainly need knowledge. They need to be told of God's love and never-ending forgiveness. They need to be shaken free of the rigidity of their views about obedience, law and authority. They could be enlightened about the less than healthy influence of authority figures in their early life, etc. But none of this will do much good, no matter how loudly preached or how often repeated, unless such people also have the experience of feeling worthwhile, of feeling that they are loved for their own sake and not for what they can do or contribute. They need to experience the gospel as liberating good news, setting them free personally, and not just as another message in words. They need to experience a community of people who really care about them individually as persons, people who can mediate God's love to them in a way that can be really felt, people who can truly become incarnations of God's love for them.

Are we free?

If super-ego people need so much in order to be freed from the shackles of their neurotic guilt, it might well be asked, how many people in the world are really free? If they are not free, there can be no talk of sin. There is, in fact, a great deal of unfreedom in the world. There are limitations that come from our physical make-up. For example, a connection has been found between the presence of an extra Y-chromosome in men or an extra X-chromosome in women and an exceptionally high incidence of delinquency, schizophrenia and homicidal behaviour. There are internal pressures operating on the psyche, from mental retardation to severe emotional disturbances. There are people so blinded by racial or religious prejudice from their infancy and childhood that they are incapable of recognising the human rights of the people they judge inferior. People who are socially and culturally deprived are less free than their more privileged neighbours. The vast majority of prisoners and mental patients come from the crowded ghettos of our cities, from broken homes and inadequate parents. It would be a mistake, however, to judge that the majority of people in our prisons are sinners. Certainly, they are people paying a penalty for legal guilt, but only God can measure the degree, if any, of their moral guilt. It could be concluded from these facts that people are not really free, that all their actions are in fact predetermined by character, environment, upbringing and a host of physical and psychological factors. But against this, there is the firm conviction from the beginning of human history that we are accountable for our actions, that we are responsible for the choices we make. By nature, we resist any kind of compulsion, and we insist on our right to free action. Our awareness of freedom is also shown in the experience of conscience resisting temptation, going against the tide, saying No to convention and authority.

Taking these two sets of facts together, we conclude that human freedom is not absolute, but relative. Our actions are conditioned by the various forces mentioned above, but they are not forced by them. If an action is performed without any motive whatsoever, it is not deemed a human action, even though performed by a human being. It is the act of a person, but not acting as person. Human action, responsible action, however, is always done for a motive, and the person decides which motives will determine the action. This is the experience of freedom. In the normal person this experience is accompanied by an awareness of responsibility. If one acts for a reason, one can be asked to give a response, explaining the reasons for one's decision and action, and one can be called to account for the consequences that flow from them. Children arrive at the use of reason when they begin to use the word 'because' in a meaningful way, when they begin to give a reason for their behaviour, and when they do this they can be challenged about the reason.

Degrees of freedom
It is clear that among human beings there is a whole scale of different degrees of freedom, from the lowest to the highest. But it would be a mistake to picture the different degrees applying to different people and fail to realise that in each one of us there are large areas of unfreedom. Just as the divisions between saint and sinner, believer and unbeliever are not simply between groups of people, but cut through each one of us, in the same way the line between free and unfree passes through each person. Each one of us is a mixture of saint and sinner, free and unfree. These pairs of terms are not put together simply for the sake of literary apposition. There is a deep truth hidden in the connection, namely that few human beings are as free as the saint, and that few people are as unfree as the sinner. Sin is not only an abuse of freedom, but is itself a danger to freedom and a limitation of freedom. In what sense is this so?

Love and sin
The mature conscience can understand St Augustine's words: 'Love God and do what you will.' Theologian Bernard Lonergan was echoing this thought when he said that the continual formation of conscience is as simple and as complex as falling in love. If you really love somebody, you do not have to be constantly referring to laws and rules written somewhere outside of you to guide you in your behaviour towards your beloved. Of course

we can be, and often need to be, helped by the experience of the wider community of family, friends and church, in order to discover what counts as truly loving behaviour, especially in serious and complex matters. Conscience is always personal, but it cannot be isolated from community, and for Christians it can never be cut off from our love of God. If I really love God with my whole heart, mind, soul and strength, he becomes the centre of my life, gives meaning to it and to the whole of creation. My hope is in him, my future is safe in his hands. He who cares for the birds of the air and the lilies of the field will see that I do not want. This gives me enormous freedom of mind, will and action. All my powers and energies become available for others, for love, for growth. By committing myself totally to God I seem to lose myself, but this is the Christian paradox. Dying to the sinful, self-centred self, I come alive to a better, fuller, freer self. Losing my life in service and love, I grow into a greater life of freedom and God's own love.

But when I sin, the meaning goes out of my life, and I have to search for a meaning of my own. When I put God aside and self occupies the centre, I become aware of my needs, become preoccupied about meeting them, worry about the future and spend all my energy building up security for myself, whether in terms of wealth, power or reputation. In choosing to put self first I narrow the range of my freedom. Since I have decided to serve self, and the self has such voracious needs, I am no longer free for others. Since one of my most basic needs is to be loved, and I have cut myself off from the love which gives me life and meaning, I am no longer free to decide how I am going to spend my life. The decision is already made for me by the need of my sinful nature. There is a never-ending compulsion to pursue my own interests and desires, and so more and more I concentrate on self. The narrowing horizon lessens my options, so in a very real sense my freedom is diminished, and I am really enslaved.

Freedom of the children of God
When I choose God instead of self as the determining factor in my life, I experience true freedom as a gift from the source of all freedom. Paul speaks of 'the glorious freedom of the children of God' (Rom 8:21), and pictures the whole of creation being set

free from its slavery to decay, groaning in its expectation of fulfilment. 'But it is not just creation alone which groans; we who
have the Spirit as the first of God's gifts also groan within ourselves, as we wait for God to make us his sons and daughters
and to set our whole being free' (Rom 8:23). We wait to receive
the gift, but it has already been given to us in Christ, so we really
possess it, though we do not possess it fully, so the battle between grace and sin, freedom and unfreedom is fought out in
the course of our lives. We respond to God's gracious invitation,
but it is not a single Yes, an isolated decision. Rather it is a life-
long process of growing in his love and service, a history of generosity and failure, of repentance and repeated conversion.

All that has been said of the mature and immature conscience, the various degrees of freedom and unfreedom, the
multiplicity of influences at work in us, and the continuing battle between grace and sin that is the pattern of our lives, should
warn us against the false clarity and lust for certainty that constantly tempt us. Life is a messy business. There are many grey
areas and there are mysteries we cannot fully understand. But it
is in the bits and pieces of everyday life that God comes to us,
and he comes to each one of us where we are and as we are. He
does not answer all our questions or solve our problems, but he
gives us the ultimate meaning of it all and his grace provides us
with the power to cope. By committing ourselves to him we gain
a new freedom, but that freedom includes the possibility of saying No. We can sin, and we must accept our burden of guilt.

Guilt is real
Psychiatrists have much to tell us of neurotic guilt, so much in
fact that there is a popular tendency to think that guilt itself is
not a reality, but something purely subjective and imaginary.
When we can point to authoritarian parents and the rigid conventions of society in the building up of the super-ego, there is a
temptation to think that our guilt feelings are nothing but an
over-active super-ego. A psychoanalyst, after hours of inter-
views, may dig up mountains of psychic garbage to probe the
roots of the problem. As we have seen above, there is much we
can learn from a study of the super-ego and the immature conscience. But it would be a pity if, whatever about the flaws in our

early training and the psychic and social influences at work on our subconscious, we overlooked the definite and obvious possibility that we *feel* guilty because we *are* guilty. If our guilt feelings are a symptom of a personality disorder we may get help from a counsellor or psychiatrist. There is no need for repentance. But if our guilt is real sin, no amount of counselling or psychiatry is of any help. What is needed in this case is repentance, conversion, atonement. The remedy is simple and easily available. God has given us the means to cope with sin. His forgiveness is there for the asking.

Sin is real

But even in the case of guilt as symptom of illness, there may be need for repentance and atonement. When the gospels quote Jesus associating illness and sin, perhaps they were not simply reflecting the simple, unsophisticated culture of the time. There can be a connection between the two insofar as human personality is all of a piece, and sin can have its effects on physical and mental health. I can nurse feelings of bitterness, resentment, anger or revenge until they come to possess my whole being. They literally take possession of me and dominate my life. Given the psychosomatic unity of the human person, this experience can spill over and show up in one or other of the well-known psycho-somatic illnesses. People in such a situation may benefit from the insights of a counsellor or psychiatrist, but they will not get to the root of their problem until they are reconciled with their brother or sister. More than one psychiatrist has admitted: 'I envy priests their power to say: I absolve you from your sins.'

While it is not the business of therapists to take the place of a patient's conscience and make moral judgements for the individual, they ought to realise that it is good therapy to restore a person's sense of responsibility, insofar as possible. While it may interest patients to be told that their present suffering and erratic behaviour can be traced to faulty potty training or inadequate identification with the appropriate parent, this information may only aggravate their problem insofar as they then feel that they are no longer responsible for their actions and there is nothing they can do. Such a conviction may totally undermine people's morale.

One of the deepest needs in human nature, apart from the need to love and be loved, is the need for respect. To tell people, even by implication if not in so many words, that they are not really responsible, may give them momentary relief, but in the long run it is a failure to respect their personhood. It is much better to help them to accept their responsibility to whatever degree is possible, and to support them in their efforts to make amends. When real guilt has been discovered, even under a mountain of super-ego-produced fear and anxiety, it should be dealt with rationally when the patient is ready. Repentance and atonement can be real therapy, even though the neurotic guilt may still have to be dealt with by the professional therapist.

Love casts out fear
But some psychiatrists are coming to see that they are very limited in what they can do, that perhaps they would be better employed as researchers, theorists, or resource-people for counsellors. For one thing, they are far too few for the vast numbers of people needing help. Many of those few simply cannot afford the time that each patient would require, so they settle for a quick diagnosis and chemical prescription. They are not in a position to provide the affirming, supportive therapy that, in many cases, must continue for several years. Ordinary people with some skill and training in counselling, who are prepared to really love the sufferer, can provide more lasting help than the high-powered psychiatrist who is only partly available. What the mentally and emotionally crippled people in our society need most of all is someone who really cares, in a personal and committed way, as Jean Vanier has so brilliantly proved, someone who can really touch them, physically, emotionally, intellectually and even spiritually. This is the great challenge to our Christian community. Christ promised the gift of healing to his church, so it ought to be a place of healing. Looking at people weighed down by such burdens of anxiety, fear and guilt, we might ask where is the love that Jesus said would be the hallmark of his followers? St John tells us: 'There is no fear in love; perfect love drives out all fear. So then, love has not been made perfect in anyone who is afraid, because fear has to do with punishment' (1 Jn 4:18).

CHAPTER EIGHT

Does God punish sin?

A major ingredient in neurotic guilt is the fear of punishment. The super-ego-ridden conscience tends to produce a super-ego type of religion, which not only pictures God as a lawgiver laying down rigid rules, but also fears him as a hard taskmaster. His all-seeing eye can penetrate one's actions to discover hidden motives, and his never-failing memory can recall forgotten or only half-confessed sins from the past. There is no avoiding his strict accounting, and though his justice may be tempered by mercy, it is still divine justice, reaching beyond the grave. Psychiatrists are familiar with the extreme forms which this irrational fear can take, and there are many people who suffer from it.

But even apart from the extremely neurotic cases, there were large numbers of good, conscientious people whose religion contained no small amount of fear. Until recently there were Catholics whose attendance at Sunday Mass was largely assured by their fear of mortal sin and eternal damnation. On the other hand, because many people no longer believe in hell they are less inclined to take sin seriously. An important element in the traditional notion of sin was not only that it was a transgression of God's law, but also that it was punishable by God. Can we still speak of punishment for sin? Are we still bound to believe in purgatory and hell?

Punishment in the Bible
The biblical notion of sin certainly involved punishment. The author of Genesis speaks of God destroying the whole human race except Noah and his family because sin had spread everywhere. The cities of Sodom and Gomorrah were likewise wiped out. Throughout the Old Testament God is pictured as rewarding the good and punishing sinners. Since there was no belief in an afterlife for most of that period, the rewards and punish-

ments were bestowed in this life. Health, long life and prosperity were counted as blessings from God for good behaviour, while illness, defeat in battle or any other calamity was looked upon as an expression of God's judgement and anger. The picture that emerges is quite clear: God is really offended by sin, his wrath is aroused and he punishes the sinner. The New Testament continues this picture. God's anger is manifest in the treatment given to the servant who showed no mercy (Mt 18:34), to the unfaithful servant (Mt 24:51), to those who killed the messengers inviting them to the wedding feast (Mt 22:7), and to the man without a wedding garment (Mt 22:13). It is evident in Jesus' condemnation of the unbelieving towns: 'You can be sure that on judgement day God will show more mercy to Sodom than to you!' (Mt 20:24). It is clearest of all in his description of the final judgement: 'Away from me, you that are under God's curse! Away to the eternal fire which has been prepared for the devil and his angels!' (Mt 25:41).

Punishment in the church

The Old Testament people of God, the New Testament Christian communities and the Christian Church through the centuries have all believed that God punishes sin. They believed in God as the just judge who would deal with each one according to their merits. The sinner upsets the order of justice, infringes rights, and must be made to pay. Divine justice judges and condemns sinners. While it was recognised that God would punish the sinner, the authorities in the community often took it upon themselves to mete out punishment in his name. Death, mutilation, excommunication were among the penalties inflicted by the community for various sins. Indeed, zeal for the rights and dignity of God led authorities to do the strangest things in his name and in his defence. The book of Leviticus commands the whole community to stone a blasphemer to death. The New Testament recommends that he be 'handed over to Satan'. The church's Inquisition gagged him and dragged him through the streets in disgrace. In seventeenth-century England, blasphemy was punished by boring a hole in the culprit's tongue. For a second offence, he would be stigmatised by having the letter B burned into his forehead, and for a third offence he would be sentenced to death. This notion of vindictive justice, that a sinner deserves punishment, and that it is imposed or inflicted from without, makes little sense in today's world.

Throughout most of the Old Testament, God's reward or punishment was experienced this side of the grave. In this context, there was no solution to the problem of innocent suffering. The book of Job simply acknowledges the mystery, but cannot explain why so many of the wicked prosper and go unpunished, while the faithful Job has to suffer so much. In the centuries immediately before Christ, belief in a real afterlife, as distinct from the shadowy underworld of Sheol, gradually began to take shape. The book of Daniel explicitly says: 'Many of those who have already died will live again: some will enjoy eternal life, and some will suffer eternal disgrace' (Dan 12:2). Paul told the Corinthians: 'All of us must appear before Christ, to be judged by him. Each one will receive what he deserves, according to everything he has done, good or bad, in his bodily life' (2 Cor 5:10). The words of Jesus about Gehenna, the flames of hell and the weeping and gnashing of teeth provided the basis for the fire-and-brimstone preaching of later centuries.

Catechism picture

The doctrine of hell and purgatory had quite a complicated theological history, but took definitive shape during the Middle Ages. We need to remember from chapter two that the Bible is not a book of history, geography or science, but the written account of the religious experience of the People of God, of the Jews in the Old Testament and of the Christians in the New. It is not to be taken literally in a fundamentalist way. There is no objective, a-historical, a-cultural word of God to be taken literally. God's word comes to us in human words, and these are always culturally conditioned, reflecting the thought-patterns and culture of the speakers. If we accept them uncritically we can easily create a picture of God reflecting our own all-too-human and imperfect ideas and experiences. Biblical statements and church teaching about faith reflect the culture of the period in which they were formulated. Thus, the book of Genesis is not a scientific description of how the universe came into being and where human beings fit into it, but gives us a religious understanding

165

of its deeper meaning, and of our own nature and destiny. The colourful language and metaphorical imagery are not to be taken literally. When Jesus spoke of Gehenna and everlasting fire he was simply using the language and images of his place and time. The challenge is to discover his meaning in terms that make sense to our contemporary world. This is also true of the statements in catechisms and popular preaching through the ages, and particularly so in the case of hell and purgatory. Catechisms generally were a digest of theology textbooks, presenting an uncritical, undifferentiated picture of 'the teaching of the church'. The short, concise answers gave the impression of perfect clarity and absolute certainty. The overall picture was so logical and consistent, with the various parts interlocking so perfectly, that some people now fear that the whole system will collapse because various items in it no longer make sense. They need to be reassured that the essentials of the faith remain intact, but they have to be expressed in modern terms if they are to carry conviction in today's world.

For people who may never have seen such catechisms or heard such preaching, it may be useful to recall some of the simplistic views of the past. Christian morality is the effort to do God's will as manifested in scripture, the teaching of the church and the dictates of one's conscience. Deliberate failure is sin. This can be mortal, which destroys the divine life of grace in the soul, or venial, which diminishes it but still leaves one in God's grace. To die in the state of mortal sin is to be excluded from the blessed vision of God in heaven, to be condemned to hell. Since the human soul is immortal, its punishment in hell will be eternal. Should one die in the state of grace, but not sufficiently pure to merit heaven, purgatory would provide the necessary purification to enable one eventually to see God. In the forgiveness of sin, even when the guilt had been remitted, there remained a 'debt of temporal punishment' still to be paid. Should any of this remain outstanding at the moment of death, it could be taken care of in purgatory. The souls in purgatory were considered 'holy souls' because they were already sure of heaven (which is more than could be said of the living), and they could be helped in their expiation by the prayers of those still alive.

Hell and purgatory

This brief summary is hardly fair to the full teaching of the church, but it is an accurate enough description of what was generally taught and believed. Popular imagination embroidered it with details not in the church's basic teaching. Many thought of purgatory as a kind of hell at a lower temperature or hell with the back door open. Teachers were often quite eloquent in describing the particular torments that would afflict different kinds of sinner, both in hell and in purgatory. A widely-read pamphlet still current up to Vatican II spoke of a certain holy religious spending eighty years in purgatory for a minor imperfection, and of others languishing there for years because they had no one to pray for them. In discussing the resurrection of the body, theologians explained that each person was judged individually at the moment of death, that the 'separated soul' went to its appropriate place of reward or punishment, heaven or hell, and that the body would be raised on the last day for a general judgement to rejoin the soul in joy or torment.

Many people took all of this to be a literally true description of fact, ultimately revealed by God, and were hesitant to question it. With equal simplicity they accepted accounts of visions by saints who claimed to have seen souls falling into hell like leaves in wintry weather. They did not understand that even canonised saints reflect the culture of their time and can talk nonsense. St Pius X in an encyclical raged against 'that most pernicious doctrine which would make of the laity a factor of progress in the church'.

In actual fact, the official teaching of the church is quite sober in this area. It says nothing whatever about the number of people in hell. Indeed, there is no statement to commit us to believing that anybody is there, even Judas, Hitler or Stalin. All that the church in its official statements is committed to on the subject is: that hell exists as a possibility for every human being, that it is the consequence of a person's final and total rejection of God, that it begins immediately after death, and that it lasts forever. There is no way of knowing the details. The most solid, and indeed consoling, statement we have about the after-life is the beautiful affirmation of St Paul to the Corinthians: 'No eye has seen, nor ear heard, nor the human heart conceived, what

God has prepared for those who love him' (1 Cor 2:9). Anything beyond that is mere guesswork and theological opinion. We really know nothing about the geography or furniture of heaven, hell or purgatory.

Church teaching about purgatory is that there is a purification needed for all who die truly penitent in the love of God before sufficiently satisfying for their sins through acts of penance. It adds that these people can be helped by the prayers of the faithful, and especially by the sacrifice of the Mass. Nothing more. There is no official statement of the church obliging us to believe anything about the nature of the purification, its location or its duration. Whether purgatory is a place, a state or simply a process is not mentioned, nor do we have to believe in a purifying fire or specific torments. Purgatory is simply a purifying process of final preparation before entering into the blessedness of heaven. It may be totally instantaneous, experienced in the very moment of meeting God. An example of the experience might be a loving couple who have separated because of the infidelity of one partner. When they decide to re-unite, the erring partner moving towards the re-union will be overjoyed at the prospect of the meeting and reunion, but still carry an element of fear and guilt which can be intensely painful but will disappear in the ecstasy of the actual meeting. The level of fear and guilt might determine the intensity of pain, but the purification itself would be instantaneous and total.

In his recent encyclical, *Spe Salvi*, Pope Benedict XVI refers to recent theologians who are of the opinion that the fire which both burns and saves is Christ himself, our Judge and Saviour. He beautifully describes the experience: 'The encounter with him is the decisive act of judgement. Before his gaze all falsehood melts away. This encounter with him, as it burns us, transforms and frees us, allowing us to become truly ourselves. All that we build during our lives can prove to be mere straw, pure bluster, and it collapses. Yet in the pain of this encounter, when the impurity and sickness of our lives become evident to us, there lies salvation. His gaze, the touch of his heart heals us through an undeniably painful transformation "as through fire". But it is a blessed pain, in which the holy power of his love sears through us like a flame, enabling us to become totally ourselves and thus totally of God ... At the moment of judgement we experience and we absorb the overwhelming power of his love over all the evil in the world and in ourselves. The pain of love becomes our salvation and our joy ... The transforming "moment" of this encounter eludes earthly time-reckoning – it is the heart's time, it is the time of "passage" to communion with God in the Body of Christ' (n 47).

New approach
In chapter two above we noted that the book of Genesis tells us nothing about what happened at the beginning of time, but gives us the deeper, religious meaning of what is happening all the time. We have long since stopped asking the Bible and the teaching church for answers to scientific questions about the shaping of the universe or the age of the human race. Scientists tell us that our universe began 13.7 billion years ago. Our imagination cannot cope with such a figure, but if we think of it as one calendar year we would discover that our earth was born on 14 August and first life appeared on earth on 4 September. Our first human ancestors appeared on 31 December about 7.00 pm, while the first human beings as we know them came just two minutes to midnight on that same last day of the year. On this calendar, Jesus of Nazareth was born at two seconds to midnight. On this timescale, the two thousand years of Christian history are the equivalent of just two seconds of the existence our universe. Awareness of these facts should make us a little more humble in our assertions and in the way we understand our religious faith. The Bible is not a book of science, but it gives us the deeper meaning of it all. It is time people realised that the same principle applies at the other end of our life. Biblical statements and church teaching on purgatory and hell are not meant as advance coverage on the details of our future life. They are not so much statements from the final chapter in the history of salvation as basic truths which help us to a better understanding of our present life and of the seriousness of the struggle between good and evil, grace and sin, freedom and unfreedom. It is a trivialisation of heaven, hell and purgatory to think of them simply and solely as future states, as reward and punishment for present behaviour.

It is true that Jesus himself used the language of reward and punishment: 'Well done, good and faithful servant ...' and 'Depart from me, you cursed ones.' He could hardly do otherwise than use the language of his time. He was a first-century Jew and used the words and images of his time and culture. But the idea of God sitting in judgement at the end time seems to drag him down to our level, and the very concept of vindictive justice is alien to the notion of a God who is infinite love and wills all people to be saved. It can be a frightening thing, frightening in the sense of awesome, to fall into the hands of the living God, and reverential fear is the beginning of wisdom. But God wants our love, and this will not come from fear. St John reminds us that fear has to do with punishment, but 'perfect love drives out all fear' (1 Jn 4:18). Too much in our understanding of the punishment for sin came from our experience of penal laws in civil society. The social element in sin, the harm done to others, calls for compensation or restitution, but it is difficult to imagine God gaining anything by punishing us simply for the sake of his justice. Just as we found a meaningful way of understanding God's will without thinking of a law extrinsically imposed, so we can speak meaningfully of punishment for sin without picturing God inflicting punishment from without.

Judgement is not God's condemnation

While allowing for the use of metaphor in the Bible and in Christian tradition, it would be wrong to dismiss references to 'God's anger' as mere anthropomorphism, speaking of God in human terms. Behind such phrases is the firm belief that God is a personal being who is not indifferent to our behaviour, that he is the All-Holy, that he is a loving Father/Mother who really cares and is concerned about our welfare. All references to the anger and judgement of God in both Old and New Testaments, however, need to be balanced against the emphasis on God's love. The key to a more satisfactory understanding of punishment for sin is to be found in the words of Jesus himself: 'If anyone hears my message and does not obey it, I will not judge him. I came, not to judge the world, but to save it. Whoever rejects me and does not accept my message has one who will judge him. The words I have spoken will be his judge on the last day' (Jn

12:47-48). There is no need for a judgement by God extrinsically decreed, nor for punishment inflicted from without. We are continually being called to judgement, continually being faced with the challenge of Jesus and his word. We cannot be neutral towards his invitation. We must decide whether we will serve God or Mammon. Our own decision is our judgement. It is our own personal act, and punishment is simply the inevitable and natural consequence of sin. It occurs in the very moment of sin and continues throughout the state of sinfulness.

Sin is its own punishment
Sin does indeed bring punishment, not from without, but from within itself, in terms of alienation and disintegration. When we sin seriously we are no longer the integrated, Christ-centred people God invites us to be, people growing in love, reaching out more and more to others, but disintegrated people, divided within ourselves, cut off from our true selves, from others, from the world about us, and in all of this from God. This, of course, refers to the state of mortal sinfulness, which excludes God and enthrones self at the centre of life. In this state, as explained in the last chapter, we still have freedom of choice, but the range of our freedom is radically diminished, and on the deepest level we are enslaved to self. Having rejected God's love, we lose our own power to love, though we may keep its appearances. If our life is really dominated by self instead of God, we will be incapable of loving others for their own sake. Others will be desired, exploited or dominated as objects for our own selfish interests. Since a basic need of our nature is the need to love and be loved, the sinner's inability to love is a loss at the most fundamental level of our being. We are not only strangers to ourselves, but we are estranged from our brothers and sisters, and no matter how much we surround ourselves with company, our heart experiences a profound loneliness. The very presence of others only aggravates the searing pain of our utter aloneness. The sinner is the only one who can echo with conviction Sartre's famous words: 'Hell is other people.'

Hell begins on earth
It is a mistake to picture hell simply as a punishment coming at

the end of life, a sudden shock of a new experience. Hell after death is simply the continuation and the logical consequence of a selfish, sinful pattern of life, the definitive state of mortal sinfulness. To experience the basic need for love and yet find it totally and continually frustrated is to be in hell already in this life, and to have it go on endlessly is worse than the hell-fire of medieval theology. Sartre's play *Huis Clos* is a brilliant imaginative picture of what hell may be like. The three characters are presented as having just died. They are in hell, pictured as a drab drawing room without windows or mirrors, and it is clear that they have become the kind of people they are because of the way they lived. They are pathetically reaching out to each other looking for sympathy, understanding and love, but each is so preoccupied with self, so totally locked up in self, that there is no love to give, and yet they cannot give up the effort, so there is the hell of constant striving and longing for love continually frustrated. In this kind of approach, hell is a state of mental anguish prepared for and begun in this life, but reaching a point of no return in death when the sinner says a total and definitive No to God. If hell is prison, there is no greater hell than to be locked up within oneself when that self has become infinitely small through rejection of God.

Some theologians would go so far as to say that since sin is negative selfishness, we can, by the way we live, become so turned in on self and so totally negative, that we have nothing to carry over into eternity, that we simply disappear or cease to exist. Growth in Christ and living for others, on the other hand, is a positive reality enabling us to live on forever in the intimacy of God's family. Then we can love fully without the barriers that at present tend to keep us apart.

There is no need to picture judgement at death in terms of God searching his account books or computer records to see whether we have a credit or debit balance. He has only to look at us to know whether we belong with him. If we have lived the Christ-life (known explicitly or only implicitly), reaching out in genuine care and concern for others, he sees the image of Christ in us and recognises us as his children. Heaven means being at home with God who is infinite love. It begins in this life insofar as to live the Christ-life is to increase our capacity for love, to grow in the likeness of Christ, so that in the moment of death we move into the fullness of life, a state we call heaven, where we will be at home with God and all those who love him.

This approach is beautifully expressed by James Michener in *The Fires of Spring*:

> Then from a side bench a man in grey rose and began to speak. Neither David nor Marcia knew this Quaker, nor would they ever know his name, but his words fell over the ugly architecture of their past like snow upon the buildings of Washington Square. He said: 'The most misleading concept in religion is that of the recording angel. I cannot believe that God remembers or cares to remember a single incident of our lives. I am the recording angel. My spirit and my body are the record. My good deeds show in me, and my wrong deeds can never be hidden. My spirit either grows to fullness or declines to nothing. God has no need of recording devices. We must not think of him as a vengeful or shopkeeping dictograph. He has created a better instrument than a strip of all-recording film. He has made me. He needs only look to me, and all is recorded.
>
> Therefore, we must conclude that we retain the privilege of erasing past mistakes. Sometimes I think we Quakers do not attend carefully enough to the teachings of the Catholic Church. I refer especially to their doctrine of final salvation. I know it is repugnant for some Friends to contemplate a totally evil man's being saved in the last gasp of life, but if what I have just said about God's establishing us as his immortal recording devices is true, I for one believe this to be possible. (p 445, London, 1949).

Fear of hell

All our talk of future existence, of course, is simply guesswork and very much an over-simplification. There are difficult philosophical and theological problems about the details of life after death and the resurrection of the body. Our belief in bodily resurrection stresses the essential fact of continuity and personal survival, but the church is in no way committed to any particular theological opinion about the details. Our faith does not oblige us to believe that anyone is actually in the state of hell as

173

final, irrevocable separation from God. It does require us to believe that God who is all-powerful and infinite love wills everybody to be saved, but that we humans are capable of rejecting God's love. Hell in this sense is a real possibility for each and every one of us, precisely because we have free will. To fear it is not to be terrified by an unChristian avenging God waiting to punish us, but rather to be conscious of the seriousness of life, to be concerned and awed by the fact that we can sinfully refuse God's gift of love, and to be constantly reminded of the need for repentance and conversion. Our traditional imagery of souls tormented by fire for all eternity in hell is beyond belief, and in no way part of our faith. In more innocent (ignorant?) times, preaching this kind of threat might have helped simple people to keep to the 'straight and narrow' path, but it is mind-boggling to imagine God creating this kind of parallel spiritual universe in which to punish his enemies for all eternity. When Jesus spoke of punishment for sin he naturally used the words and images of his time and culture. Only fundamentalists who read the Bible literally understand him as describing the geography and furniture of hell. We should have the humility to say that we have no way of knowing the details of the after-life, but we believe in the infinite love and forgiveness of our God.

The healing process begins now
Heaven and hell are not simply states of life after death, but realities prepared for and already begun this side of the grave, eschatological conditions with all the tension of the 'here and now but not yet' about them. In the same way, purgatory as a purifying process has its beginnings here on earth. As we have just seen, the punishment for sin, beginning even in this life, is really the effect of sin itself on our being. Even apart from the consequences our sin may have for others, injuring their person, their property or their reputation, poisoning the moral climate of the community or damaging the physical environment, all sin has an effect on ourselves. Apart from the harm particular sins may do to our health, every sin leaves its mark, deep or shallow, on our personality, making us the kind of person we are. Since all sin is selfishness, every sinful decision increases the selfish streak in our nature. It affects our relationship with God, neighbour and environment, and disrupts our inner harmony.

When we repent and receive God's forgiveness, we are healed by his grace at the core of our being. It is possible that our repentance and conversion will be a dramatic experience, turning us inside out and shaking us to the foundations. But it is seldom like that. It is not often, if ever, that we are capable of taking the whole of ourselves into a single act. Our conversion is a reorientation of our life back to God, but it takes time for this to be worked out fully so that it penetrates all areas of our lives, all levels of our heart. The sin itself is forgiven and is now no more, but its effects (which are not sins) still need to be dealt with. Repentance is more than just sorrow for sin. To be genuine, it must involve atonement, and this means restoring 'at-oneness' between ourselves and God (by prayer and prayerful love of neighbour), between ourselves and our neighbour (by restitution and loving service), and within ourselves (by mortification, discipline, self-control). It should be obvious that these are not three watertight compartments that can be taken care of in isolation. Work in any one area will not be genuine unless it reaches over into the others. Even prayer can be an escape, and it is an illusion unless it also finds expression in service.

Repentance takes time
What all this means is that repentance is not just a decision, but also a process that takes time, that must reach into the different levels of our being. God's forgiveness heals the root of our problem, transforms us into new creatures, but he expects us to cooperate with his grace in healing the effects of sin. This is what penance is all about. Should death intervene before the process is complete, the remainder is taken care of by what we call purgatory. This is the instantaneous purification in the moment of death enabling us to become whole persons, purged of the last traces of selfishness, and ready to enjoy the happiness of heaven. There is no need to think of it as a place in which people have to spend time until they are released. Those undergoing such a painful, but purifying experience can be helped by our prayers, not in the sense of having others pay the fine for their release, but in the sense that they are supported by the solidarity of the communion of saints in their transition from this life into the fullness of life with God. Pope Benedict XVI puts it very well

when he says that the faithful departed 'can receive solace and refreshment through the Eucharist, prayer, fasting and almsgiving. The belief that love can reach into the afterlife, that reciprocal giving and receiving is possible, in which our affection for one another continues beyond the limits of death – this has been a fundamental conviction of Christianity throughout the ages and it remains a source of comfort today. Who would not feel the need to convey to their departed loved ones a sign of kindness, a gesture of gratitude or even a request for pardon? ... The lives of others continually spill over into mine: in what I think, say, do and achieve. And conversely, my life spills over into that of others: for better and for worse. So my prayer for another is not something extraneous to that person, something external, not even after death. In the inter-connectedness of Being, my gratitude to others – my prayer for them – can play a small part in their purification. And for that there is no need to convert earthly time into God's time: in the communion of saints simple terrestrial time is superseded. It is never too late to touch the heart of another, nor is it ever in vain' (*Spe Salvi*, n 48).

The future is here

Christian faith will always be curious to know more details of the great truths of faith, so we will continue to search for ways of making them meaningful in each new age. Whichever theories of heaven, hell and purgatory we find most helpful, we need to remember that they are only theories, guesswork, and must be constantly checked against the basic teaching of the church, however bare and sober this may seem to be.

The mystics often speak of the acceptance of a certain degree of ignorance, *docta ignorantia*, as a mark of wisdom. The reminder is especially necessary in our present context. We know nothing of the details of life after death, and perhaps it is just as well. Our Christian faith has to do with the meaning of life rather than with the geography or furniture of heaven and hell. Preoccupation with future states could distract us from the business of everyday living and let us forget that the realities of heaven and hell begin here on earth. Jesus came, as he tells us, that we 'might have life, life in all its fullness' (Jn 10:10), not simply as a future reward, but as a here and now possession. When

we look forward to the fullness of that life beyond the limitations of our present existence, there is no need to fear, because
the God we meet is not the God who punishes, but the loving
and faithful God who wants all people to be saved. It is not at all
true that God punishes sin, but sin is its own punishment. What
we need to fear is our own sinfulness, what it can do to us, and
most of all our refusal to repent, to be converted and to accept
the gift of God's forgiveness. The phrase 'eternal life' does not
mean just more of the same, one day at a time going on forever,
but the fullness of life, of all that is good and true and beautiful,
without limit, beyond imagination. Paul's beautiful words to the
Corinthians are all we need to know: 'No eye has seen, nor ear
heard, nor the human heart conceived, what God has prepared
for those who love him' (1 Cor 2:9).

CHAPTER NINE

The Gift of God's Forgiveness

Whatever about the therapy required to deal with neurotic guilt, there is a sure-fire remedy available for real guilt and sin, namely repentance, atonement and forgiveness. On the level of human relationships there is a sense of new life and fresh start when an apology has been accepted and the broken strands of love brought together again. But when the forgiveness comes through the sacramental action of the church, backed by the authority and power of Jesus himself, it can bring a peace not of this world. Christians through the centuries have experienced sacramental confession as a real safety-valve for their accumulated burden of guilt, and received the words of absolution as a healing balm for mind and heart. But, like so many other elements in the life of the church, our experience of God's forgiveness in the sacrament of penance had its own historical development through the centuries. Christ empowered his church to forgive sins in his name, but it took over a thousand years for the sacrament to develop into the form in which we know it today. Most people would be surprised to hear that St Augustine never went to confession, and that for centuries the saintly bishops of Gaul preached that one should do penance, but go to confession only on one's deathbed.

It would be a mistake to imagine that we have nothing to learn from the past, or to think that developments in the church have always been for the best because they were directly under the guidance of the Holy Spirit. In fact, history is there to show that Christ's promise of being with his church until the end of time is no guarantee against its making mistakes. The church is not only a community of sinners needing constant reform and continual conversion, but a human family subject to the ordinary laws of human growth. This growth has its share of groping and stumbling, experimenting and learning. It brings into the future not only its successes, but also the traces of some of its less happy experiences and even its mistakes and failures. Thus, our present understanding and practice of the sacrament of penance is not all that it could be and we have no idea of what the future may bring. The new rites of celebration are an attempt to improve it, but they will have little effect unless the faithful (including bishops and priests) have a proper understanding of sin, repentance, conversion, reconciliation, penance and the sacramental celebration of God's forgiveness. Such an understanding, of course, will be coloured by our notion of God, of the church and of sacraments in general.

Problems

Too many people still have a taboo notion of morality and a magical idea of the sacraments. The impression is still abroad that only in confession are sins really forgiven; an act of perfect contrition is supposed to achieve the same result, but one needs to be almost a saint to make one, in which case it would not be needed in the first place. Some confessors are still preaching the 'gas-station' concept of grace: one can never get enough of a good thing, and frequent confession keeps one continually 'topped up'. Few people see any intimate connection between the sacrament of penance and the penitential elements of prayer, fasting and almsgiving involved in conversion. Many use the sacrament simply as a 'guilt-shedding process' with little real experience of reconciliation or spiritual growth. Some confess the same 'laundry list' each time and yet are dissatisfied because it does not enable them to cope with all the sinfulness they are conscious of. The present practice of private confession cannot deal with communal responsibility for the sinful structures of society or a sinful climate of opinion. Others are so concerned about law and measurement that their confession leaves large areas of morality untouched because there are no specific laws covering them, or they are not easily measured. Since the *Humanae vitae* debate, many people who feel free in conscience to practice contraception nevertheless feel guilty about not mentioning it in confession. Those who do confess it 'shop around' for a sympathetic priest, and they feel the variety of views and attitudes confusing. They wonder about the priest's precise role as confessor.

Many people think of sin simply as an offence against God, and see the priest as his representative, so that the church as community is almost totally bypassed both in the confession and in the absolution. Present practice can foster an individualistic piety. Besides, the idea of penance as reconciliation is obscured by equating obligatory and devotional confession, since it is difficult to speak of real reconciliation with the church in the case of minor daily sins. Although the Council of Trent's demand for integral confession of sins according to number and kind referred only to mortal sins, children were trained to think of it as applying to all sins, so that many adults still engage in a frantic search for everything they can possibly think of, and their almost neurotic preoccupation with self sometimes blots out all awareness of the tremendous gift that is God's forgiveness. Likewise, too much emphasis on the priest's role as judge can give the impression of a criminal court where every last ounce of guilt must be accurately measured and ultimately paid for.

Forgotten truths

Even before we look to the new rites, there are some 'forgotten truths' about the sacrament of reconciliation that we need to be reminded of: the theological nature of sin; a more nuanced presentation of the distinction between sins, including the dropping of the over-simplified 'mortal-venial' division; the importance of the 'time' or 'process' element in both sin and reconciliation, so that confession is simply the 'sacramental moment' in a whole process of repentance; the fact that there are various forms of penance (ordinary, everyday ones and liturgical ones, sacramental and non-sacramental); that the obligation of private confession applies only to those who are conscious of sin which is subjectively serious; that confession of necessity and confession of devotion ought to be clearly distinguished; and that grace and spiritual benefit are not increased in mathematical proportion to the frequency of confession. Church authorities at present voice concern about the dramatic fall in the numbers going to regular confession. A knowledge of history can be a sobering experience. For centuries Catholics had such reverence for the Blessed Sacrament that they rarely went to communion, so the Council of Trent obliged them to receive at least once a year. When at the beginning of the last century Pope Pius X encouraged frequent communion, people felt that they needed confession before receiving it, so this brought in the custom of frequent (weekly or monthly) confession. That practice is barely a century old.

Can we prove that when thousands queued in churches every Saturday (within living memory) to confess impure thoughts or distractions at prayer, they were closer to God than in today's world when it is a major problem for people to find quality time for their families while they struggle with problems of mortgages, health and education? But we need to go to a deeper level, to notice the contrast between the handful who still go to confession and the high percentage (up to 80%) who go to communion although many of them practice contraception. Another problem for God's holy people who are the church is the inadequacy of official teaching on divorce. Those who fail in their marriage (and they may soon be 50%) and do not qualify for a church annulment are condemned to celibacy for the rest of their lives, and if God does not give them this special gift and grace they are denied the Eucharist, leaving them with all the burdens and obligations of being Catholic but without this divine food for which they long to nourish their faith. Theologians for centuries have taught that the Eucharist brings forgiveness of sin, healing for the wounded, but church law has made it a reward for good behaviour. Confessors concerned about this ministry should ask if reviving literally what was the church's practice for less than 5% of its history would contribute to the health of God's holy people who are the church. Even if we did succeed in bringing back the weekly queues, where would we find the priests to absolve them? We would begin to experience what hundreds of thousands of our fellow-Catholics in Latin America have been enduring for centuries. If these points are properly understood, a reduction in the numbers approaching the sacrament or less frequency of individual confession need not cause alarm.

Ordinary means of penance
In speaking of God's forgiveness, the impression should not be

created that the sacrament of penance is the only means or indeed the only safe or sure way of receiving it. People need to be told of the importance and efficacy of the ordinary, everyday means of reconciliation. We saw that sin weakens or destroys our relationship with God, alienates us from our brothers and sisters, and disrupts the inner harmony of our lives. Penance is not just paying a fine for wrongdoing, accepting punishment inflicted by a vengeful God. Rather, it is a reversal of the sinful process that turned us from God and neighbour and left us divided within ourselves. We are reconciled to God by prayer, particularly the Our Father. If we can say this prayer with our whole being, really mean every word of it and try to live the attitude it reflects, then we are once more children of God. Our reconciliation with each other can be brought about by restitution where necessary, and by almsgiving, not merely the giving of money, but of our time, talent, energy, sympathy, in a word, by our giving of ourselves. We can be healed within ourselves from our weakness and self-indulgence through fasting and self-denial. Traditionally, these three: prayer, fasting and almsgiving, are the main forms of penance.

The New Testament gives special emphasis to mutual pardon as a necessary condition for divine forgiveness, and later tradition singled out the Our Father and holy communion as means of reconciliation. Daily work can have a penitential value. The penalty mentioned in the Genesis account of sin: 'You will have to work hard and sweat to make the soil produce anything' (3:19) could be seen not simply as a result of sin, its punishment, but also as a means of reconciliation. Our daily work can associate us with God's own creativity in improving the world, enable us to co-operate with others and give us a sense of fulfilment and inner peace. The whole Christian life should be a spiritual sacrifice offered for sin. It is a pity that these ordinary, everyday means of pardon have been so neglected in the last few centuries, as though confession were the only way. Without minimising the value or usefulness of confessions of devotion (where no sin is involved), we need to realise that God's grace and pardon come to us through the events of daily life. These ordinary means of pardon are always available, and they can be a safeguard against the formalism of mere good intentions and

182

the too easy 'three Hail Marys' so often handed out for sacramental penance.

Penance and confession

If sin is a process brought about by, and given expression in,
concrete actions, the same is true of repentance; it is a process involving time. Like the lost son in Christ's parable, the sinner
'comes to his senses', realises his tragic situation and repents. At
the first genuine turning towards God, the heavenly Father
reaches out in forgiveness, and the wandering son is once more
at home. On God's part, the act of forgiveness is instantaneous
and pure gift, not an earned reward. But on the sinner's part,
this return to God's friendship is only the beginning of a
process. It will take time to repair the harm done to others and to
let conversion have its full effect on mind, will and emotions.
This is the area of asceticism, of prayer, almsgiving and penance.
In the case of more serious sins, sinners must be so disposed that
they are willing, at an appropriate time, to confess these sins to a
priest. To refuse to be confronted with the incidents which broke
our relationship with God calls into question the sincerity of our
repentance

The reason for confession as part of the process of reconciliation is that sin is never a purely private affair. Even our most
secret sins affect our brothers and sisters in the community, and
when we sin grievously we cut ourselves off not only from
Christ, but from his mystical body, the community of his followers. For repentance to be genuine, therefore, it must be not merely
a turning back to God, but a firm desire to be reconciled with the
community. Private confession to the person offended may rec-
oncile us to that particular person, and where possible this
ought to be done. But reconciliation with the church as such can
only be effected through bishop or priest empowered to act on
behalf of the community. It is this official reconciliation with the
community which has been singled out by the church as the
sacramental moment in the process of repentance and forgiveness. This is the sacrament. In this encounter between priest and
penitent the mystery and gift of God's forgiveness reaches a
focal point of special intensity and meaning. Reconciliation with
the community is the outward sign of reconciliation with God,

and the absolution given by the priest is the concrete expression of God's forgiveness.

It is in this wider context of penance, the penitential process and community, that we should consider the sacrament. Keeping this background in mind may provide a safeguard against slot-machine absolutions and a magical approach to confession. To take some of the emphasis off the listing of sins may help people towards a more Christian notion of the God of infinite love, especially those people who continually confess doubtful sins or incidents from their 'past life'. One gets the impression that they confess these 'just in case' God might have something on them, fearing that God might present them at judgement day with a list of sins they had somehow committed without being aware of it. They use confession almost to insure themselves against God. Many of these attitudes owe their origin to distorted notions or exaggerated emphases on different aspects of the sacrament in the course of its history.

New Testament
It would be naïve to imagine that the sacrament as we know it came directly from Christ himself. In its modern form it is nowhere to be found in the New Testament, but penance and the forgiveness of sins are at the very centre of the preaching of Jesus. He began his ministry with the call to 'repent and believe the gospel' and he took leave of his disciples with the command that 'in his name the message about repentance and the forgiveness of sins must be preached to all nations' (Lk 24:47). Jesus himself forgave sins (Mk 2:2-12; Lk 7:36-50), and he expressly entrusted to his church disciplinary power over believers who fall into sin (Mt 18:15-17). After a fruitless private monition or before two witnesses, sinners are to be denounced to the church, and, if they will not accept correction they are to be treated as heathens and publicans, i.e. to be excommunicated. In Jn 20:22-23, Jesus told his disciples: 'Receive the Holy Spirit. If you forgive people's sins, they are forgiven; if you do not forgive them, they are not forgiven.'

Penance plays an important part in the epistles of Paul, and he makes clear that the church's decisions with regard to a sinner have supra-temporal consequences. James and John speak of the universality of sin and of its power, but they both emphasise that divine forgiveness is universal, that even the gravest sinner can count on forgiveness. The only exception is the 'sin against the Holy Spirit,' which would seem to be the sin of final impenitence, total rejection of God, the radical closing in on self that makes the sinner incapable of responding to grace.

Early centuries
In the first few centuries it was left to the bishop in each area to determine the way in which the gospel principles of forgiveness would be implemented. Gradually set forms of administration took shape. A sinner could go to a spiritual counsellor to confess secret grave sins, and the counsellor would decide whether the sins were grave enough to warrant public penance, but he did not give absolution. This came only after the penance was completed, and was a solemn reconciliation, usually on Holy Thursday. The public penances became quite harsh, including fasting and sexual abstinence, lasting for years, sometimes for life. The severity of these penances, especially the prohibition of the use of marriage for so many years, resulted in the postponement of penance for as long as possible, and a stage was reached when the church actually forbade the admission of young people to penance lest they be unable to continue it. More and more it became simply a preparation for death. The church became a victim of its own rigidity, so that for centuries no sacraments at all were available for the long years of a person's life when sins were most frequent.

So fixed was this attitude that a council of bishops at Toledo in 589 condemned repeated confession as an abuse. But the practice was already fairly widespread, coming from the Celtic churches, and by the seventh century frequent confession was common. In Ireland, penance was private, consisting in confession, the acceptance of the penance prescribed by the priest, and finally reconciliation. Many penitents did not return for reconciliation, so gradually the practice developed of granting absolution at the time of confession and the penance was done afterwards. This eventually became the common practice of the church.

To help confessors in the administration of the sacrament,

the Irish church invented the so-called penitential books, which listed the penances for various types of sins, graded according to severity, hence called tariff penances. Prayer, fasting, abstinence from marital intercourse, pilgrimage or exile were all imposed. Some were for life, others for years, from thirty down to one. For lighter sins: forty days down to one day. Seven days fasting was the penalty for drunkenness, one day for immoderate eating. A long penance could be exchanged for a shorter one of greater intensity. This kind of substitution was often necessary because several lifetimes would not be sufficient to carry out the accumulated burden of penance in some cases.

Of course these penances must be judged against the general harshness of life in those centuries. The penitential books stressed the need for contrition and conversion, and in spite of the emphasis on penitential works, the ecclesiastical and sacramental aspect of penance was quite clear. The obligation of annual confession was laid down by the 4th Lateran Council in 1215, which also imposed the strictest secrecy on the confessor. The Council of Trent added the obligation of integrity, that is, that all mortal sins be confessed in detail according to number and kind. In 1576 St Charles Borromeo decreed that every church was to have a confessional box, a step which completed the privatisation of the sacrament.

Confession and communion
Until the beginning of the twentieth century the vast majority of people rarely received holy communion. In 506 the Council of Agdes imposed the obligation of communion three times a year (Christmas, Easter and Pentecost), but in 1215 the universal law for the church decreed simply 'at least at Easter'. There were two traditions with regard to the need for confession. According to one, the Eucharist itself included forgiveness, hence the penitential rite at the beginning of the celebration (general confession of sinfulness and a form of absolution), but after the 4th Lateran Council more and more theologians insisted on private confession of grave sins as a requirement for the reception of communion.

Inevitably, confession came to be seen as preparation for communion, so that when Pius X in 1905 recommended frequent and even daily communion, the practice of weekly or monthly confession quickly followed. This is the pattern most of today's Catholics are familiar with. But the pattern has dramatically broken up in the last few years. Some of the reasons for dissatisfaction with the recent tradition have already been mentioned. We need to ask: what can be learned from the history of the sacrament, even in the brief outline we have just glimpsed? For one thing, it might relativise some of the elements we have tended to look on as absolutes, and at least it can shake us out of the rigidity that so often stifles development.

Various forms

The sacrament took many forms down through the centuries, and some of them continued side by side for years. Jesus spent much of his time with sinners and outcasts and had harsh words for the self-righteous religious establishment. He forgave sin and empowered the community of his followers to do the same, but he did not spell out the ways in which it was to be done. The church, responding to people's need for forgiveness, created new forms of penance as they were needed to meet the needs and understanding of a particular age. In the first two centuries the church consisted of small, closely-knit communities centred on the weekly Eucharist. Christians confessed to one another, admonished one another, forgave each other. For serious sin, a brother or sister would be excluded, put out of the community by excommunication, but the community continued to pray for them until they could return. The community felt responsible for the sinner. When it was feared that reconciliation was becoming too easy and Christians might grow lax, the practice of public penance was introduced. This served its purpose for a while, but then hardened to the point where pardon was not available until immediately before death.

The good sense of the community gradually moved away from this extreme practice and developed private penance and more frequent confession. For the convenience of the faithful, the order of penance and absolution was inverted so that forgiveness was granted before the penance was carried out. But with the loss of community awareness, the role of the confessor increased; he was spiritual father, teacher, physician and judge.

He was seen as God's representative, and sin was more and more considered simply as a personal breaking of God's law. Private and frequent confession did wonders for the spiritual life of the faithful, and people travelled miles to avail of holy confessors like the Curé of Ars, but the practice also encouraged an individualistic piety. The detailed listing of sins and the minute examination of degrees of guilt often gave rise to scruples, and on the other hand it totally ignored the social dimension of sin.

New rites
The 1974 legislation on the sacrament of reconciliation allows for four types of celebration: 1) individual confession and absolution, which was the common tradition, 2) individual confession and absolution, but fitted in between communal preparation and thanksgiving, 3) communal penitential services to promote a spirit of repentance, but which do not forgive serious sin, and 4) general confession of sinfulness, followed by general absolution, but with the obligation to confess privately at a later date. This last form is restricted to quite exceptional circumstances, which, in the opinion of many bishops, are not likely to arise outside of some missionary countries.

These new rites are an attempt to recapture some of the best insights of the past. The sacrament is described as reconciliation rather than just confession. Some prominence is given to sacred scripture, emphasising its healing power as well as the fact that it calls us to judgement and repentance. Communal celebrations allow for a homily and also enable the community to acknowledge responsibility for the general sinfulness of society. They bring home the fact that we are a community of sinners needing God's healing and pardon. However, many theologians cannot see why actual forgiveness is still restricted to private individual confession except on occasions so rare as to make them not worth counting. They maintain that sins are indeed forgiven in the third form of celebration, without private confession and individual absolution. This is not necessarily 'cheap grace', because most people who have had this experience also use and appreciate private confession when they feel they need it, and for many who had not been to confession for years it was the step that helped them to return. The second form, combining communal and individual, is clumsy and impractical except for well-organised, small groups with no shortage of confessors. Many feel that it has an element of 'magic' about it.

The new rites are an attempt to revitalise the sacrament, but the restrictive way in which they are interpreted means that they may make it just a little more meaningful, and then only for the devout. They are not going to work wonders. They will make little difference to the large numbers who have real difficulty with traditional confession practice. One wonders if the words of Jesus about leaving the ninety-nine and going after the one lost sheep have any application in this context. Perhaps the new legislation is simply a holding operation, a slow, tiny step in the direction of a better understanding of the sacrament, which will evolve further when church leaders are ready. But much more needs to be done to help people towards not only an understanding, but an actual experience of the mystery and gift of God's forgiveness. Surely an essential element in development is to listen to the actual experience of penitents, and most of them find general confession and general absolution the most meaningful as a spiritual exercise to which they are willing to give time, whereas the one-by-one 'quickie' feels more like an artificial exercise merely to satisfy canon law.

Need for balance

It would be a pity to encourage one form of penance at the expense of the others, or to see the sacrament in isolation from the whole process of reconciliation. Both communal and private celebrations of the sacrament are necessary and should complement each other. We need to trust people a little more, and the only way to trust them is to actually trust them. St Paul tells us to examine ourselves (1 Cor 11:28). Much more could be left to the personal responsibility of individuals with regard to self-examination and self-discipline. They could decide which forms are more appropriate for them at any given time. On the other hand, the faithful have a right to expect guidance and help from the church. The two need to be kept in balance.

It is understandable that authorities in the church should feel the weight of their responsibility before God for the spiritual welfare of those entrusted to their care. They also feel responsible for sacred scripture, the sacraments and for the things of God in general, which they must safeguard. But occasionally they give the impression that they are defending God, in which case it needs to be asked whether it is really God or a particular unhealthy notion of God that is being defended.

History shows how often the church tied itself into a straightjacket of immobility with too much legislation, how laws intended to bring people closer to God actually kept them at a distance from him. Jesus pointed out that the Sabbath was made for people and not *vice versa*. In the same way, theologians constantly remind us that the sacraments are for the faithful, not the other way round. But it is not clear how far this is accepted in practice.

Forgiveness God's gift
Reference has already been made to the 'forgotten truths' about penance that need to be recalled. Perhaps the greatest and most forgotten truth of all is that God's forgiveness is sheer gift, unearned, unmerited. In our concern to see that God is not mocked or even slighted, we may have lost our perspective. Though we speak of the gift of his forgiveness, most people feel that they must earn it, be worthy of it, that it comes only after they have done their penance, paid their fine. But this is not the impression we get from Jesus. Both in his own ministry of forgiveness and in his preaching he makes it clear that the initiative comes from God, that forgiveness is the gift of his love, and that the works of penance are the result of it, not the condition for its granting. This is particularly evident in his words to Simon the Pharisee about the sinful woman: 'I tell you, the great love she has shown proves that her many sins have been forgiven' (Lk 7:47). She was not forgiven because of her great love, but her love was the effect of forgiveness. In the many descriptions of Jesus telling people that their sins were forgiven, not a single one suggests that he asked for a list before granting his forgiveness.

The parable of the lost son (Lk 14:11-32) is the classical sermon on God's mercy, but how many people appreciate it fully? The younger son is the average sinner, independent, wanting to go his own way, to cut loose from home and community. When 'at last he came to his senses,' he decided to return to his father with the confession: 'I have sinned against God and against you.' But the original motive for his change of heart was selfish enough: the contrast between the comfort of home and his own sad situation. The father did not wait for him to prove his worthiness. He did not give him a trial period as slave, then hired worker, before accepting him again as his son. He had never ceased loving him. His love respected the young man's decision to leave home and trusted him with the money. Without even listening to the son's confession or lecturing him on his behaviour, the father received him with open arms and celebrated his return. In our own experience of the loneliness and alienation of sin, our motives for repentance may be quite mixed. But God takes care of that. His love is always there, freely offered as gift. No matter how often we turn away from it, he never withdraws it. We have only to reach out. When we experience his forgiveness, we understand all the more our sinfulness, and we respond by trying to live as his children. Works of penance and atonement naturally follow.

God's prodigal love

Not a few in our Christian community fit more easily into the role of the elder brother, annoyed at the possibility that sinners get off so lightly. But the father has forgiveness and healing for this kind of sin too. The parable is often called the story of the 'prodigal son', but the central figure is really the father illustrating the absolute prodigality of God's love, poured out spontaneously and without measure. In a sense, the words spoken to the elder son are addressed to each one of us, in spite of our sins: 'All I have is yours.' God's love is not conditional on our being worthy of it. Unlike some parents, he does not say: 'I will love you if you behave properly.' His attitude is rather: 'If you accept my love, you will not want to sin.' This beautiful parable can be very consoling when we look for forgiveness, but even when we are just struggling with the loneliness and routine of everyday living we can be spiritually lifted up in hearing those comforting words of the prodigal father: 'All I have is yours', his strength, his goodness, his abiding presence of comfort and love, and of course his endless forgiveness.

At this point, however, it is important to warn against trivialising sin and God's forgiveness. One can become almost senti-mental picturing a grandfather God who overlooks our misde-meanors and loves us out of our badness into his own wonder-ful goodness. Sin is more than mere personal wrongdoing for which we can ask pardon and try to make amends. There is a deep mystery of evil in sin which is rooted in our human condi-tion. Our human nature has dark forces and mysterious powers within itself which are not simply the effects of social depriva-tion, of mental or physical disorder, but are rather stirred up and released by these. We are all sinners in the very depths of our being, and so we all need healing. There is so much we do not understand about the mystery of evil, and sin is essentially evil. Forgiveness on this level is more costly than we can appreciate. God, in Jesus, entered fully into our human family and took upon himself our burden of sin. He 'became sin' for our sakes. His very presence provoked and brought out the evil in people, to be soaked up and neutralised in his silent, suffering body as he went to the cross and accepted the criminal's death. A mod-ern symbol of Jesus on the cross is the lightening conductor on tall buildings. When an electric storm is raging in the atmos-phere with all its lethal danger, it is attracted to the tallest metal lightening conductor and shoots into the earth where it is neu-tralised and rendered harmless. Jesus on the cross could have protested his innocence, rebuked his enemies, but his silence soaked up and neutralised all that evil. This is the cost of our healing. There is a deep awareness of the mystery of sin behind the church's joyful song at the Easter vigil: 'O happy fault which gained for us so great a Redeemer.'

Message of salvation
The first preaching of the apostles was that in Jesus, God had reconciled all people to himself, that in him we have the forgive-ness of sin. This is salvation and liberation present in the church as a here and now reality, the first-fruits of the resurrection of Jesus, the beginning of new life in the Spirit

People need to bear this message of salvation, but more im-portant still, they need to experience it. The real test of the efficacy of any of the various forms of the sacrament of reconciliation is that it brings about real reconciliation and healing. In the ministry of Jesus forgiveness and healing went hand in hand. In a certain sense, should we not ask: Where is the healing that will prove that the church has the power to forgive sins? (Mt 9:5). If the church is to be a light to the world, it must be a credible witness to the love of God incarnate in Christ. It must give a continual example of mutual pardon, of fraternal love. If the church is truly Catholic, it must be a home where all the members feel at home, a fellowship which overcomes the barriers and divisions of sin and selfishness. If the church is the sacrament of Christ, it must be the visible sign of his forgiving love. Not a sign pointing elsewhere, but an open invitation to a community in which people are healed and made whole, reconciled to each other, made friends with each other, and with God. We are familiar with the various theological definitions of the church, and especially the central one emphasised by the Vatican Council as the People of God. But the most telling image of our church is that of the great big tree in which all the birds of the air can find shelter, the weak and wounded finding protection and healing and the strong and healthy at the top, singing out God's praises.

CHAPTER TEN

Can morality be taught?

The new thinking on many of the topics touched on in the previous chapters has been a source of confusion and upset for many people since the Council. But what many serious-minded people, particularly parents, teachers and pastors, are more immediately concerned about is what is sometimes called the 'breakdown of morality'. They can accept the 'sinfulness' of the 'world', but they feel helpless when faced with the seeming rebellion of the younger generation of Christians. They find it hard to understand how children of good, church-going parents can so easily reject the moral standards they were taught at home, in school and in church. The immediate reaction of a father or mother to a teenage member of the family on drugs, having a baby before marriage, or going for an abortion, is to ask: How did it happen, why did it happen? So often they insist: But I told them it was wrong, they know they shouldn't behave like this. Sometimes the reaction becomes an agonising self-recrimination: Where did we go wrong, did we fail them in any way?

Is it so bad?
It has always been the mission of prophet and preacher to point to the sins of society, to alert people to the immorality of the times. We need such reminders. But the moralising can be overdone. It has become almost a cliché to speak of the permissiveness of today's world and complain about the church going to the dogs. It is natural too to look for scapegoats. Some bishops blame theologians for 'confusing the people' (as though they were never confused by bishops), priests blame parents for not exercising control in the home, parents blame teachers and pastors for their failure to give clear moral principles, and everybody blames the 'world' or the 'media'.

Each group pointing a finger at a particular scapegoat should realise that there are three other fingers on the same hand pointing back at themselves. 'Passing the baby' is part of the psychology of sin described in the Genesis story at the beginning of the Bible. Adam blamed Eve, who in turn blamed the serpent. Since each one of us is, whether we like it or not, 'our brother's and sister's keeper', we all have a share in the responsibility. The failure may be unconscious, and therefore without sin, but our unwillingness to accept responsibility or to do anything about it can indeed be sinful. It is not the purpose of this chapter to point a finger in any one direction, but rather to raise questions that will stimulate reflection. As in so many other areas of Christian faith and living, perhaps there are many things we have taken for granted in the area of teaching morality that need to be looked at a little more critically.

First and foremost, the facts must be seen in perspective, without panic. It is simply not true that the world is in a worse state now than ever before. Only people who know nothing of history speak like this. We may feel that we are further off from heaven than when we were children, but this is generally no more than feeling. The myth of the golden age is as old as human history; we all tend to look back nostalgically on the past and see it through rose-tinted spectacles. A generation or two ago perhaps there was less gang violence or sexual promiscuity in our immediate neighbourhood, but it is a very large assumption to claim that the overall moral climate was better. Social conditions were different, sanctions were stronger, and for many people the possibilities for wrongdoing were extremely limited. The old sailor with little material for confession after several years at sea could give as his excuse: plenty of temptation but little opportunity. For previous generations, even the temptations were limited. The fact is that the world has changed more in the past fifty years than in all of previously recorded history. Today's youngsters have to cope with pressures far more subtle and complicated than those known to their parents, and they are faced with a vast variety of choices that were simply undreamed of in the past.

Culture-gap

There is simply no way of comparing generations in any worthwhile way. The parent who begins a lecture with the words
'When I was your age' is liable to be told by the teenage son or
daughter: 'But you were never my age.' James Michener's novel
The Drifters is a graphic description of the vastness of the culture-gap between today's adults and their teenage offspring. It is
no longer simply an age-gap or a generation-gap. It really is a
culture-gap. Many aspects of the cultural shift are highlighted
by Alvin Toffler's fascinating *Future Shock,* but philosophers and
theologians claim that for the past few decades the human race
has been undergoing one of the greatest cultural changes in its
entire history. They describe it in terms of the shift from classical
to historical consciousness. This change involves a whole new
outlook on reality, and reaches into every area of experience.
Vatican II adverted to it, for example, in the document on *The
Church in the Modern World*: 'The accelerated pace of history is
such that one can scarcely keep abreast of it ... and so we substitute a dynamic and more evolutionary concept of nature for a
static one, and the result is an immense series of new problems,
calling for a new endeavour of analysis and synthesis' (n 5).

Part of the problem in today's church is that people talk
about morality and the teaching of morality with practically no
reference to this change. But the change affects both our notion
of 'morality' and how it can be 'taught'. It is taken for granted
that there is a revealed and timeless morality that has only to be
taught or handed on, but in fact there are question-marks over
both the content of morality and the ways in which it can be
taught. So many people look to the past or to some revelation
from above as the source of moral teaching. But it is significant
that even in the area of dogmatic truth, the Vatican Council
speaks of revelation as an ongoing process, continuing into the
present. It says that 'Christ reveals us to ourselves and gives
meaning to the riddles of sorrow and death' (*Church in the
Modern World*, n 22). 'Believers, no matter what their religion,
have always recognised the voice and the revelation of God in
the language of creatures' (ibid, n 36). In his self-revelation 'God
spoke according to the culture proper to each age' (ibid, n 58).
Speaking of revelation as a continuing process to be newly ex-

pressed for every age in prophetic witness, it says that 'It is the task of the whole people of God, particularly of its pastors and theologians, to listen to and distinguish the many voices of our times and to interpret them in the light of the divine Word, in order that the divine truth may be more deeply penetrated, better understood and more suitably presented' (ibid, n 44).

Changing morality?

With regard to the 'content' of morality, enough has been said in previous chapters to make clear that no moral problem can be solved simply with a quotation from scripture or an ecclesiastical document. There is no 'package' of detailed moral truths to be merely preserved and handed on intact to later generations. The church's function is to remain faithful to the spirit of Christ, to preach in word and deed the good news of salvation and the liberation we have in Jesus, and try to live out his commandment of love. But how the commandment of love is to be understood and implemented will depend on our understanding of ourselves and of our world in each culture. There have been radical changes in the church's moral teaching through the centuries. There is no shortage of examples: with regard to slavery, property, usury, war, women, sexuality, marriage, responsible parenthood, organ transplants, social justice, church-state relations, conscience, conscientious objectors, freedom and human dignity, peace. It is a false loyalty to the church, and no loyalty to God or to truth, to pretend that the changes were all minor modifications. Changes on all of these subjects were substantial, and often radical.

Had people been aware of the provisional character of most of the church's statements on moral matters, they would be less upset and confused when faced with change. But if the statements themselves had been presented less dogmatically there would be less need for humility in admitting that they needed to be modified or perfected. The Vatican I statement that the Pope is infallible when teaching as head of the church on matters of faith or morals, is frequently quoted in support of a particular 'teaching of the church', but it is seldom recognised that the church has never made an infallible statement on a matter of morals. The point being made here is not that one can lightly dismiss the church's moral teaching because it is not infallible, but simply that people need to understand the changeability of morality. As already explained, this does not mean a morality without norms or a private conscience cut loose from objective standards. It simply emphasises the cultural conditioning of all concrete norms, and the fact that answers from the past cannot always solve new problems.

While we can rightly claim to have high moral teaching in the New Testament, a knowledge of history should keep us from boasting too much. Only too often through the centuries the church imbibed and reflected the prevailing values of the times, and its record in the fight against colonialism, slavery, anti-Semitism, racism or anti-feminism is nothing to be proud of. Though we can make allowance for historical context, the church was no better than the secular state when it justified torture and the death penalty for heresy. Please God, we have come a long way since then.

Common search
When it comes to discovering solutions to new moral problems, the whole people of God, pope, bishops, theologians, priests and laity, simply have to work towards them with their God-given human reasoning power. The simple commandment 'Thou shalt not kill' will not solve the intricate problems of medical ethics, nor have we any formula of solution for the new questions arising from the population explosion, genetic engineering or brain transplants. In this common search it should be stressed that in a sense the whole church is a learning church and the whole church is a teaching church. Married people have a lot to teach celibates about the experience of marriage, and priests and laity can learn from each other. Likewise, the church learns from its past, from its mistakes, from other Christians, who have their own experience of the Holy Spirit, and from the surrounding world. Bishops and theologians have special teaching functions and they collaborate in promoting faith, and both groups serve the church.

As part of their pastoral responsibility, the pope and the bishops have a special authority in the area of teaching, though they are by no means the only teachers in the church. For Vatican II a central teaching was the principle of collegiality, that the church is governed by the college of bishops, with and under the pope. They exercise a shared responsibility with the pope and are not simply his delegates. In carrying out this responsibility, pope and bishops have a grace of state available to them because of their responsibility, but it does not operate automatically. To access it they have to take the ordinary means of research, study, consultation and prayer to discover and formulate their teaching. But they have no access to sources beyond the reach of the body of the faithful, nor are they empowered to produce 'new teaching', to tell the faithful things they would not otherwise know. In the area of infallible pronouncements on matters of faith, pope or council can only 'define infallibly' what is already the faith of the church. In the question of categorical morality (i.e. teaching in particular areas of morality), right and wrong cannot simply be 'decreed' and 'accepted'. It can only be preached and urged, backed up by persuasive reasoning inspired by the gospel and the tradition and experience of the church. In this area, the support of the Holy Spirit does not guarantee the truth of the teaching, but simply prevents the church from falling finally and definitively into error.

Teachers of freedom?
When Jesus took leave of his disciples, he commissioned them to 'Go to all peoples everywhere and make them my disciples' (Mt 28:19). Thus, he entrusted his teaching function to his church, to the whole community of his followers, to be shared in different ways by all. There are bishops, theologians, scholars, teachers, missionaries, counsellors, parents and friends. But the most important teachers for those born into a Christian community are their parents. It is from them that we get our faith and our understanding of morality. Their work is continued by teachers in school and by priests in church. Parents, teachers, priests, all have their part to play in the teaching of morality, and in a sense all are extensions of the teaching church embodied in the pope and bishops. But some questions arise about the teaching process today which may give food for thought to the various teachers in the chain.

Speaking of education, the Second Vatican Council affirms

that 'children and young people have the right to be stimulated to make sound moral judgements based on a well-formed conscience and to put them into practice with a sense of personal commitment' (*Christian Education*, n 1). It urges those responsible for educating others to try to form 'people who will be lovers of true freedom, who will form their own judgement in the light of truth', and it stresses that 'one of the key truths in Catholic teaching is that our response to God by faith ought to be free' (*Religious Freedom*, nn 8, 10). Paul frequently speaks of 'the glorious freedom of the children of God' (Rom 8:21). He urged the Galatians to 'Stand as free people, and do not allow yourselves to become slaves again' (5:1). He told the Corinthians that 'where the Spirit of the Lord is present, there is freedom' (2 Cor 3:17). Jesus himself promised his followers: 'If you obey my teaching, you will know the truth, and the truth will set you free' (Jn 8:31-32).

These quotations come from a variety of contexts and would need careful explanation, but there is no denying the emphasis on freedom. The salvation we have in Jesus means liberation from the slavery of sin and from the imprisonment of ignorance and fear. A basic concern of Christian formation, therefore, should be to enable people to grow as free persons, to encourage personal responsibility and moral maturity.

Inhibited growth

But our teaching has frequently been unsuccessful in this, and large numbers of people are imprisoned by an immature conscience, live in constant fear, and have seldom experienced true freedom. This is not the place to discuss the various methods of catechesis, but a point may be raised for those who hanker after the clarity and security of the old catechism and the black-and-white absoluteness of the moral rules that went with it. The traditional catechism was largely a condensation of the theology textbook, a summary of grown-up beliefs. It was taught to children to prepare them for life, as though they were simply adults in miniature. We looked for an adult response of faith from adolescents and young children, and in many cases we took it for granted that they had such faith because they had learned the answers to our questions.

In the area of morality, we did not make quite the same mistake, because we taught them rules reinforced by rewards and punishments, which is what they understood in those early years. In the same way as they learned behaviour acceptable to the parents (toilet training, table manners, etc), they learned a list of 'sins' punishable by God in hell and good deeds rewarded by God in heaven. God was used as a cudgel to ensure that they would conform. Indeed he was sometimes used as a threat to have them conform to the social prejudices of the parents. Children were told that 'God would not like' certain things, although there was no way of knowing whether he had ever even expressed an opinion on them.

Many people outgrew the childish fear provoked by the 'God as threat' as they matured morally. But much of the church's practice continued to rely on this fear in getting people to 'behave', and many were thus kept at a childish level of response. In the area of dogma we treated even small children as adults in the material we taught them, while in the area of morality we continued to treat grown-ups as seven-year-olds. Missing Sunday Mass was declared to be a mortal sin, punishable by hell-fire, while for centuries we did nothing to make the Eucharistic celebration a meaningful experience. For some people, it is still a matter of 'obligation'. Like any large society, the church needs law, but the multiplicity of laws attempting to provide for every foreseeable eventuality would seem to imply that people are not to be trusted to do the right thing in a given situation. It was forgotten that people only become trustworthy through the experience of being trusted.

Less than a hundred years ago Pope Leo XIII wrote to the Archbishop of Paris: 'To the pastors alone is given the power of teaching, judging and ruling; the people must allow themselves to be governed, corrected and led to salvation.' In spite of the insights and ideals of Vatican II, this paternalistic attitude is not quite dead in the church. It is traditional Catholic teaching that parents must make decisions for their children, but they can be guilty of sinful neglect if they do not help the children to grow towards freedom and autonomous decision. This is particularly true in the area of morality. Is it not bordering on the sinful when church practice tries to guarantee morality by pressure and sanctions, apart from those cases where sanctions are absolutely necessary? So often there is an appeal to 'loyalty' and 'obedience' to accept a particular ruling instead of an effort to convince and persuade people's conscience. Authority is too frequently substituted for reason.

Challenge from youth

People who are accustomed to having most of their moral decisions already made for them, who have been trained to think of morality in terms of obedience to rules handed down, are ill-equipped to make conscientious judgements when they are suddenly told to 'follow their conscience'. This is the dilemma of many parents at the present time when they are challenged by their teenage children. They do their best to 'hand on' the moral truths they themselves received from home, school and church. They grew up in a society where conformity was rewarded and questions seldom allowed. But their children live in a different world.

The 'traditional teaching' can be passed on in terms of moral precepts, but it is much more important that children be taught the mechanics of moral evaluation and personal conscientious judgement. With methods appropriate to each stage of their psychological development they should be helped to see what factors need to be considered in any given situation, how they are to be balanced one against the other, and how one decides on what is morally the best thing to do. The answer cannot be given in advance. But once they leave childhood, nobody can make their decisions for them. It may be upsetting for parent, teacher or priest to see the youngsters decide on and do things we consider 'wrong' or 'sinful', but unless they have the freedom to make mistakes, whether or not they actually make them, they will not grow in moral maturity. God respects our freedom in the initial act of faith, and we must respect it in each other. The person who is prevented from ever making a mistake may also be prevented from ever growing up.

Sharing values

Parents, teachers and church leaders may hand on the moral wisdom of the church enshrined in commandments and rules, but the real problem is to communicate the values behind such norms. Information is not enough. Likewise, mere conformity, or obedience to an external law (thou shalt not steal, kill, etc), is not virtue. The virtuous action is the one done out of the conviction that it is the right thing to do. But it is too easily assumed that values (like truthfulness, sincerity, justice, etc) can be 'transmitted'. In fact, values are not personal values unless they are 'discovered' and personally chosen as worthwhile, as something worth striving for, paying for, making sacrifices for, as values one wants to live by. The challenge is to create an atmosphere and environment in which children and young people discover moral values as truly valuable.

They will not be convinced by exhortations from parents or others to tell the truth, go to church, or be fair to others if they find those same authority figures continually telling 'white lies', being careless about church attendance themselves, or boasting to each other of 'good' business deals which patently involved unjust practice. Even small children are highly sensitive to such inconsistency, and what they follow is not what they are told verbally, but what they see 'done' and what they think 'works'. Parents sometimes complain of the 'materialism' and 'permissiveness' of the younger generation, but are quite unaware of how much these things are part of their own thinking and how much their practical judgements are influenced by them in spite of theoretical attachment to the principles they preach. Our own double-think in many areas of morality may be partly responsible for the moral confusion or rebellion of the younger generation.

Moral development

There is a vast amount of research by developmental psychologists from which valuable lessons can be learned by those concerned with moral formation. The lessons are not only for parents forming their children, or teachers dealing with students, but also for holy mother church itself helping the faithful towards the freedom of the children of God. Kohlberg and practically all the experts in this field have found a consistently direct connection between conscience and parental punitiveness. Punitive aggression by the parent leads to aggression by the child, but it does not lead to moral learning. The old pattern of lecturing, rewarding and punishing may produce conformity, which may have the appearance of virtue, but it does not lead to moral development.

Even the lecturing has its weaknesses. Parents often admonish their children for bad behaviour with the complaint: 'You should know better!' In many cases, the youngsters do know, and the gap between knowing and doing is one we all experience, and even St Paul admitted to it. But over and above this tension, which is simply one of the effects of original sin, there is the fact that so much of our moralising is cerebral, limited to abstractions, and presented in words that are not meaningful to young children. An eight-year-old sees no connection between the principles he is taught about respecting other people's property and taking fruit from a vendor's basket. The reason why our efforts at moral training so often meet with disappointment is that they rely too much on the intellectual approach. Children are sometimes called 'little liars' at an age when they haven't the faintest idea of what a lie is in moral terms. They tell lies out of fear or as an enjoyable exercise of creative imagination, but they have no intention of deceiving anyone, much less of harming. Adults who read moral meaning into quite innocent events or insist on extracting 'confessions' under threat of punishment can be guilty of mental cruelty to children. Such attitudes not only do a great deal of psychological harm, but actually stunt the moral growth of children.

Lack of love
There is considerable statistical evidence to show that delinquents tend to come from homes where an excessive amount of corporal punishment was administered. When children who suffered in this way are old enough, their reaction to the blind, unreasoned way in which they were handled is expressed in anti-social aggression. They have not learned respect for authority and show no signs of a healthy conscience. The excessive nature of the punishment and the inconsistency of its application leaves them feeling a lack of love and of basic trust, thus depriving them of two of the essentials on which mature moral living depends.

Strange as it may seem, the children of totally permissive parents are deprived in precisely the same essentials. The parents may give them money and seemingly endless freedom, in fact everything except what the children need most of all, namely the gift of themselves and their genuine care. Such children may boast to their peers that their parents do not care how much they spend or where they go, but when they get into trouble the boast sounds very hollow. Deep down, they know that what they are really saying is that their parents don't really 'care'. Of course, it may well be that the parents do in fact care, but their neglect or ignorance of what caring really means can prevent the children from discovering and feeling their love.

It follows that some form of moderate punishment can be an element in moral training. It can help in the development of responsibility as young people learn to accept the consequences of their actions. Likewise, rules have their part to play insofar as children discover that even limitations on their freedom are for the sake of a greater freedom. But neither punishment nor rules will result in moral development unless the individual gradually discovers personally that it is good to do the right thing.

This discovery is a slow process. In fact, developmental psychologists, as was mentioned in chapter 7, have discovered at least four clearly-defined stages of moral awareness that the young person passes through from childhood to late teens. Some adults progress a further stage or two, but many never even make it to the fourth and are still stuck on a lower level. How many grown-ups still have the childish attitude: 'If only God didn't exist, what a great time I could have!' Any efforts at moral formation must take account of the gradual nature of this development, with special emphasis on the word 'growth'. Moral formation is a lifelong process of growth, not merely in knowledge, but in sensitivity, imagination and feeling, a growth in wholeness.

Whole person
The moral response must be a response of the whole person, so the formation of conscience cannot ignore the emotional and affective aspects of life. Reasoning, will and emotions are all involved. Reason is essential. Knowing the good is not just a

matter of being told what is right, but of understanding and being convinced that it is right. The efforts of all educators of conscience, therefore, should concentrate on raising the level of people's reasoning in moral matters rather than imprinting rules and regulations. Many parents are at a disadvantage insofar as their own experience was largely the acceptance of rules, so they cannot be blamed when they feel helpless as they see their rules and values questioned or rejected by today's youth. It is not their fault that they were not encouraged to question or reason, that they were simply told what was good for them. A one-sided preaching on obedience, dependence and humility made them feel guilty at the mere thought of questioning. They deserve a great deal of sympathy, but they need support and help.

 One of the greatest needs in the church for many years has been for adult education, with a programme whose content and methods are geared for adults, not a repeat of childhood learning. It is too easy an excuse to claim that 'people are not ready for it', that the 'simple faithful' do not want to be disturbed. It can be sinful neglect on the part of the church to continue a policy that actually keeps people at a lower level of moral development, one that prevents them from giving more of their intelligence to God. This need is being met quite successfully at the present time and the lay men and women who respond are excited and enthusiastic in their commitment to courses. But the weakness is in church structures which fail to take advantage of this enrichment of the faithful for the health and development of local communities. A sobering thought for church leaders is the comment of Belgian Cardinal Godfried Danneels, now 75 years old, in an interview published in the London *Tablet* when he said he was distressed that there are not brighter men in the church hierarchy. He attended every meeting of the synod of bishops since 1980 and said: 'When I look at the synod assembly, so many good people are there with really pastoral hearts. They are good shepherds, But from time to time I think it would be good if 5 per cent of them were also thinkers, that don't lack hearts. We need among the bishops and cardinals some really intelligent people.'[1] One of the great advantages of Vatican II was that

---

1. *The Tablet*, London, 31 May 2008.

it had the assistance of many of the world's top theologians all during its work.

Personal values

Raising the level of people's reasoning in moral judgement is one of the essentials of moral formation. But since the reasoning will be not only about facts, but also involve a response to values, people need a community and atmosphere which will enable them to discover real values for themselves. They need a community at home, in school and in church in which they discover for themselves how good it is to live by the principles of justice, truth, sincerity, fidelity to promises, concern for the weak, respect for persons. It is difficult for them to discover such values if they have never experienced them in a meaningful way in their own lives, or if these values are clouded or betrayed by the institutions or standards of society. The real values in our lives are the standards we live by, not the abstract ideals we verbally subscribe to.

Since the whole fabric of Christian living is simply the putting into practice of Christ's law of love, the basic value underlying all the others is love. Children and young people need to see that there is real love behind all the rules and regulations, that to search for solutions to moral problems is really to look for the best way to respect each other's rights, to love each other, and to enable each other to grow. The love in question is not conditional love, in which the parents love the child only insofar as it is an extension of themselves, reflecting their opinions and meeting their demands. It is genuine love, reflecting God's own love, in which the child is loved for its own sake, in spite of its faults.

This is the test for many parents today, when their teenagers experiment with drugs or sex, neglect or reject their religion, or become total drop-outs. A good practical definition of love is 'staying in relationship'. It calls for a great deal of selfless love and real concern to keep open the lines of communication with a son or daughter who seems to reject everything we stand for. But to reject them is to reject the future generation of the church. To close our hearts against them is to teach them that the church is simply a club for nice people, not the community of the followers of Jesus in which forgiveness and reconciliation can be experienced as a gift from God. Prayerful reflection on the figure of the father in the parable of the lost son (Lk 14:11-32) may remind us of the Christian ideal in this kind of situation

Maturity the goal

The purpose of this chapter was not to outline a programme of moral formation, nor to criticise the methods of the past, but to draw attention to the need for a critical look at the simple phrase 'teaching morality'. It is understandable that those in authority, parents, teachers, priests and bishops, should feel responsible for those in their care, feel the impulse to guard and protect them, and worry when they seem to drift away or show signs of becoming independent. They also feel responsible for the institution they represent, family, church, society, and they naturally tend to conserve and protect the wisdom and traditions of such institutions. A static society tends to have a static Christianity. But in both cases there should be less concern about conservative protection and more emphasis on growth and development. If they have the emphasis in the wrong place, church leaders can too easily become preoccupied with control rather than moral influence, and imagine that they have no authority unless they have power, hence the recourse to threats and sanctions.

The differences are important and far-reaching in their consequences. Preoccupation with power and control leads to a negative, condemnatory attitude to new ideas, an intolerance of pluralism, a deadening uniformity, an oppressive centralisation, and no consultation in decision-making, all of which militate against the personal growth of individuals and communities. Too much control can stifle initiative, and power easily provokes fear. The challenge to all teachers of morality is to release the God-given potential that is in each person, to create the encouraging, supportive community in which every individual is helped to grow towards ever greater self-autonomy and self-esteem. When Paul speaks of the variety of gifts in the church, 'apostles, prophets, pastors, teachers', he stresses that they are for the building up of the body of Christ, to enable all of us to 'become mature people, reaching to the very height of Christ's full stature' (Eph 4:13).

CHAPTER ELEVEN

Let's Rehabilitate Sin!

It would be a total misreading of this book to conclude that recent developments in scripture studies or theology have done away with the notion of sin or in any way minimised its importance. Nor can it be said that they have so altered its description as to empty it of meaning. On the contrary, running through all of the preceding chapters is an implicit plea for a rehabilitation of the word 'sin'. It has fallen on hard times, and it needs to be rescued. In the world at large it is an empty word, generally avoided, or used in the most superficial sense. In the churches it has become so trivialised that it touches only the surface of people's minds, no longer finds an echo in their hearts, and fails to help people change their lives. There is no need to find a substitute word to sound more modern, because it is one of the basic words of our religious tradition, a word as fundamental as 'grace' or 'God'. In order to rehabilitate it, we need to rescue it from the oversimplifications that keep people from taking it as seriously as it deserves.

Neither symptom nor crime
To emphasise sin is to re-affirm moral responsibility, to do people the honour of respecting their personhood. Society's superficial reaction is to reduce sin to symptom or crime, so that all that is needed is to treat the neurotics and punish the criminals, leaving the rest of us with an easy conscience. But this is very much an over-simplification. In the chapters on guilt and punishment we drew attention to the need to recognise real guilt in whatever degree it is found, and to help people accept the consequences of their actions, which is the element of punishment. God does not inflict punishment, and we might do well to follow his example by seeing to it that penalties, either in civil society or in church community, are therapeutic, working for the offender's im-

provement, or in extreme cases affecting the common good, simply a deterrent. But vindictive punishment is simply collective revenge, and should have no place in Christian thinking.

To have dealt with the neurotics and criminals is not to have finished with sin. The big sin is to refuse to accept that we are our brother's keeper, that in fact we are responsible for our brothers and sisters, to close our eyes to the fact that we are part of the system which encourages people to behave neurotically or criminally. So many of these people are more sinned against than sinning. To draw attention to their unsocial or antisocial behaviour is to distract from our own responsibility, to forget that many of our own attitudes and actions are far more harmful to society.

Recognise sins

We are continually sinning, but we prefer not to think about it, and the fact that so many people are in the same boat makes the evasion all the easier. The fact that dishonesty, tax evasion, pilfering, malingering are so common, means that the honest person is made to look and sometimes feel eccentric. For the health of society we need a new awareness of the seven capital or deadly sins, plus a few more: pride, greed, covetousness, lust, envy, gluttony, anger, sloth, waste, cheating, stealing, lying, cruelty, alcohol and drug abuse, drunk and dangerous driving. These are not simply diseases for which we are not responsible, pathological conditions we can do nothing about. There is no need to catalogue the harmful results to society of any or all of these, nor to describe the basic unhappiness and lack of wholeness they bring to the sinners and their families and friends. But it would be a good thing to remind ourselves that they are bad, that we need to be converted from them and try to avoid them.

Society at large needs such a reminder, and the churches too need to have their conscience stirred. It is the function of preachers to keep the Christian community aware of the sins in our midst, to call us to repentance and atonement. But the purpose of this book was not to moralise about particular sins, nor indeed to enter into discussion as to whether different forms of contraception or sexual behaviour are sinful or not. Rather it was to stir the conscience of Christians to reflect on the seriousness of sin, to re-think some of the assumptions and uncritical views that tend to trivialise it.

Trivialising notions

Thus, we saw how narrow and crippling is the influence of an over-simplified notion of moral law; a preoccupation with precise measurement; a disproportionate concern with sexuality, particularly physical actions, without reference to their full human meaning; judgement of isolated bits of behaviour divorced from the overall pattern of moral living; an inflated and morbid super-ego taking the place of conscience; neurotic guilt feelings smothering the experience of real moral guilt; the punishment of sin seen in terms of an angry, vengeful God; the sacrament of reconciliation used mainly as a guilt-shedding process with little experience of real conversion; the notion of God's forgiveness as something to be worked for and earned rather than accepted and celebrated as healing gift; morality presented simply as rules to be obeyed; unthinking conformity praised as obedience; the teaching authority of the church used simply as power to command; the over-protective caution of those in authority, bishops, priests, teachers, parents; the failure to raise the level of people's reasoning about moral issues; the reluctance to promote autonomous moral decision; the lust for clarity and certainty beyond what is possible or appropriate.

To this list could be added more general factors like concentration on private morality to the exclusion of any awareness of responsibility for community sinfulness like prejudice or discrimination; a gigantic blind spot with regard to sins of omission, and particularly the sin of simply not caring, not being concerned, and of not being concerned at our lack of concern; an artificial separation between church and world, spirit and matter, soul and body, worship and service, love of God and love of neighbour, future life and life here on earth; a water-tight division between teaching church and learning church; a failure to realise that the church is not only an institution with its structures and laws, but also a fellowship of brothers and sisters in the Lord, a sacrament of Christ, a herald of the kingdom of God, a servant of the world God so loved; the refusal to read the 'signs of the times' in the light of the gospel as an ongoing revelation of God's will; a failure to recognise the presence of the Holy Spirit in other Christian communities and indeed in world religions, and to admit that we might learn something from them; a complacency that prevents us from realising the wealth of new insights in the documents of Vatican II and from admitting how radical a change in thinking they call for.

Call to change

This is not meant to be a list of sins, though it could provide material for a fruitful examination of conscience. Failures in these areas may not only be sinful, but they can narrow our concept of sin and indeed our understanding of Christian morality. To speak like this may be upsetting to some Catholics who claim that they do not wish to be disturbed in their faith. This reaction merely underlines once again the need for adult education in the church, how necessary it is to explain that our faith is in Jesus Christ, but that our understanding of it will be coloured by the culture in which we live. To want a 'simple faith' in a world that is no longer simple is a failure to hear God's call in the complexities of daily living, an escape into a fantasy world in which even God can be fashioned in our own image and likeness.

The irony is that those who complain about 'innovations', *à la carte* Catholicism and a 'new theology' undermining their simple certainties and relativising their false absolutes appeal to the 'teaching of the church' and fail to realise that it is the church itself which is calling them to change, through the authority of an ecumenical council. The documents of the Second Vatican Council are the 'official teaching of the church', more 'official' than any catechism produced before or after the Council. That they represent, in many cases, a combination of different theologies and leave some questions without satisfactory solutions should warn us against false clarity and misleading simplicity. The effort to lessen their importance by quoting earlier 'teachings' or previous papal teaching against them is the worst of bad theology.

Without going into detail on the more intricate moral problems, they have much to tell us that is relevant to morality in today's world. Their insights and approach throw new light on many of the topics discussed in the previous chapters. First of all, it is significant that the Council totally rejected the special document on *The Moral Order* drawn up by the Vatican preparatory commission, a document which reflected literally the legalistic and casuistic approach of the old textbooks. Instead of a separate document, the Council spread its teaching on morality over many documents as the need arose. This is not the place for an extensive treatment of Vatican II moral teaching, but we need to recall its new perspective and the radical departure from a tradition that was at least a few centuries old. It looked to the Bible, dogma. and the life of the church as sources for renewing moral theology. Ignoring the old 'blueprint' notion of natural law, it gives a clearer picture of it as God's plan; it presents Christian life as a gift from God, a fruit of the Spirit (*The Church*, n 7). It stresses the dignity and freedom of the children of God, in whose hearts the Holy Spirit dwells as in a temple, and whose 'law' is the new commandment 'to love as Christ loved us' (ibid, n 9). It uses the word 'law' more in Paul's sense of a framework or principle of faith rather than as a precise and detailed code (e.g. *Church in the Modern World*, nn 22, 24, 28, 32, 38, 41, 42, 43, 48, 50, 51, 78, 89).

God's call in today's world
The relativisation of external law is an immediate consequence of the Council's teaching on conscience, discussed in chapter 6 above. It emphasises that conscience is not omniscient or infallible, and we are reminded of the fact that it can be blunted by sin. But there is a firm insistence throughout on individual responsibility, and on the freedom of our response to God. Faith is conversion from sin and a turning to God, not once but continually as we grow in personal relationship with Father, Son and Holy Spirit. But nowhere does the Council suggest that the gospel, church teaching or even the presence of the Spirit give us solutions in advance. Though the people of God believe that they are led by the Spirit of the Lord, and get inspiration from their faith, they still have to 'discern in the events, the needs, and the longings they share with other people of our time, what may be genuine signs of the presence or of the purpose of God' (ibid, n 11). God's call is to be heard in the here and now, in the bits and pieces of everyday life, and to be sought afresh as each new problem arises.

The world and earthly values are no longer looked upon as temptations and distractions from spiritual life, but are recognised as part of the basic goodness of creation. The moral challenge to us is not simply to keep the law in order to get to heaven, but to develop our full potential, to grow into the likeness of Jesus, who is not only God made visible, but the human person made perfect. As Jesus did not drop out of the sky as an alien from another world, but was a man of his time who had to grow in age, wisdom and strength; so too the Christian is rooted in this earth, belongs to the human family and is part of its culture.

With this kind of vision, the Council resolutely rules out any kind of individualistic or otherworldly morality and piety. The document on *The Church in the Modern World*, whose opening sentence speaks of joy and hope (*Gaudium et spes*), emphasises human solidarity, cemented by love extending even to enemies (ibid, n 28), and lists the principles or basic truths that should guide moral decisions: inter-dependence, co-responsibility and participation, respect for human rights and social justice (ibid, nn 25, 31, 24, 29). It lays particular stress on the rightful autonomy of earthly affairs (ibid, n 36).

Values before rules

The second half of this Council document is a treatise on values that ought to be a sourcebook for Christian thinking on morality, dealing as it does with family, cultural, economic, social and political values, and questions of international life, war and peace. This is a very far cry from the rule-morality and listing of sins with their varying degrees of sinfulness so characteristic of the old manuals, but it is now the 'official teaching of the church'. In practice, therefore, the church would not merely be faithful to its own teaching manifested in the principles of Vatican II, but also it would be more effective as a teacher of morality if it were simply to drop all attempts to draw a sharp line between mortal and venial sin, both objectively and subjectively. Concern about such a division has been a mental straitjacket of scrupulosity and fear for millions of Catholics, preventing their growth towards moral maturity.

Likewise, the church in future will have much fewer and far less detailed moral rules than in the past, and will focus more on fundamental principles of moral reasoning, a deeper insight into human and Christian values, and a heightened sense of personal responsibility among the faithful. After all, a central insight of Vatican II is that the church is first and foremost the People of God. This could be upsetting for those pastors who fear that they may lose 'control' of their flock and experience a diminution of 'power' in their ministry, but it will be a big step forward for the church when such leaders can stop worrying about 'putting people straight' or 'making them good', and instead concentrate on their primary function, which is to preach the good news of Jesus.

'Christian' morality?

With so much talk of the 'autonomy of earthly affairs' and the recognition of 'human values', it could be asked 'What is Christian morality?' or 'Is there such a thing?' This question has occupied moralists for some years past, and there is growing consensus on the view that, in terms of content or specific commands, there is no Christian morality distinct from basic human morality. The Ten Commandments of the Old Testament and the virtues preached in the New Testament are all simply moral demands of human nature, applicable to all human beings. The insights of the Council make clear that Christians and humanists have the same grounds for knowing the difference between right and wrong, and should therefore collaborate in seeking solutions to the world's problems. It was for this reason that Pope Paul could address his encyclical letter on fostering the development of peoples, *Populorum Progressio* (1967), which is certainly a document about morality, not only to Catholics, but to all people of good will.

Once again, this could be upsetting to those accustomed to thinking of the church as 'possessing the truth,' almost 'owning the truth' to be handed out to others, but again they need to be reminded that the Vatican II documents are now the official teaching of the church itself. However, there is something different and special about Christian morality. Just as the religious faith of the people of God in Old and New Testaments saw the obligations of human morality in a new context, in the context of the covenant-relationship with God and as a consequence of the

215

new life in Christ, our faith today enables us to view the demands of being fully human as a response to the call of God in the person of Jesus, in the light of his teaching and his example.

Faith makes a difference

Our faith provides us with a new stimulus and motivation to act morally, puts before us the attractive, impressive and challenging model of Jesus in his humanity, and through his Holy Spirit gives us the power to cope with our sinfulness and respond to his call. Furthermore, the teaching and example of Jesus may make us more sensitive to ideals above the normal, like turning the other cheek, going the extra mile, forgoing our rights, loving our enemies, and remind us of a theology of suffering, of failure and the cross. Likewise, our belonging to a Christian community, a community of faith, service and worship, can make demands on us like participation in the Eucharist and celebration of sacraments that are not operative for non-believers. Also, our belief in a personal relationship with God leaves us open to the possibility of experiencing a personal invitation from him not merely to continual conversion and greater intimacy, but also to a special way of service in the community, for example in the priesthood or religious life. Finally, belief in a God of infinite love, caring for us personally, can bring healing, growth and wholeness that will colour our attitude towards our neighbours and the world about us. Faith also makes a difference in the understanding of sin. It considers sin not simply as selfishness, letting oneself down, disappointing or hurting others or breaking a law. Sin is all of these, but for the believer it is much more. It is the refusal to behave like a child of God, a failure to reflect the mind and heart of Jesus our model.

The human person fully alive

These are all important differences, but they should not allow us to forget that underlying them all is the basic moral demand to become *actually* what we are *potentially*, to become fully human. If we are called to follow Jesus, who is not only God in human form but also the perfection of humanity, the more Christ-like we become, the more fully human we become. There are individuals for whom the external expression of their growth in

Christ will be blocked by obstacles beyond their control, so we must beware of a too-easy identification of holiness and psychological wholeness. There are forms and degrees of holiness known only to God. But the normal pattern is that our growth in Christ is a development of our humanity. St Irenaeus describes this ideal in his beautiful claim that 'The glory of God is the human person fully alive.'

But nobody grows alone. Our roots are in the earth, whose stewardship God put into our hands, and our life, health and growth are determined by our relationship with those around us. We are what our relationships enable us to be. To respond to God's call to grow, to be fully human, therefore, is to be in a correct relationship with these realities. In fact, we have no way of knowing whether we love God, whether our prayers are more than words, apart from the test of service, of love of our fellow human beings, as Jesus himself tells us: 'unless you did it to one of these my least brethren'. Certainly, we need to pray and worship. Like Jesus himself, we need to be alone with our heavenly Father from time to time and we also need to praise and thank him together as a community. But, without the touchstone of service, we cannot be sure that this is not mere escapism, that our contemplation is not simply talking to ourselves about ourselves. There can be no love of God except through the neighbour. When Jesus calls us to serve God rather than the mammon of wealth, power or reputation, he is really telling us to live for others. But since we are to love them as we love ourselves, a certain healthy self-love and self-esteem is essential to being human and being Christian. This strand of our Christian vocation needs to be more openly acknowledged and developed against an exaggerated and one-sided preaching on humility and self-abasement which did so much damage in the past.

Reality of sin

It would be easy to get carried away by the optimism of the positive picture of our dignity and call as presented in the Vatican II documents. But a too optimistic picture is bound to be shallow. The full picture must include the dark side of our nature, equally emphasised by the Council, namely the evil in our depths that can turn self into God, the pride, avarice, lust and aggression

217

that are the effects of serving that false god. Our exaggerated self-love is a dis-orientation at the very centre of our being. It is what we call 'sin', and it expresses itself in all kinds of broken, distorted and destructive relationships with those around us and with the material world in which we live.

The purpose of this book was to focus attention on the seriousness of sin, to rescue the notion from the many elements in our tradition that tend to trivialise it, and to remove the misunderstandings that tempt people to dismiss it as a reality. We need to see it not simply as misdemeanour, law-breaking, or surface action for which we can easily make amends, but as a mysterious, ever-present reality in the church as a whole and in individual members. It is a reality to be concerned about, but not to be unduly afraid of. 'Where sin increased, God's grace increased much more' (Rom 5:20). In Christ Jesus we have the forgiveness of all sin, but unless we are convinced of our sinfulness in all its depth and complexity, how can we realise how much we need him, or fully rejoice in the pardon, healing and new life he brings us?

The future?

It is no accident that the chapters on law and sex are much longer than any of the others. It simply shows how much these areas of Christian morality were crying out for critical examination and renewal. The legalistic and abstract approach could not be sweetened by piety, since references to God's love were often so spiritualised in the past that they made little connection with the reality of people's daily lives. There was no theology of sex worth speaking of. For older Catholics it was an endless source of scruples and temptation. For far too long the primary purpose of marriage was seen as procreation, with the secondary purpose as the 'relief of concupiscence'. Official church teaching still insists that every act of intercourse must be 'open to procreation', whereas God himself has arranged that a woman is fertile for only 48 to 72 hours every month, which means that procreation is essentially linked to the marriage relationship itself and not to every act of intercourse. The church's traditional attitude to sex is only one of the factors contributing to the haemorrhaging of church attendance at the present time, but it is a very important one. Thanks to gifted and prophetic lay writers, men and women with personal experience of married life, we are developing a new and meaningful theology and morality of sexuality. They make good use of the insights of the Second Vatican Council, but they feel that the most central insight of that wonderful Council receives only notional assent by our leaders, namely the nature of the church itself and the manner of its organisation and functioning.

Vatican II totally abandoned the description of the church as a 'perfect society' and defined it first and foremost as 'the People of God'. Of course it is also an international institution, an organisation, with its civil service and administrators, but this is secondary. As People of God we are all equally members, with the same baptism and dignity, but in practice clericalism still dominates our experience of church, and the laity, God's holy people, still feel this. They are never consulted in any meaningful way and they are disheartened that their children have so much difficulty in relating to the church. Those children, who can be as caring, generous and loving as their parents were in their time, are not impressed or happy to hear their world described simply in terms of materialism, personalism, and relativism. From their point of view they are tempted to add 'Catholicism' as a negative experience. They look in vain for the joy and hope described by Vatican II in its presentation of the church in the modern world. Our church is indeed undergoing a tramatic experience. Mass attendance has dropped dramatically in developed countries, and vocations to priesthood and religious life are at an all-time low. We are accustomed to thousands in Latin America having no Eucharist for months because they have no male celibate clerics to lead it, and in Europe and North America churches are closed and parishes are 'clustered' to keep the dwindling church ticking over. But this is a one-sided emphasis on the church as organisation, and moving the furniture is only a small part of what may need to be done.

The church in developed countries is forced to close churches or to cluster them in groups to be serviced by a 'flying padre', a mobile priest to visit them in turn but without a Christian community of which he himself is part. How long can a celibate priest who really belongs nowhere survive as a human being, and what kind of old age can holy mother church provide for him? This kind of 'vocation' will not attract new vocations. The Vatican recently ordered bishops around the world to appoint a priest to organise special prayer meetings and adoration of the Blessed Sacrament to pray for vocations. We have been praying for decades for more priests in Latin America and now in our home countries, but we fail to see that perhaps God has already answered our prayers: that he/she is not interested in 'more of the same'. God is asking us to use our God-given reason and common sense to search for new answers. There is no need to close or sell the church building. We could ordain a working man or woman or a recently retired person to celebrate the Eucharist and bring the sacraments to the sick and dying. Everything else can be taken care of by a well organised Christian community of lay people with their various gifts. For the first hundred years after the death of Jesus Christianity was not recognised as a religion and there were no churches. The Eucharist was celebrated in private houses and the leader was somebody appointed by an apostle or a man elected by the community. More often the leader of the celebration would be the owners of the house, who could be a married couple or a rich widow. Only later was the leader prayed over by the laying on of hands, and only very slowly did our present notion of priesthood develop. Many people imagine that at the last supper, after the withdrawal of Judas, Jesus ordained the remaining eleven men as priests, giving them everything except Roman collars. But in fact there is nothing in the gospels to show that Jesus consciously founded the church, or even *a* church. Nor did he ever ordain anyone a priest in the modern sense, or even think of a cultic priesthood. Inspired by the early history of our Christian communities and the division of ministries, we should be free to devise a healthy and human re-organisation that could revitalise our parishes.

The church as all God's holy people
The church as People of God needs more attention. They need to hear the good news of the gospel in terms that make sense of their ordinary everyday lives, with a vision that enables them to recognise the basic goodness of God's wonderful, beautiful creation, and helps them to feel his loving presence in their human relationships.

Some people are inclined to look to the ever-increasing numbers of Catholics in the developing world as hope for the future. There is no doubting their enthusiasm and the quality of their faith, but they are affected by the same social factors that were part of our own experience in the past. It is a step up socially to opt for priesthood or religious life, with the prospect of education and foreign travel. But when these countries reach relative prosperity they will face the same problems we have to cope with today. There are no simple solutions. We may do our best to re-organise our structures and make the best use of our personnel, but the deeper renewal is a bigger and more important challenge. Current efforts at evangelisation focus on liturgy, prayer and sacraments, but these are the very practices that Catholics are abandoning.

The interesting fact is that the surveys which indicate dwindling numbers in church attendance tell us that huge numbers still believe in God and there is a great interest in spirituality. The challenge is to respond to this opportunity, to feed this hunger by helping people to find God in a meaningful way in their relationships, in their experience of sex, in the bits and pieces of everyday life. In today's world people are not going to fill the churches in their thousands if all they find is 'more of the same'. Large numbers of enthusiastic lay women and men have done courses in theology and scripture that have opened their eyes to the deeper meaning of church and they are only too willing to share in its renewal. In their search for new ways forward they are open to new possibilities in which God could renew his holy church: more meaningful lay involvement, married clergy, women priests, real accountability of church leaders to their communities of parish, diocese, and world church. If Jesus were to visit us in person today we might be consoled by his customary greeting: 'Peace be with you', but probably shocked at his little bit of reality therapy 'Why are you afraid?' We should not be afraid to admit how much unhealthy, useless and even dangerous baggage we have been carrying for far too long in our theological past. We should leave it in the past and open our eyes, our hearts and our minds to the liberating and challenging insights we get from the Second Vatican Council calling us to renewal.

While the topics just mentioned are means towards effective renewal, we also need radical change in our understanding of Christian religion and our image of church. Karl Rahner in 1979 drew attention to the fact that the Christian Church began as a form of Judaism and then developed over two thousand years into the church of European culture and civilisation, but with Vatican II it realised that it was really a world-church. Instead of hankering after the glories of the past, the challenge now is to adjust to the new reality of there being no future Christendom, but rather a diaspora-church, a little flock, a *pusillus grex*, a church equally at home in all cultures, in every part of the world. This would take us into uncharted waters, but it might help us to become a more humble and more convincing church, rather than a world organisation proud of its efficiency.

There is far too much fear in the church. We need to get rid of our fear, and one way of doing this is to feel that we are trusted. We need to trust each other more. After all, God trusts us: with his Son (in spite of what we did to him), with his word in scripture, with his sacraments, indeed with his church (and what have we made of it?). An incredible mystery, if only we could believe it. Perhaps God is telling us that the only way to trust people is to trust them, as he trusts us.

In spite of the many unattractive elements in our church at the present time, I have no hesitation in declaring that I am passionately in love with it, and I am very much at home in my Catholic faith. A pessimistic Catholic is a contradiction in terms. I find the goodness, truth and beauty of God in the wonderful world he has created and entrusted to our care, and I feel his love most strongly in the precious gift of friendship. As for the church, it is my home. It brings me so much of the endless compassion of Christ; the kind strong gentleness and refined sensitivity of Mary the Mother of Jesus; the consolation from God himself to help us through the many dark nights of the soul; the strength of grace in the midst of weakness; the deep-down conviction of the mystical meaning of all reality; the deeper meaning of living and dying; the magic of enjoying the earth as the home God gives us out of love, and at the same time realising that we have here no lasting city.

Dom   872/611
Publication

? why no dtr Sean Rogers in Ire?